INVISIBLE*

*JUKEBOX

Published in Great Britain by Quartet Books Limited in 1998
A member of the Namara Group
27 Goodge Street
London W1P 2LD

A catalogue record for this book is available from the British Library

ISBN 0 7043 8046 3

Phototypeset by The F.S.H. Group, London
Printed and bound in Great Britain by C.P.D. Wales Ltd

Contents

Interviewers

Barry Adamson, Gavin Bryars, Harold Budd, John Cale,
Future Sound Of London, Diamanda Galás, Bruce Gilbert,
Philip Glass, Peter Hammill, Ice T, Mixmaster Morris, Alex Paterson,
John Peel, Courtney Pine, Jah Wobble and Robert Wyatt were
interviewed by Mike Barnes

Steve Albini was interviewed by Jakubowski

Jack Bruce, Elvis Costello, Ali Farka Touré and
Paul Weller were interviewed by Phillip Watson

Neneh Cherry was interviewed by Ian Tucker

Coldcut and Sonic Youth were interviewed by Mark Sinker

Holger Czukay was interviewed by K Martin

Anne Dudley was interviewed by Louise Gray

Goldie was interviewed by Julie Taraska

Lydia Lunch was interviewed by Hopey Glass

James MacMillan was interviewed by Kenny Mathieson

Graham Massey and Mark E Smith were interviewed by Dave Haslam

Henry Rollins was interviewed by Steve Holtje

Introduction

In June 1991 *The Wire* magazine published an interview feature with the ex-Rip Rig & Panic pianist Mark Springer under the section heading Invisible Jukebox. The format of the interview was a new one for the magazine, but the idea, as outlined in the feature's strapline, seemed simple enough: each month, sit a musician down with an interviewer, play them a series of records, and ask them to identify and comment on them — with no prior knowledge of what they were about to hear. Over the last seven years *The Wire* has continued to run a monthly (well, more or less) Invisible Jukebox feature, opening its mysterious listening booth to a wide array of musicians from the worlds of Electronica, avant rock, drum 'n' bass, HipHop, jazz, modern classical and World Music. 32 of the best of those interviews are now collected in this current volume (Mark Springer didn't make the final cut, unfortunately, but Neneh Cherry, another former Rip Rig & Panic associate, did).

From early beginnings as something of a journalistic curio, the Invisible Jukebox feature has become one of *The Wire*'s most popular and provocative regular sections. Each month, the Jukebox selections are programmed to fit the profile of the latest subject. And more often than not, in articulating the appeal (or otherwise) of other people's music — that of their own contemporaries, heroes from the past, or the unknown 'wild cards' which we slip in from time to time — the Jukeboxees end up revealing more about themselves and their work than they would through any amount of direct grilling, dispensing a series of priceless insights, barbed asides, and the kind of dropdead pronouncements typified by Jack Bruce's reaction upon recognising Led Zeppelin's "Custard Pie": "Why are you playing me session musicians?"

Tony Herrington, Editor/Publisher, *The Wire*

Special thanks to *The Wire*'s Rob Young and Chris Bohn for additional edits and research.

The Wire is the UK's most adventurous independent music magazine, offering in-depth monthly coverage of a wide array of non-mainstream and experimental music, from Electronica, avant rock and breakbeat culture to jazz, modern classical and World Music.

For more information, contact:
The Wire, 45-46 Poland Street, London W1V 3DF
Tel: 0171 439 6422 Fax: 0171 287 4767 E-mail: the_wire@ukonline.co.uk
Website: http://www.dfuse.com/the-wire

Justin Quick

001 >

Barry Adamson first came to prominence in 1977 as the bass guitarist with Magazine, one of the pivotal groups in Manchester's post-punk era. The group split in 1981 after releasing five albums. That year, Adamson contributed to The Birthday Party's *Junkyard* LP. After a liaison with Steve Strange in Visage, he became a founder member of The Bad Seeds alongside Nick Cave, Blixa Bargeld and Mick Harvey. Feeling restricted by the rock group format and wanting to explore his multi-instrumental talents, Adamson split from the group in 1987, embarking on a solo career. He released his first solo single, a reworking of Elmer Bernstein's 'The Man With The Golden Arm', in 1988, followed by a series of EPs. His solo albums for Mute Records, *Moss Side Story* (1989), *Soul Murder* (1992) and 1996's *Oedipus Schmoedipus* (which features contributions from Cave and Pulp's Jarvis Cocker, among others), were all conceived as soundtracks to imaginary films. Adamson is also a bona fide soundtrack composer, writing music for a number of films including Carl Colpaert's *Delusion*, Allison Anders's *Gas, Food, Lodging* and David Lynch's *Lost Highway*. The Jukebox took place in London.

ARTIST
A Certain Ratio
TITLE
The Fox

SOURCE
The Fox 12″

label

Factory

OK, this is A Certain Ratio. The title escapes me. It's very early. I think it's from 1980.

It's *The Fox* from 1980.

[After a conspicuous bum bass note] I always remember that bit, thinking how great it was.

[As the track ends] I find the ideas really exciting. I think at the time they would have been seen to be executed in a really great way as well. I think I was affected most by the first A Certain Ratio, where there was just the four of them strumming guitars and basses before drummer Donald Johnson joined. It was beautiful, it just ached. The lyrics were just so morose and down, but exactly right for the music and these noise effects from the guitars. I wish I could be more detailed about the memories of that, but I used to really like seeing them, hearing them play.

It was strange because they were almost beautifully untogether, and he [Johnson] was as tight as anything. He was doing incredible things. When I saw a later version – when they were tight together, all of them, and [Johnson] was playing samples and stuff – it was pretty amazing.

Although this was recorded 16 years ago, it doesn't seem to have dated. Perhaps it was somehow out of time when it was recorded?

I thought at the time, 'That's pretty way out.' After the punk thing, dance music was commercial-minded man's saviour, the polar opposite to punk. But to the commercial man it's still pretty way out to have a guy who can only play three notes on the trumpet and then play effects. The instrumental ghettoisation is about: You have to be beautifully skilled on this instrument. But here they were with a punk approach: 'I'll just blow this trumpet and put it through all these effects because it *sounds* wicked anyway.' That is ahead-thinking because it's also a place where the commercial-minded man would not go.

The trumpet sounds like it's trying to mimic the sounds Miles Davis got on *Bitches Brew*.

I'm going to do it next week. I tell you, next week I'll have my trumpet out and effects boxes! When you put it on I first thought it was live Miles Davis; I expected to hear John McLaughlin coming in. Then I realised it was closer to home, and everything was phased as well.

ARTIST
Henry Mancini
TITLE
Extract from Background To Murder

SOURCE
A Touch Of Evil: OST

LABEL

Varese Sarabande

I recorded an extract from halfway into the piece to make it more difficult.

I know this. . . OK, Henry Mancini. *A Touch Of Evil.* [Adamson whistles along] Genius.

This Mexican style of music seems to have been used in the film to make your average Middle American viewer feel more threatened and stranded than if ethnically-ambiguous music was used to build the tension.

Yeah. What's going on with that border area? Why is Charlton Heston Mexican? [Laughs] Orson Welles was very clear with his direction of the music in this film. This is one of Mancini's moments, but he was a bit bemused why Welles got him to compose what was called 'Music of the Day'. [Welles] said, 'I want you to compose music of the day and I'm going to have it on the radio.' There's a lot of rock 'n' roll music in the film. That was the music of the day that Mancini was instructed to compose so they could put it out of bars, cafes, out of the radio. And it works great just being quiet and coming out of the bar rooms, so we stay with the action really up front.

There's not much main score: the opening theme with the long shot, the murder scene and perhaps some other moments. I think Welles was actually a bit concerned that Mancini made things too grand, because he wanted it to be as mysterious as possible. Is this off the soundtrack CD? It's a beautiful combination of setting the scene, describing where we are in the world; a border town with the influence of the percussion and the mystery and the excitement of...[He sings a motif]. Beautiful.

What are the differences between writing actual and imaginary soundtracks?

I guess it's about direction. With my own stuff I'll go: OK, this is the scene, this is what it's all about, this is what I'm trying to say, this is what I'm trying to convey. With *Touch Of Evil*, they might bring Mancini in at the end of the picture, or he might see the script. [Welles] might say, 'I'm doing a picture. I want you to work and think: "Border town". "Danger".' And he might go away and just hear this rhythm. That's very much the way I approach my own things. So in *Moss Side Story* I'm thinking, 'What's in the air? How can I set this up?' The opening track on *Moss Side Story* is trying to provide a scene which is dangerous – the psychological manner of it is slightly out-of-kilter.

For *Gas, Food, Lodging*, Allison [Anders] might say, 'OK, the character in this scene is carefree, flighty and has a certain thing about them.' She might want me to underscore the tone of that – to give it that lightness. All of it is to stir something in here [he points to his torso], all the way across the board from my stuff to that stuff [Mancini/Welles] to *Gas, Food, Lodging*. It's the same approach but different direction.

I've just done some work with David Lynch [on *Lost Highway*] and he was very clear about what he wanted from the emotion of the scene, so he'd direct me in certain ways. Once I got in the ballpark, he'd say, 'Now I want you to go in a little further. Look at the eyes there. What are they saying, even though they're talking about this?' Then you start to underpin the emotions so it becomes three-dimensional.

When I first went to see Lynch's *Eraserhead* in my teens, I found Alan Splet's sound design extremely draining.

Incredible, incredible. This new film is as draining, I tell you. I left the screening of it so worried. [Laughs] One scene is not too far from that [*Background To Murder*] in terms of the orchestration, lots of bass trombones and stuff, then it goes into other areas that are pure horror-*noir*. It's scary. I couldn't listen to this music for very long because things would start happening to me. I'd go home and people would start ringing the door bell at two in the morning and I'd think, 'That's never happened to me. What's going on?'

ARTIST

The Beach Boys

SOURCE

Here Today

TITLE

LABEL

Here Today (*Backing Track*) Sub Pop

[Immediately] The Beach Boys. [At the end of the track] I've no idea what it's about other than it's The Beach Boys.

It's a recently released outtake, just the backing track, of *Here Today* from the *Pet Sounds* sessions.

I like all the brass work. It's almost like the *Good Vibrations* sound with the organ and the plucked bass and the out of tune piano. Interesting one – sound innovators, the search for something new.

Good Vibrations was the first record I ever bought. I bought it for my sister's birthday and then kept it. [Laughs] I was totally taken by the possibility of sound. I couldn't identify what was doing what, so it all seemed futuristic and weird. And at the same time I recognised certain things like church organs and bass and I guess the vocal harmonies. I knew The Beach Boys in terms of "Fun Fun Fun" and all that sort of stuff. I didn't know of course that there was such a thing as a psychedelic period going on where people were trying to expand their minds; and Brian Wilson was trying to find something not unlike Phil Spector.

For me *Good Vibrations* spoke volumes on the possibility of what happens with sound. I'm thinking particularly of when I was in Magazine for some reason; there was a little bit of reference to that in terms of trying to do things with sound, and going back to A Certain Ratio, putting things through effects.

Funnily enough, I was working on a piece the other week and I used that sound of the bass being plucked very close to the bridge, tight. There's a mystery about it. As well as underpinning the sound, the melody makes it percussive. It works very much as a guitar. A fascinating sound with the trombones as well, which are almost like lead instruments, and it's quite a dark instrument to use on something that seems quite light. And I love the use of 20 tambourines or whatever it is.

ARTIST

Massive Attack vs The Mad Professor

SOURCE

No Protection

LABEL

Circa

TITLE

Eternal Feedback

[Immediately] Massive Attack. Mad Professor remix. Beautiful. I think this is the quintessential modern day record. I think that all records should sound like this. [Laughs] I think everybody should have a Mad Professor remix. It should come with each record. I can understand it from the technical point of what's going on, therefore some of the mystery is taken away. When I don't allow myself to get involved in that, and just listen to it as a work of art, I think it's incredible. It's an inspired move on both sides to do the record like this. It's what we all want – I think that's the key as well.

A lot of people are doing dub remixes using different methods, but still in that spirit of dub.

It's about a feeling and about being able to be very spiritually connected. We can go really far with this. I remember watching [On-U Sound's] Adrian Sherwood work and he was talking to me about not really getting into anything until the track is breathing. And if we take the Latin meaning of 'spiritual', spirit means breath and life. So if the life is breathing in the music. . . I can hear how all these effects are set up, but there's something very connected spiritually to a breathing sensation, and a life thing, and things are moving randomly, just happening: it's almost like it's mixing itself; it's like the outside things, the spirit, the breath of life, are helping it along. I can really feel it with this.

ARTIST	SOURCE
Isaac Hayes	Joy
TITLE	LABEL
Joy	Stax

I don't know who this is but I'm trying to see if I can work it out from the phrasing of the horns and stuff. I'm homing in on Isaac Hayes for some reason. [Starts singing along when the vocals come in] Yeah, of course.

It's from *Joy*, released in 1973.

I was pinning down some of those horn phrases and the way he uses those alto flutes at the top end, which is very traditional, but it's also a filmic orchestration again to give this visual power. He's talking about joy but he has tremolo strings which is a mysterious thing and quite dark, disturbing. It's moving the skin around so he's trying to get to this emotion. There's some mystery with it about this woman he's maybe talking about. So he's creating quite a picture within the orchestration, I feel. It's beautiful. I actually know this track. I'll have to buy it now.

What do you think about his movie music, specifically *Shaft*?

Mindblower. Why? Because it's a pop song but it's able to touch people on such a broad level. It's got really amazing hooks. Every time we think of wah-wah guitar, for some reason everyone goes, 'Shaft', because of the way it was used. But the orchestration is incredible. All the teachings of orchestration in the world won't suggest to you what colour you should use for a certain thing. I think his choice of instruments to orchestrate those passages really go 'boom' like that, and then we're open to all this cool stuff.

I've got *Shaft*, the double album, and I was really affected by the way he was able to suggest what was going on in the same way as Mancini, through the use of contemporary orchestration, but giving it something of the time, *and* saying: these characters are black. I think he's a brilliant musician, a real genius. My fantasy is that the guitar part wasn't written. Maybe they had this funky thing working with the strings and maybe the guitar player had a wah-wah in his case and said, 'Let's try it.'

Barry Adamson

Hector Zazou

Songs From The Cold Seas

The Lighthouse

Columbia

It's Siouxsie And The Banshees. Or with Budgie.

It's Siouxsie on vocals, but the music's by someone else.

It's with somebody German, maybe?

He's French Algerian, actually.

These are getting harder! [Laughs] OK, fill me in, what's the deal?

It's Hector Zazou, *Songs From the Cold Seas*. There are all sorts of people on this track. Mark Isham's on trumpet and there's a shaman chanting in the background. Zazou started the project by collecting field recordings and source material from places like Greenland, Finland, Iceland, the Orkneys.

[Adamson looks at the CD] I didn't know of this record at all. It's good. He obviously dreams this material, therefore opens it out to call in these other people who put it together in his own visual way. Just lately I've been drawn in a little bit with the whole Icelandic thing, particularly with film makers and how they do it over there. I'm reading a book at the moment that's set there and it's a world that's not been contemplated so much. There are pages of descriptions of the different kinds of snow and the textures and the depths of the ice.

Zazou is a composer who orchestrates singers and musicians as much as anything else, bringing in different people on each track, which is something you do on *Oedipus Schmoedipus*. How do you select which musicians to use?

A lot of the time the music tells you who you need and what you need. And if you've met this person before it goes into the subconscious while this music is being created and that's like the finished picture in a way. I think it's possibly what's going on here. In my own experience the thing is there already and you have to find what it is that's needed there – if it's a certain voice, I hear it in the same way that you might hear a horn line or a trumpet line.

There is a dreamlike element to this music for me, and I think the dream element is about putting together worlds to create a world that wouldn't necessarily be there.

Barry Adamson

Roxy Music

Virginia Plain 7"

The Numberer

Island

Roxy Music. Funky! It's called "The . . . something".

The Numberer.

That's the one. It was the B-side to *Editions Of You*. No, *Virginia Plain*. I went from the beginning up to *Country Life*. The first album just blew me way. I come back to Magazine in some ways: experiments with sounds around a song and the individual interpretations by members of the group: [guitarist] Phil Manzanera, [saxophonist] Andy Mackay and of course Eno with the electronics, the synth fall-out. And the drummer [Paul Thompson] was fantastic; Johnny Gustafson's bass, always amazing.

Actually, the bass on the Roxy Music records was one of the things that drew me into bass. They had different players but it was always an approach that anchored the section and played around with melody as well.

Magazine were often compared to Roxy music.

I think Roxy Music did provide a background of early teenage experience, just this mystery, this idea of a life that was being lived in a way, working-class Manchester life, and hearing this music there was almost a punk element to it. The thing I really liked about it was the songwriting depth, *In Every Dream Home A Heartache*, *For Your Pleasure*, and the way they set up moods that didn't rely on any convention. Bryan Ferry comments on this world that's removed from the world that he was familiar with in the beginning but always aspired to and then reports on the delusion of that world. And then some of the great things of that world too, where you can do The Strand and go to this place because we're rich and beautiful. I love the risks that are taken in these early tracks. That goes back to other things we've been talking about with A Certain Ratio and The Beach Boys – those elements of finding something that's slightly off, but it's haunting and it gets you.

ARTIST
Squarepusher
TITLE
Bubble

SOURCE
Bubble And Squeak EP
LABEL
Worm Interface

It's so weird, that programmed drumming. [Fretless bassline comes in] Wow! Weather Report meet drum 'n' bass. I love that sound, though, I've got to be honest, that snare. I was never much on fretless bass actually. . . [He tails off, distracted by the music]

This is Squarepusher, Tom Jenkinson. He programs and plays bass as well – with an obvious jazz rock influence.

Nice. Star record. I love drum 'n' bass programs. It's beyond what the human mind is capable of working out. When I first heard drum 'n' bass it seemed a natural machine-drum progression into what we would call jazz. If you think about jazz drumming, like when a jazz drummer takes a solo, I think there are similar elements. One day, just to confirm this in my mind, I took a drum 'n' bass rhythm and put it under a straightforward jazz piece and it fitted. If you imagine that written out for a really great jazz drummer, he could play it with a snare and cymbals; apart from there being an underlying consistent beat, it really is like a jazz drummer workout – I think of solos I've heard by Elvin Jones. I don't think the worlds are that far apart, and therefore it's no coincidence that Squarepusher would play his later jazz-style bass and have that jazz connection going on somewhere.

Was your bass playing ever influenced by jazz or jazz rock?

I had a similar sound in some ways, but I didn't play fretless very much. I didn't like fusion, I didn't like the guitar. I don't know why. It made sense to me later when I heard people like The Lounge Lizards, when it became more of a punk thing, and some aspects of Lydia Lunch, *Queen Of Siam*, which was basically a jazz ensemble big band with electric guitar. I liked Sly And The Family Stone: Larry Graham using the bass to underpin the rhythm, the odd melody, walking up the top and expressing the instrument in that way.

ARTIST
Herbie Hancock
TITLE
The Naked Camera

SOURCE
Blow-Up: OST
LABEL
Premier Soundtracks

Herbie Hancock. *Blow-Up*. I actually enjoy this as a jazz piece but it doesn't really make me think of *Blow-Up* to be honest with you. I think it's the kind of jazz that wouldn't necessarily exist in a film. The opening track and The Yardbirds and some of the other pieces do, but that track is beautiful as a piece of jazz music, and Herbie Hancock is a genius composer. There's a great mood to it, I think it's really clever. It's almost more jazz than film, if you get my meaning. That [bass] refrain has a platform to put a visual image on the top of, but I think it's a fine-line one. I would listen to that one outside of the film.

What prompted your interest in soundtrack music?
I think it's where I first really discovered the emotional value of music. My sister was playing a lot of rock music in the 60s. I liked it, but then going to see a movie and hearing music as well and seeing what was going on and feeling the music move me left a real thing that I chose to stick with in some way. It kept resurfacing as well through punk rock and jazz. But then there would be this root that always led back to film.

The modern soundtrack is whatever fits. Who would have thought that Al Green's *Let's Stay Together*, which we all kind of visualise in our own ways in whatever romance we've had in our lives, is now stuck to a film and it becomes, 'Oh, that track from *Pulp Fiction*.'

Pulp Fiction sold shitloads. And there was a time at the beginning of my career when I might have gone, 'Oh no, it's the death of the composer when you start putting those songs together.' But it's getting people into seats and also making them open to the modern day soundtrack. Which is what I try to do with *Oedipus Schmoedipus*, almost make it like the modern day soundtrack, not have orchestral themes, but a series of pieces, like *Oedipus: The Album*. There's that Jarvis Cocker song, that Nick Cave song, there's a Miles Davis piece on the same record: how come? Because that's the soundtrack, the modern day Oedipus soundtrack, as I see it.

Does knowing that a piece of music is linked to a film alter the way that a person listens to it?
I think it really does, because the mind is then open to the idea of visual interpretation. And I think that we're very sophisticated these days at visual interpretation. We know wad sad music is, we know what happy music is, we know what mystery music is. It sets a mood, that's the license that it gives the listener.

What's your favourite soundtrack?
Well, this month I'd say it has to be Quincy Jones, *In Cold Blood*. I think that has to be a slice of genius and a half.

Barry Adamson

C. N. Launt

US guitarist and producer Steve Albini's first group, Big Black, shot to prominence in the mid-80s as one of several underground American post-hardcore groups (others included Dinosaur Jr, Sonic Youth, Butthole Surfers) on the UK Blast First label. The trio (with a lethal drum machine) recorded two full-length albums, *Atomiser* and *Songs About Fucking*, before calling it a day. Albini's next project, Rapeman, attracted considerable controversy in the UK for their name (the title of a Japanese Manga comic), all of which obscured the fact that *Two Nuns And A Pack Mule* (1988) was a massive advance into the beyond, Albini's trademark metallic-sounding guitar married up to the former Scratch Acid rhythm section. After Rapeman split, Albini embarked on a second career as a producer and engineer, most notably with Nirvana, PJ Harvey and The Pixies, but also working with underground acts from America, Europe and Japan as disparate as The Ex, Scrawl and Zeni Geva. In the early 90s he unveiled his latest group, Shellac, another trio (with Bob Weston and Todd Trainer on bass and drums). At the time of the Jukebox the group had recorded two singles for Touch & Go. Unsurprisingly for a former journalist (mainly for the US fanzine *Forced Exposure*), Albini seemed to relish discussing the selections he disliked as much as those he enjoyed.

Bo Diddley

Mumblin' Guitar

Bo Diddley Rides Again

Pye

I can't immediately identify it, but it sounds like it's one of the Hazel Atkins wild party boogie music school.

It's Bo Diddley.

Ah. Makes perfect sense. I'm not terribly literate in old boogie music specifics, but I've always liked stuff of this kind of energy and clotty rhythm. Obviously stuff like Jon Spencer Blues Explosion would not have been possible without somebody like this laying the ground- work.

Why is Jon Spencer so popular with American underground musicians?

Well, for a while now it has been uncool to acknowledge rock 'n' roll, probably because it has so many revolting stepchildren, like the whole Bruce Springsteen bar-room school of practitioners. And hating those people is so easy that you end up hating all their forebears by association. So people who started liking music around the time of punk rock, like I did, in a bald reaction to that way of thinking, basically just ignored music like this. And that has carried over as that generation became the dominant culture in the rock music scene. I guess in a way having someone like Jon Spencer play music like that removes that affected rock star hippy appreciation of the blues and washes the bad taste out of people's mouths.

Throbbing Gristle

Hamburger Lady

DOA – Throbbing Gristle's Third Annual Report

Industrial

I'm tempted to blurt out Kraftwerk right away, but it isn't. No, this is Throbbing Gristle. This was a staple on a college radio station in Chicago called WZRD. They used to use *Hamburger Lady*, and other utterly inappropriate Industrial music, the way some stations use the chatter of teletype machines behind newsreaders. Right after I moved to Chicago in 1980 is when I started being exposed to just about every kind of music. Having grown up in Montana I didn't have a lot of exposure, and WZRD was absolutely instrumental in educating me about what was available.

It's strange how your perception of things changes over time. While I was in college I thought minimalist, unsettling electronic music like this was about the weirdest, most extreme, coolest thing you could do. But most of the people involved in the early Industrial music movement have not acquitted themselves well over time, like Cabaret Voltaire degenerated into just an absolutely tasteless disco band. The entirety of Psychic TV's output, I think, is absolutely trivial in comparison with the content and quality of Throbbing Gristle.

Steve Albini

Fugazi
23 Beats Off

In On The Kill Taker
Dischord

Again, I'm tempted to blurt out Fugazi. This is *23 Beats Off*, about a celebrity who becomes an unwitting poster child for HIV, and what I get from the subject matter of this song is that a person of some significance can lend his significance to something else, and often does so without ever knowing he's done it, as in the case of a celebrity who's HIV. Fugazi are first and foremost an outstanding live rock band. They play so much and under such diverse conditions that they could pull off an outstanding show in a mine-shaft or underwater.

Black Sabbath
Supernaut

Paranoid
Castle Communications

Is it Black Sabbath? There's a large number of seminal Chicago punk rock guitar players who absolutely worship Black Sabbath. I've always hated them. They really mean nothing to me.

What about their impact on everyone else?
There are a couple of things. One is tuning the guitar real low. That's so prevalent now that when you hear a Heavy Metal album, if it's performed in normal tuning, it sounds speeded up, as though it's a chipmunk version of a hard rock band. But they've had a lot wider influence than just the hard rock scene. They would have these folk and classical moments on their records – absolutely excruciating – and those in a way legitimised equally unendurable moments on records appearing nowadays. The entire *Unplugged* movement, I think, is directly traceable to the folk and classical moments on Led Zeppelin and Black Sabbath records. *Unplugged* to me is such a sodomising of rock music; I really can't stomach it.

011

Steve Albini

The Ex & Tom Cora
The Big Black

And The Weathermen Shrug Their Shoulders
RecRec

Is this Tom Cora? Is this with The Ex? I just saw a show Tom was playing with The Ex, and I was really impressed at how successfully he integrated his cello playing into a rock band, especially because The Ex play in such an abstract manner to begin with. Their songs don't necessarily have a structure where it would allow him to write a part to fit into the song; he actually has to start thinking like them and playing in their spaces.

I've always been a huge fan of The Ex, I think again more as a live band and cultural experience than a recording band, but I think they represent the absolute giddy enthusiasm for music and completely unrestricted aesthetic that most punk rock bands were hoping would be the development after the punk rock era.

ARTIST
Naked City

TITLE
Perfume Of A Critic's Burning Flesh

SOURCE
Torture Garden

LABEL
Elektra Nonesuch

Sounds like it could be either The Boredoms or a Japanese band that loves The Boredoms.

Nearly. It's Naked City with John Zorn and [The Boredoms'] Yamatsuka Eye.

Oh. John Zorn's kind of an interesting character in that he's managed to make a career for himself by assembling groups of outstanding musicians and blowing a duck call over them, and taking a royalty off the record sales. I have to say it's a pretty unique way to earn a living. I can't say I have that much respect for something that at its core seems parasitic, but he does assemble interesting arrangements of people.

One of the things I've thought about the way John Zorn operates is that it is impossible to believe fully in something that changes constantly. It is impossible for me to believe that he is absolutely committed to any of these aesthetics that he seems so comfortable hopping between. It's conceivable that someone could have that broad and that deep an emotional foundation, but I've never met anyone like that.

Zorn could be considered an outgrowth of that enforced eclecticism and self-conscious multiculturalism that I think has dragged an awful lot of musicians down. I can't help but think if he would form a three-piece that would develop its own aesthetic instead of trying to pirate them from other people, that he could make music of substance and quality that would endure. But instead it seems like he's more of a middle-management type where what he does is direct underlings and exploit their abilities. I have trouble appreciating that as a way of working.

ARTIST
Band Of Susans

TITLE
It's Locked Away

SOURCE
Love Agenda

LABEL
Blast First

Band Of Susans? I think Robert Poss, the guitar player and lynchpin, is an enormously underrated guitar theorist. A lot of his approaches to the density of guitar are completely overlooked in any discussion about guitar. There's a lot of people who use guitars in a droning fashion, but the way he structures the song around a drone instead of finding a drone to fit into the song, I think, is wholly unique. And these days, in the studio, every band has layer upon layer of guitar playing identical parts. But in Band Of Susans, formally there are three or four parts that are playing; they're not embellishments on the song, they are fundamental parts of the composition.

ARTIST
The Raincoats

TITLE
Shouting Out Loud

SOURCE
Odyshape

LABEL
Rough Trade

Is this Ut?

Nearly. Earlier.

Raincoats? There was a flash of recognition; I was going to say Raincoats but then I thought: no, he wouldn't be playing *me* The Raincoats, he'd be playing Kurt Cobain The Raincoats. I think it's obvious that this band laid the groundwork for so many other bands, like The Sugarcubes. I mean, people always talk about the importance of them being women in the punk or rock scene. I think that's trivial; the music they were making is so singular and unique that they opened a lot of creative avenues for everybody.

Which male groups have assimilated The Raincoats?

Men that have made music that has been influenced by this stuff? Oh, well . . . I have, for example. There's a whole new school of what I would call low-key rock bands in America, playing fairly intricate, nerdy, largely instrumental music. I don't think it would be unfair to lump bands like Slint in with the cultural stepchildren of The Raincoats. In terms of the sparseness, the brittle quality, there's a tenuous nature to the rhythm so you're never really certain if they've started playing the song yet. It's as though this piece is an introduction to something else.

ARTIST
The Beatles

TITLE
Helter Skelter

SOURCE
The White Album

LABEL
Parlophone

Steve Albini

Is this in fact The Beatles doing their *Helter Skelter*? For The Beatles, I would have to say that this is OK. If I were listening to this in the abstract, I would say, yeah, this is an all right song. I don't own any Beatles records, they never meant a thing to me. I really have almost no appreciation for hippy music, except for certain bits of Neil Young. If The Beatles over the course of, what, seven or eight albums, managed to produce that one good song, I really don't know that the rest of the trouble was worth it. But that kicks ass more than the Black Sabbath you played earlier.

ARTIST
The Sex Pistols

TITLE
Holidays In The Sun

SOURCE
Never Mind The Bollocks

LABEL
Virgin

I have to say that this record is one of the first punk rock records that had an impressive sound, that wasn't just thematically impressive. I really like the sound of this record; it was a benchmark for how a rock record could be powerful and idiosyncratic at the same time. I probably haven't listened to this in ten years; I don't think anyone has. This is one of the few records I would actively associate with a period in my life: yes, this is when I was a teenager and punk rock happened, when I started buying records, listening to music, smoking pot, fucking women, all the things you start to do at a certain time. But even now I can appreciate it as a great rock song and as an outstanding recording.

ARTIST
Nirvana

TITLE
Smells Like Teen Spirit

SOURCE
Nevermind

LABEL
Geffen

[The tape chews up on the first attempt at playback] Actually it sounds better with the tape warble. This song, of course, was totally unavoidable. I'd never listened to this entire album until very shortly before I was slated to work with them, and I remain unimpressed. [Albini produced *In Utero*, the 1993 follow-up to the multi-platinum *Nevermind*]

This song means nothing to me, other than there was a period of about nine months when you couldn't go to a public place without being sure of hearing it. It's a catchy pop song produced in a style that was just waiting to explode. They're the archetype Grunge band. That style was sitting there waiting, ripe and pregnant, to give birth to a new era of MTV. I don't begrudge them their success in the slightest.

014

Steve Albini

Jak Kilby

He will only admit to it jokingly, but singer, bassist, composer and multi-instrumentalist Jack Bruce is a rock 'n' roll legend. He first came to attention in 1962 when he joined Alexis Korner's Blues Inc, quickly becoming an integral part of the 60s British R&B scene in groups led by Graham Bond, John Mayall and Manfred Mann, among others. But it was Cream, the trio he formed with Eric Clapton and Ginger Baker, that really propelled him into the stratosphere. In their three years together the trio (reportedly) sold 30 million records. Cream split partly because Bruce wanted to return more to his jazz and blues roots. Since 1969, he has explored these and other paths, including rock, Latin and classical, in a wide variety of settings, and worked with Tony Williams, Carla Bley and Kip Hanrahan among many others.

Joni Mitchell with Jaco Pastorius and Charles Mingus

Mingus

Asylum

The Dry Cleaner From Des Moines

It's Jaco. Joni Mitchell. Is it a James Moody song? Oh, it's the *Mingus* album. Charles is definitely the biggest influence on me as a musician, partly because he was a bass player, but also because he was a composer bass player. He was a very early fusion musician if you like, because he fused country blues to jazz, and all of those things have stayed with me. The very first person I listened to was Percy Heath. When I was about 11 or 12 my father took me to see The Modern Jazz Quartet at the St Andrew's Hall in Glasgow and even though I was sitting in the back row, Percy just had this fabulous tone and that turned me on to want to play the bass. Then I listened to Scott La Faro, Charlie Haden, Ray Brown, of course – the list is endless – Oscar Pettiford, Leroy Vinnegar, Jimmy Blanton. But when I became aware of Mingus it changed my whole life. It was his total approach as a band leader and a bass player and a composer that appealed to me, and really touched me.

And Jaco?

Jaco was a fabulous player, and he certainly made his mark on the bass, but he was a very tormented person. I spent a night playing with him in a little club in New York shortly before he died, and half way through the jam he just sort of said me, 'Oh, you've got to come with me,' and I went outside with him and he just ran away. He just literally sprinted down the block and around the corner and I never saw him again – ever. At the end of his life he seemed to be going in all directions at once: he was kind of up for a second, then really down. There was no calmness there at all. I can certainly relate to it, but it's very tragic that he didn't hang around any longer.

Lightnin' Hopkins

Last Night Blues

Prestige/Bluesville

Last Night Blues

Should I know who this is? It sounds like Little Walter on harmonica, but it isn't him. Is it Sonny Terry? [l   ] But it's not Brownie McGhee.
No, you'll have to tell me.

It's Lightnin' Hopkins.

Oh God, yeah, but I don't know this at all. I consider myself lucky for recognising Sonny Terry. I wouldn't claim to be anything like an authority on blues music, but Lightnin' Hopkins – you can't really say anything about liking him or not; he just is. Any slight knowledge I have of the real blues, the country blues, was gained through Eric. I knew about Muddy Waters and Howlin' Wolf, but Eric introduced me to people like Robert Johnson and Hopkins and Skip

James. I think it's the reality of it that I liked. It's the link with Africa: you could imagine that music almost unchanged played in West Africa a couple of hundred years ago. It's like a little hint back to where we all come from, because no matter what colour we are, we all come from there. It's like a race memory, something that echoes in our souls, that exists in all music – like a common language. It has to be the basis of the music I play – that search for the common thing, that something that cries out in the music. God, that's a bit philosophical. Let's move on before I get any worse.

ARTIST
Led Zeppelin

TITLE
Custard Pie

SOURCE
Physical Graffiti
LABEL
SwanSong

Pah. Obviously I should know this. It's not Led Zeppelin, is it? Why are you playing me session musicians?

Do you want to listen to any more?
No. Oh, I'm only joking, but I never listened to them to be quite honest – it just didn't interest me. Funny enough I got asked to join that band. But I didn't – I don't know whether you noticed. I was more interested in the jazz rock fusion thing, especially with Tony [Williams]. I'm not putting them down as musicians, and the lads have done well and everything, and it's not jealousy, but it's just the fact that their audience was created by us lot [Cream] and Jimi [Hendrix], and we threw it away. I don't envy what happened to them. I've been through the rock 'n' roll madness as much as I really want to. That was part of the reason why Cream came to an end: when it got really big, I soon stopped being interested in it, I thought it had got out of hand, so I went deliberately in the opposite direction and played small jazz clubs. But Robert Plant – what was it that [Cream lyricist] Pete Brown said about him? Oh yes: he uses the wrong kind of fertiliser.

Jack Bruce

ARTIST
John Coltrane

TITLE
Mr PC

SOURCE
Giant Steps
LABEL
Atlantic

Coltrane. What can I say?

Do you want to listen to this more?
Yeah. It's Paul Chambers on bass, isn't it? Again a tragic much-too-short life. He was a wonderful player, but the thing about him was that he was so influenced by Coltrane and the approach he had to impro- vising. I love great bass soloists, but that wasn't something I ever tried to emulate. I was more attracted to people like Mingus or Charlie Haden – the grooving approach as opposed to tremendous technique and soloing. To me the bass has always been more of a functional instrument – a catalyst really. But I always, obviously, loved Coltrane's playing. It's amazing to listen to him now: Coltrane changed the world for tenor players and his sound has become so much part of the language. Miles made some criticisms of Coltrane in his book [Miles's autobiography], but I think Miles didn't like him because he didn't dress sharply enough. It was the same with Tony and Larry [Young]. Miles would tell his bands where to buy clothes – it

was a store called Parachute in New York – but, of course, Miles wouldn't buy his clothes there – he went somewhere better.

Do you think it's overstating the case to say Coltrane's music has a spiritual dimension to it?

No, I think we all get that from Coltrane – that's what it's all about. And that's the great thing about jazz or blues. It's that link to what we are and where we come from. I don't know if I would put it any higher than that, otherwise it gets difficult to talk about. But certainly it's something that strikes a chord. And that incredible *Ascension* album he did towards the end, which was put down, but I love that. Although it's maybe a little more difficult to listen to, it's still very happening. *Very* happening.

ARTIST
Jah Wobble

TITLE
Visions Of You

SOURCE
Rising Above Bedlam
LABEL
East West

I've definitely no idea who this is. It's not Donovan. That's a joke. . .

It's Jah Wobble.

I actually should have recognised that old-fashioned bass sound, yeah. I know of him, and I've heard a couple of things by him, but he's not somebody I know much about. And it's Shinehead on vocals, isn't it? I thought it might be. It's quite interesting really. I would have to listen to it more I guess . . . erm . . . but it's not really my kind of thing.

Let me play you another track. [*Soledad*]

It's sort of pleasant, but to me there's not a lot to listen to. It just sounds like backbeats with reverb. It's almost New Agey, background stuff, which I have problems with, I have to say. It's even like a lot of the straight music that they're pushing at the moment, like [John] Tavener. I went to see his new opera the other day and it was kind of hypnotic, but I kept waiting for the music to happen. I like great rhythms and great melodies and shattering chords and Stravinsky and Messiaen – stuff that grabs you. Messiaen's music just has big chunks of sound – I love that – and it seems to have this very deep meaning in the way that Coltrane's music does. It's not like Beethoven where you get a theme and then 20 minutes of twiddly bits. I'm not trying to be controversial, but Beethoven only knew three chords as well. I haven't heard this whole record, obviously, but it has that feeling of mood music. And although there's a place for it, I would say it's probably the elevator.

ARTIST
Bootsy Collins

TITLE
Jungle Bass

SOURCE
Jungle Bass EP
LABEL
Island

I don't know.

What if I was to say Parliament/Funkadelic?

Oh God, I wish I'd said it now. It's Bootsy Collins. Again I've got links with Bootsy because I know George [Clinton] quite well and Bernie Worrell. Bootsy's great if only because his basses are better looking than anyone else's. He has that star-shaped one, remember? I like all this stuff, I mean I love it actually. There are probably better players than Bootsy technically, but he's solidly in the tradition of Larry Graham who really invented the slapping bass I guess. There's a lot of humour in that whole area. That particular track didn't grab me, but this is the funk . . . the real funk.

ARTIST

Jacqueline Du Pré

TITLE

Elgar's Cello Concerto in E Minor

SOURCE

Elgar's Cello Concerto in E Minor

LABEL

EMI Classics

I know this. Give me a while. It's Jacqueline Du Pré – the Elgar. I've got chills – it's the sound, the tone. She had the most sublime sound. Tragedy. [Long pause] Yeah. It's the real funk. If you want to talk about spirituality, then it's right here in the same way it is with Coltrane. It's just a different way of approaching and achieving it. This must be the ultimate recorded performance of this piece and she very much made it her own. I was in love with her in the 60s, and followed her career, because I can't think of anyone that I know – even Casals and Fournier – with a more appealing cello sound, or more moving. I'm glad that recording exists.

You seem genuinely moved listening to this piece.
Yes. Initially by the sound, but then by her life. Although she was very brave and an inspiration to everyone, I still feel a loss.

ARTIST

Blind Idiot God

TITLE

Stravinsky/Blast Off

SOURCE

Blind Idiot God

LABEL

SST

I've never heard of Blind Idiot God.

Although you might not think so, there's a classical link with the last piece: this track's called _Stravinsky/Blast Off_.
[Laughing] Erm, yes . . . Stravinsky might have liked it, I don't know. I've nothing to say about it.

But you like the guitar trio format?
Yeah. The first jazz group I really liked was Ornette Coleman's trio, and the first jazz things I was involved in was just saxophone, bass and drums. So I keep returning to trios because there's a lot of freedom there – it tends to be more linear than harmonic which I like, and it gives you a lot of space to play. I'd have to listen to the whole thing, but it seemed deliberately undisciplined, which is fine.

Cream were quite noisy at times weren't they?
Yeah, very noisy. But if you listen to the records there was also a lot of delicate playing. Ginger can be a very sensitive, filigree, melodic player. There was a certain amount of crashing guitars, but there was also dynamics. Good name though – Blind Idiot God.

Jack Bruce

ARTIST
Jimi Hendrix

TITLE
Come On (Part 1)

SOURCE
Electric Ladyland

LABEL
Polydor

Well, what can I say? We all know who that was. Great. He was a great guy and I wish he was around now. Around the time of his death we were planning a band with Tony [Williams] and myself, and I think it would have been pretty great if it had happened. Like all creative people he was always developing, but at the end of his life he was up against a brick wall. He seemed to want to go towards playing with people more on his own level. I mean that with all the respect in the world to the people he played with, but they were very much background players. Jimi opened up the possibilities of the electric guitar, but he was raw, wasn't he? A lot of things you've played have this spirituality in common – this depth and reality, whether it's Jacqueline Du Pré or Jimi Hendrix. They tap into something that is almost beyond human music. There are too many people in my musical life who I miss because they are no longer here. And Jimi is certainly one of them.

Jack Bruce

Iris Garrelfs

021 >

Composer Gavin Bryars was born in Goole, Yorkshire in 1943. In the 60s he played double bass in a Sheffield-based jazz trio with Derek Bailey and Tony Oxley – an association which developed into the improvising trio Josef Holbrooke. He has spent many years concurrently composing and lecturing. His work has always been closely linked with conceptual art and has drawn on sources as diverse as football and pataphysics. One of Bryars's most notorious side-projects was the formation in 1970 of The Portsmouth Sinfonia, an orchestra of musical amateurs. His breakthrough came when he recorded *The Sinking Of The Titanic* and *Jesus' Blood Never Failed Me Yet* for Brian Eno's Obscure label in 1975. A 1992 re-recording of *Jesus' Blood* featured Tom Waits and was released on Philip Glass's Point label. Since his 1984 opera *Medea*, directed by Robert Wilson, Bryars has tended towards more ambitious, richly textured works. In recent years he has written pieces for guitarist Bill Frisell, saxophonist Evan Parker, The Hilliard Ensemble, The Arditti and Balanescu Quartets and cellist Julian Lloyd Webber.

ARTIST	SOURCE
Tom Waits	**Blue Valentine**
TITLE	LABEL
	WEA

Somewhere

Well, so far it's *Somewhere There's A Place For Us* from *West Side Story*. . . Ah, it's Tom Waits. A sensational version. There's one phrase where he sounds like Louis Armstrong, a little twist in his voice. Tom Waits is a genius.

What do you particularly like about this version of the song?

I like the song in any case. It must have been the early 60s, I suppose, when I first saw it [*West Side Story*]. The guy who sang it in the original, Richard Beymer, is in *Twin Peaks*; he plays the part of the guy who owns the store and the Great Northern Hotel [Ben Horne].

It's supposed to be a fairly poignant moment in the film, fairly sad and a kind of pivotal thing and there's that sort of quality of a blues singer doing it, through Tom. And although he's singing in a very relaxed way – it's probably one of his most relaxed performances – there's still that edge, that intensity and that poignancy in his voice. Tom is just a sensational singer and a great composer too.

How did you come to use him on the re-recording of *Jesus' Blood Never Failed Me Yet*?

In a roundabout way. Tom first got in touch with me in the 80s when he was touring, to see if he could get a copy of [the original recording of] *Jesus' Blood* on Obscure, because he'd lost his copy and he said it was his favourite record – which is actually high praise.

When I came to [re]do it, I think Philip Glass thought I was going to do it the length of the original, which was 25 minutes. I said, 'No, I want to do a whole CD of it.' What I had to do in making that was to have a much richer scenario, so the music goes through more phases. The way this whole piece was mapped out, everything that we'd had throughout the whole piece was accompanying the old man's pre-recorded voice; no one actually plays the tune. [*Jesus' Blood* features a tape of a tramp singing the title hymn.] It struck me that maybe at some point somebody should join in. I got in touch with Tom and he agreed to do it.

We made a promotional video and he tells this story about when he first heard it. It was his wife's birthday and the party was over and people were gone – empty champagne bottles and balloons and streamers lying about – and they had the radio playing. The piece started to play and he said, 'Holy shit, what's that?' They held hands and he was crying the whole way through. So when he sang it, it was really personal to him. And his performance of it, that was one of the great musical moments for me, being in the studio with him. He insisted that he'd just do it with me, the engineer and nobody else.

ARTIST	SOURCE
Evan Parker	**50th Birthday Concert**
TITLE	LABEL
	Leo

Not Backwards, As In Doubt

I'll probably be miles out here, it doesn't sound quite right to me, but it sounds like the Evan Parker trio [with] Barry Guy and Tony Oxley. But the sax playing sometimes doesn't sound like Evan – the early part when he was playing slightly more rhapsodically. I prefer Evan playing solo concerts and then he's playing more wall-of-sound stuff. Now I recognise it, the Coltrane tone influence; Evan always was an enormously knowledgeable Coltrane freak.

I lived next door to him. We each had a one room flat – he had his wife and son in there as well – on the top floor of this hovel in Kilburn. I heard him practising the sax all day, or playing John Coltrane records. And it was the time that I developed a kind of hatred of jazz and we had a very interesting love–hate relationship.

Is free improvisation a style of music that you'll be likely to play again, or have your other styles taken precedence?

They have really. But it nearly happened fairly recently. I was touring in Japan with my ensemble in September, and I got a message from a guy in Los Angeles that Derek [Bailey] and Tony Oxley were playing a duo set in Santa Monica and would I be prepared to fly from Tokyo to Los Angeles and play a couple of sessions with them to reform this trio [Josef Holbrooke], which hadn't played for 29 years. It was set up with a radio broadcast and everything, but I was taken ill in Tokyo and had to be flown back to England so I had to get in touch to cancel. And coincidentally, the same day Derek phoned in to cancel as he was ill in England, so it all fell apart. In principle I don't object to doing it, it's not what I'd do naturally by choice, but if it was set up I wouldn't say no. I seldom say no to anything.

ARTIST
Arvo Pärt

SOURCE
Miserere

LABEL
ECM

TITLE
Extract from Miserere

It's by Arvo but I don't recognise it.

It's an extract from *Miserere*.

I thought it might be when I heard the soprano. I thought it sounded like Sarah Leonard. I've got the recording but it's one I haven't listened to very much. I'd forgotten the percussion; that's what threw me.

It's interesting that Pärt, who's thought of as being quite solemn and austere, used electric guitar and bass on this piece.

I remember David James from The Hilliard Ensemble said he was slightly nervous when he heard that the instrumentation included electric guitar, but it's very cleverly blended in. It becomes like another orchestral instrument.

Arvo is obviously a very spiritual man and his music can sound rather austere – it can also sound very sensual sometimes. One of the reasons that he probably did this is he has a fantastic ear. He's got a very good sense of orchestration, a very good sense of how to get effects. I think that comes from the years he worked as a sound engineer on the radio in Tallinn. It was just his imagination saying, 'That is what I should do.' And his imagination is usually pretty damn accurate.

I love Arvo as a person. When his music was first heard in the West, the major impact was the ECM recording of *Fratres*, and that was just a revelation:

everyone had to re-evaluate how something that sounded almost ancient could be contemporary. Arvo is someone with modern ears and a refreshing sense of direction.

Do you think that the 'Holy Minimalist' tag that is put on Pärt, Tavener and Górecki, is a true reflection of some spiritual yearning by both composers and public, or is it simply a marketing exercise?

In some American record stores they have a bin which is labelled 'Faith Minimalism'. That's where you get those guys. A couple of times I've almost been put into that, with some of the things I've done with The Hilliard Ensemble. But when people realise I'm not a Christian, not even remotely, then I get dropped into a different bin.

'Atheist Minimalism'?

Well, it's more of a mixture of agnosticism and Buddhism really, so I'm kind of neutral. I don't deny that people have spiritual experiences and that music can be part of that, but I don't try and milk it. I think that sometimes there are some areas of musical composition where it can be slightly opportunist to write in that way: it almost became a vogue. [But] Arvo is the real thing. He's the genuine article.

ARTIST

The Beatles

TITLE

Goodnight

SOURCE

The White Album

LABEL

Parlophone

[Immediately] Oh, it's *Time To Say Goodnight*. Is it Ringo singing? It's a beautiful track, a great arrangement. That French horn there is fantastic. Is it the end of *The White Album*? Lovely album. When [producer Hal Willner] did the Walt Disney album *Stay Awake*, they finished with Ringo singing, in a similar arrangement to this, *When You Wish Upon A Star*. A very similar kind of quality. It's a nice irony: Ringo is probably the one person out of the four you wouldn't expect to be singing with a string orchestra. I think it's a stroke of genius on this one. He's not one of the greatest singers in the world, but for this he's perfect. It's a simple honesty. He's not pretending to be a trained singer, but he doesn't send himself up by singing like a duffer. This is the best he can do. It's almost like someone singing hymns at school – rather than taking the piss out of it, you do the best you can.

Were you a Beatles fan?

It's not something I particularly listen to now, but in 68/69 I listened to a lot of Beatles, because in 68 I was living in America. I remember I was very fond of *Lady Madonna* which came out over there. I did get a lot of The Beatles' albums: *Magical Mystery Tour*, *Abbey Road*, *Sergeant Pepper*, *The White Album*. I just love the invention. And I suppose a lot of that was down to the skill of George Martin and the whole team of arrangers and the people putting the package together, as much as The Beatles themselves.

My one encounter, not with The Beatles, but with John Lennon and Yoko Ono, was at a benefit concert which was given in a gallery in Piccadilly in the autumn of 68. It was in support of a lot of art students who were under pressure – Hornsey and Guildford and all that kind of thing. [Pianist] John Tilbury and I did this live electronics thing together, and immediately afterwards was John Lennon and Yoko Ono. And he used my mic. So I passed the microphone to John Lennon and he said, 'Thanks, wack.' Very sweet That's my only personal connection with The Beatles.

If this information gets out, there will be people coming round here knocking on the door.

[Laughs] Can I touch the hand that touched the microphone that was passed to John Lennon?

ARTIST	SOURCE
## John Zorn	**Spillane**
	LABEL
TITLE	Elektra Nonesuch
## Spillane	

[After listening intently for over five minutes] I'm slightly baffled by this one, I must admit. It struck me it could be one of about five different people, and all of them probably wrong. The ones I came up with were Sun Ra, Frank Zappa, Bill Frisell, Van Dyke Parks, and that's about it. It's that kind of heterogeneous mix of things which gratuitously clicks into another style. The spoken voice sounded very much like the way that Frisell used spoken voice on the Disney album. It's that editing from one style to another that you find in all those people, but it's probably none of them.

Frisell plays on it. It's by John Zorn.

Well, I thought about John Zorn but thought it was too long for John Zorn. The Zorn I know is like snapshots. Well, of course, it is snapshots, but they're all strung together. Up to the point where I started talking I was quite interested in it. Then I thought this is going to go on for quite a while and it's probably lost its way a little bit.

What do you think of Zorn's jump-cut editing style?

I think it's fine, I enjoy it. It's not something I would do myself. In fact Zorn works better on record than live. I remember seeing him play with Bill and also with Fred Frith and Joey Baron and the set was really rather frustrating because they'd play a 40 second number, stop, then look around for the parts for the next thing and wonder what they would play next. They had about two minutes between each piece and then a 30 second thrash, and it was just rather chaotic. But on record it works fine.

ARTIST	SOURCE
## Philip Glass	**Einstein On The Beach**
	LABEL
TITLE	Sony Masterworks
## Bed	

It sounds like something of Philip Glass, but I don't recognise it.

It's a part of *Einstein On The Beach*.

It was the progression which reminded me of *Einstein*, but I didn't recognise this section. I've probably never heard *Einstein* all the way through. Some parts of *Einstein* I think are really stunning. I think it is essentially a [Robert] Wilson theatre piece, his work rather than Philip's. Obviously Philip's music is what people know now, but it comes about through Bob Wilson's ideas. Philip supported them with the music, and it's now been listed as one of Philip's major operas when in fact it was a collaborative piece.

There are several text things in there that I think are really stunning, very funny, and really interesting writing. I never saw it live and I've only heard extracts of the music. When Philip played extracts in concert it was never that one, more the high octane, fast, exciting things. And the things that I like from the recording, which I tend to zap to, are the choral ones, the ensemble plus choral voices and spoken voice.

Minimalism seems to be broadening out as a catch-all category for anything that isn't over-ornate. And anything that uses repetition, as your work can do, gets put in with it too. Isn't it a redundant categorisation now?

It's become useful for selling a concert or selling an album. But for me, Minimalism was a term that Michael Nyman was one of the first people to start using in terms of music, because it was a term in fine art before that. It basically meant a kind of music which was either repetitive or single-image music, where you had a very limited amount of materials which you permutated in different ways.

Jim Tenney, a composer who lives in Canada, thought that the only true Minimalism was LaMonte Young's undifferentiated drones. He tends to refer to what most people call Minimalism as 'pulse-pattern music', which is quite an accurate description. Not quite good enough for journalism, pulse-pattern – awkward to say as well. But Minimalism was really a historical period from 66–76, and after that those composers – Steve Reich, Philip Glass, LaMonte Young, Terry Riley – all started to do different things. With *Einstein On The Beach*, Philip started to work with theatre. Steve Reich started to think about orchestration and harmonies and things like that, which take you in another dimension from Minimalism. Terry Riley started to work with string quartets.

Minimalism really became something you could use as a technique, one of the resources you could use in a piece, whereas previously it was a really hard-nosed aesthetic. So it actually has disappeared completely as a form of music, unless people are doing the old-time Minimalist stuff. What Philip writes now I'd hardly call Minimalist.

Michael Nyman has gone on record as saying that he is sick and tired of being labelled a Minimalist.

Well, if people called me Minimalist I'd react in the same way as if someone called me a thick Yorkshire git – it's reasonably accurate but not completely true.

ARTIST
Bearded Seals

TITLE
Environmental recording

SOURCE
Ocean Of Sound
LABEL
Virgin

I don't know what it is, but it sounds like one of those old rudimentary electronic kind of things. It sounds rather dated, from a particular era. It sounds like it's from the 60s.

It's actually an underwater recording of bearded seals.

Oh, right! I thought about whales, it had that sort of quality. The whales I'd know, but the seals I didn't recognise. It sounded to me like people playing with early electronic music but really not being composers. In fact they're not composers, which is quite reassuring. It's very sweet actually, it's nice. Do you know the lyrics?

It's from a compilation album put together by David Toop as a companion to his book *Ocean of Sound*.

Well, that figures. I remember years ago, 74, when I was in San Diego, people in between the physics and music departments were trying to set up doing free improvisation with dolphins. They'd analyse the sound of dolphins and then synthesise it and play it back and play with them. They'd put speakers in the ocean and play with the dolphins. The dolphins would sing with them and they'd do improvisations.

When I was in Los Angeles last week, there was a piece in the paper saying that they'd actually had to stop some sonic experiments in one of the bays north of Los Angeles because three large humpbacked whales were found dead in the bay. They were wondering if it had anything to do with the sound experiments; long-distance sound projection at very high decibels under the ocean. It could well have killed them.

Sound can be dangerous.

Especially underwater as it's actually much more efficient under there – travels four times the distance.

Is it true that you did some underwater recordings for *Sinking Of The Titanic*?

They weren't recorded underwater. What we did was to simulate it by working in a physics laboratory, simulating the kind of sounds which might have happened if the string players were playing underwater. But in fact they can't play underwater so we couldn't do that. The depth of water we needed, several miles in the North Atlantic, the speakers wouldn't have stood the pressure. So we had to calculate what would happen and then try and do it in terms of all sorts of things like equalisation, delays, all sorts of things like that.

We did the first live recording of *Sinking Of The Titanic* in a disused water tower that had a particularly interesting acoustic ambience. And then we did a performance just after that in a swimming bath in Brussels. We actually played on a raft on the water. I enjoy playing with the physical nature of the environment you're playing in and doing things which relate to that, the acoustic space you're working in.

ARTIST
Howard Skempton

TITLE
Extract from Lento

SOURCE
Lento

LABEL
NMC

I actually don't know it. It could be Górecki and could equally be Michael Nyman or Philip Glass.

It's by an English composer, a contemporary of yours.

Is it Tavener? It's not me. It's not Howard Skempton, is it? That's not *Lento*, though, is it? Gosh. Howard is one of those composers, one of my contemporaries from that same era of experimental music from the late 60s, early 70s, who's probably stayed closer to that territory than most. It's almost like a statement of faith, like a very simple way of permutating small amounts of material. It's a form of Minimalism but not in the way that we understand repetitive music – it's actually working within a miniature framework and turning things round from different perspectives.

Skempton was a member of The Scratch Orchestra, which had parallels with The Portsmouth Sinfonia: what was your intention by forming The Sinfonia?

There was no intention behind it at all. It originally started out one sunny May day in Portsmouth. We started to have a kind of Opportunity Knocks concert in the quadrangle of the art college where I was teaching. All sorts of people put together different kinds of acts, people telling jokes, jugglers, and we had this idea to form a symphony orchestra. There were only 13 of us and most people couldn't play the instruments, but we had to play something that would be recognised, no matter how badly we played it. Occasionally, if someone joined the orchestra because they wanted a good laugh, we'd kick them out, because everyone was doing their best. It was the gap between what they were achieving and what they were trying to do which became funny.

Since their knowledge of music didn't come from having studied music history, but rather what they'd heard on television, adverts and so on, we had to choose things which would be known to all of us. And so we came up with the *William Tell Overture*, because that was the *Lone Ranger* theme.

We did this as a one-off at first, but afterwards we did a tape of that piece and did one of those little floppy records which we mailed out to people all over the world who we particularly admired, like Mao Tse-Tung, [footballer] Rodney Marsh, Leonard Bernstein. Bernstein liked it, but we didn't get a reply back from Pierre Boulez.

In 73 we made our first record which Brian Eno produced – he played with us from time to time – and that was recorded in a school hall in Wimbledon. And then we did a second album which was a live album at the Albert Hall. There were some people who came thinking they were going to hear the real thing, but there were only three people who walked out from an audience of more than 2000. Then we did another album of rock classics because The London Symphony Orchestra had done an album of rock classics. This was the worst orchestra in the world, and we thought there shouldn't be a worse orchestra in the world than us, so we did an album of Beach Boys and Beatles medleys and things like that.

ARTIST
Bill Evans Trio

TITLE
Jade Visions

SOURCE
Sunday At The Village Vanguard
LABEL
Riverside

[Immediately] It's *Jade Visions*, Scott LaFaro. It's the Vanguard album. It's certainly the last thing they recorded, and may well be the last thing they played together, as [bass player] LaFaro was killed about two weeks later.

It's interesting because it's LaFaro's own composition and it's in 9/8, but it's in an unusual 9/8 time and there's two versions of it. There's one which is on that label, and a second take was also recorded. In this version, LaFaro makes a mistake in his own piece and loses a beat and Evans corrects him. It's quite touching to find someone who's undoubtedly the greatest jazz bass player of all time making a mistake in his own composition: you suddenly think, 'Thank God he is human.'

This trio for me was what ultimately got me into music full time. I realised this was what I wanted to do initially, but then I moved away from it. This track and *My Foolish Heart*, the ballad, were what I loved most. A lot of bass players after LaFaro, in order to go further, concentrated on his high, fast work, without realising that the supremely accurate choice of the right note – very solid, very in tune, really nice full sound – is what the band needs.

Charlie Haden was telling me that Scott LaFaro's bass, which was damaged in the car-crash which killed him, had turned up somewhere in a bass repairer's shop in New Jersey not long ago. Charlie used to share a flat with Scott LaFaro for a time. It's quite nice working and getting to know people who have these connections. In fact a really tenuous connection is that [composer] John Adams told me – when I first started being friends and visiting John in California in the 70s – that his first wife's sister had been Scott LaFaro's girlfriend. Not bad is it? [Laughs] Maybe Scott LaFaro was killed on his way to visit John Adams's first wife's sister. Coo, that's music history, isn't it?

029

Gavin Bryars

Gillian Campbell

031 >

Born in 1936 in Los Angeles, Harold Budd grew up in the Mojave desert town of Victorville. A meeting with Albert Ayler in the army resulted in a spell as Ayler's drummer. In the early 60s he studied composition and acoustics and produced a number of avant garde and Minimalist pieces through to 1971, including *Lino*, a 24 hour marathon for solo gong. This period was overlapped by a spell of teaching at California Institute for the Arts between 1970–76. Budd then abandoned the avant garde with the assessment, 'I'd minimalised myself out of a career.' He resurfaced in 1972 with the piece *Madrigals Of The Rose Angel*, the score of which included a topless female chorus, concentrating instead on 'existential prettiness'. A version of the piece appeared on *The Pavilion Of Dreams* in 1978, released on Eno's Obscure label and featuring an ensemble that included Eno, Gavin Bryars, Michael Nyman and saxophonist Marion Brown. In terms of recorded output, Budd came into his stride in the early 80s releasing a number of solo albums that started with *The Serpent (In Quicksilver)* in 1981, as well as collaborations with Eno (again), The Cocteau Twins, XTC's Andy Partridge, Bill Nelson and Hector Zazou. Budd's interest in spoken word yielded *By The Dawn's Early Light* (1991), which featured his own texts, and *Walk Into My Voice* (1996), on which he read pieces by a selection of Beat poets.

ARTIST
Sunny Murray Duo featuring Charles Gayle

SOURCE
Illuminators

LABEL
Audible Hiss

TITLE
Truth Queen

[Referring to the piano player] Wow, that's really good. Is it Paul Bley?

No, it's Charles Gayle.

If I could play jazz, this is the way I think I would play and sound. I like that idea a lot, where there are no pyrotechnics and no display of gratuitous technique and simply do the right notes at the right time. This is really good. I couldn't possibly pick out who the drummer is.

It's Sunny Murray.

Is it really? Yeah, he's almost the person who invented the way of doing this, so of course I would miss it! This is really an extraordinarily interesting piece. Also, if I could play jazz drums this is exactly the way I would want it to sound. He's just so damn skilful.

You did play jazz drums once, with Albert Ayler. How did that happen?

We hooked up from the out-and-out accident of being in the army together, in the same army band. I was the only one willing to take a flier at it. I thought it was outrageously wonderful music. Everyone else thought it was absolute dreck, didn't understand it at all, thought it was crazy as hell. I think we were kind of a joke, a laughing stock. But before I had gone into the army I had been exposed to Paul Bley's quintet when he had Ornette Coleman in it. And to be perfectly frank, I thought Ayler was really a spin-off from that tradition in a way. But I have to tell you my skills as a drummer were not anything to talk much about. I wanted to be Art Blakey or Kenny Clarke, but I just didn't have it.

ARTIST
Bob Wills & His Texas Playboys

SOURCE
Swing Hi! Swing Lo!

LABEL
Music Collection International/Demon

TITLE
New Spanish Two-Step

[Immediately] Wow! This must be Bob Wills. Man, oh man, I didn't expect to hear this in London. Oh God, this is lovely. Bob Wills has that funny double-string violin playing style. You just get the feeling that they went to the studio with massive hangovers and just knocked out the music.

I heard a wonderful story – I'm sure it's total bullshit – of Willie Nelson and his band before they were extraordinarily famous walking into a bar somewhere in west Texas – they were the band. Some bodyguard stops them outside and says, 'Are any of you guys carrying a gun?' Everyone says, 'No, we're not.' The bodyguard pulls a gun out and says, 'Here, you better take this then.' [Budd dissolves into laughter]

Is this the kind of music you heard when you were growing up in the Mojave desert?

Yeah, it was everywhere, the equivalent of *The Archers*, you just couldn't escape. Everybody talked like that and listened to that sort of stuff. It was an interesting phenomenon. I thought it was normal at the time, but I look back now and see that it's a sub-class or a distinct class of American who are disenfranchised, what people disparagingly call 'white trash': hard working, never successful at anything, you know. Funny times. Glad I'm not there, to be honest with you. That was a good one. Well done, man, a rush of nostalgia.

ARTIST
Allen Ginsberg

SOURCE
Holy Soul Jelly Roll: Poems And Songs 1943–1993

TITLE
Pacific High Studio Mantras

LABEL
Rhino/World Beat

[Referring to the singer] Wow, he changed chords. Whoo, dear. I presume it's LaMonte Young. No? Is it Terry [Riley]? I'd better listen a bit more, maybe. I swear it sounds like LaMonte Young sold out to a pop producer. Or a film soundtrack where they demanded from LaMonte that he changed chords occasionally.

It's Allen Ginsberg.

Oh shit, yes, of course. [Budd looks at the box set which the CD is part of] Oh my, that's lovely. This is a handsome box set. Where did you get this from?

It was released a couple of years ago. Can you guess when this track was recorded?

My guess would be. . . It would be a bad guess. I know that he was doing this thing as early as 1965, 1966. It could be from that generation, it's hard to say. Of course it would be impossible to detect a stylistic change [laughs]. This is really lovely.

I never go to concerts or clubs, never. The last time I went was about 100 miles south of LA. I went down to see Michael McLure read poetry, and there was a set by Lee Ranaldo of Sonic Youth. It was great. I thought to myself: I'm too hermetic. I don't get out enough and really hear what interesting artists are doing.

Did Ranaldo's set include spoken word elements?

It did. Mostly it was pre-recorded. I think they were analogue tapes that were just crashing into each other and then he was doing heavily processed solo guitar in front of it, but only adding to the sound, not soloing in any way. It was riveting. It was in a very staid mission town, adobe Mexican colonial-type place.

ARTIST
Morton Feldman

SOURCE
Triadic Memories

LABEL
Sub Rosa

TITLE
Extract from Triadic Memories

Beautiful piece. I haven't a clue what it is.

It was composed in 1981 and it's an extract from a 73 minute piece.

I imagine then that it would be Morton Feldman. *Triadic Memories*? Beautiful

[Budd looks at the CD] Jean-Luc Fafchamps: completely unknown pianist to me. Beautiful performance. Feldman was a sublimely beautiful artist.

Were you influenced by him?

Absolutely, yes. When I was a 'proper' American avant garde composer, I scandalously ripped him off. I was originally attracted to the notions and philosophy of John Cage. From that I spun off to Feldman, who seemed less doctrinaire and more interested in the potential of what sound can actually do to your state of mind and where you are and how you get through the world. He was responsible for some really extraordinary moments in American music. You and I could play this piece, do you know what I mean? It doesn't require the ability to play Liszt preludes. It's completely antithetical to that notion. All you need is the kind of spiritual aggressiveness to sit down and be true to what's in front of you. The hard part with a Feldman performance is the control necessary in order to continually pull it off for such a long time. So in many ways, this piece is documenting the fact that this gentleman had made the decision to do a 73 minute version of it and he did it, believing in it all the while. Not a 'gig' in other words.

ARTIST

Anonymous Javanese Musicians

TITLE

Ayun Ambing

SOURCE

Sundanese Degung Sabilulungan: Music Of West Java Vol II

LABEL

Interra

Harold Budd

It's a funny combination. It works beautifully. Gamelan and Sufi flute.

It sounds like it was recorded in a state-of-the-art studio. Some gamelan recordings I've heard feature people talking, birdsong, passing traffic. . .

I don't know if one's permitted to say this anymore, but it doesn't sound exactly 'ethnic'. It sounds like white man's magic on somebody else's language.

It's Javanese.

Yeah, it would be. This scale is called 'slendro' and it's one, three, four, five and seven in the scale. That's why it has that funny major seventh sound to it all the time. It's quite beautiful. The thing is that this music defies being captured on recording, but this music that we're listening to works perfectly. I think there may be some adjustment there for the market forces. I think this is a noseflute tune because it has a tentative breath thing at the beginning.

I'm afraid my knowledge on noseflute technique is rather scanty.

I think we are listening to one, actually. Maybe that's why they always sound so distant. It's such an appalling idea. I must say this is particularly pretty, though. Some of the pre-pop music gamelan have rhythmic cycles that force you well into the night before they run their course and you couldn't possibly document them. You could document the sounds, I guess, but you probably couldn't very accurately document the experience of having to sit through that for that long.

Once in Tokyo, my hosts asked me if there was something I particularly wanted to see. I said I wanted to see a Noh play, if it was convenient for them, and I saw the blood drain from their faces. Anyway we went, and I see what the problem was. It was three hours of absolutely nothing happening, except one guy, a narrator I guess, who's sole job was to hit a kind of hollow drum that he held and squatted on the stage. Extraordinarily beautiful costumes, almost no motion at all and an audience of about 100 people, 80 per cent of whom were quite elderly. And at moments, totally mysterious to everyone else, they would look at each other and nod in approval that it was done satisfactorily. I thought that was really charming, but it was a gruelling three hours: it really went on.

Who's the cello player? Is it anyone really famous?

ARTIST
Joe Zawinul

TITLE
The Soul Of A Village Part II

SOURCE
The Rise And Fall Of The Third Stream

LABEL
Rhino

The keyboard player's the main man.
Is this from the 1960s?

1967, but released the following year.
Well, you've got me.

It's Joe Zawinul.
Yeah, of course, makes perfect sense. Everything makes perfect sense when you know. It's great. Very strange. When you said the keyboard player is the main man, I thought it must be Joe Zawinul. But then I'd say that and you'd stand up and leave the room.

Do you like the way he uses the Fender Rhodes?
He plays it really well. It's kind of hard to find those sounds anymore, the Fender Rhodes and the [Hammond] B3. You're lucky when you run across them. It's not the same thing using a sample, and I'll tell you the reason why. It's because the key action was always anti-human on the Rhodes, you could almost never get a quiet sound. You had to hit them. It's like hammering at something in order to get a sound. As a consequence the Rhodes always sounds like itself, not because of its mechanism and all the technology, but it's so hard to get a sound from the goddamn keyboard. I think that's one of its most attractive things. Certainly it lends itself to funky blues playing. The Rhodes company should market those sounding boards that they have: the little hammers hitting those steel tubes. That's the whole point of the instrument. It's not the sound that comes out, it's *that*. Rhodes won't do it of course. I used to have a Rhodes, but with the break-up of my marriage and eventual divorce I lost a lot of things: Calvin Klein coats, Fender Rhodes piano. I could always buy another Calvin Klein, but I needed a Rhodes to make the money to buy it. Tragic!

ARTIST
John Coltrane

TITLE
Alabama

SOURCE
Live At Birdland

LABEL
Impulse!

It sounds like McCoy Tyner. That must be Coltrane. This was the last time that jazz was really magic, I think. It really took you to a place that you weren't in at the moment. You were moved out to some other place. I was originally going to say this is Pharoah Sanders, but it's obviously not.

I was saying to my son last month: can you imagine what it must be like to be a tenor sax player and continually have to confront this massive wall of Coltrane? You're always the underdog.

This is *Alabama*, from 1963.

63. What was I doing in 63? Listen to this part here. It's embarrassing to listen to music from 63 that's this fucking good. I was actually an adult then and I wasn't even close. [Laughs].

You wrote a piece for Marion Brown [*Bismillah 'Rrahmani 'Rrahmin*, included on *The Pavilion Of Dreams*] who was part of Coltrane's free jazz circle. How did that association happen?

I met Marion when he was on the road somewhere in California. I was visiting somebody and he was on the road with some academic dude and they showed up at the house for dinner or drinks or something like that. No one knew who Marion was. I did because I knew his ESP records and I was really anxious to meet him, not to collaborate or do anything of the kind, but as a fan of Marion Brown. I didn't give a rat's ass about the other guy. [Laughs]

We really got on very well and I sent him a tape of *Madrigals Of The Rose Angel*, because he asked me what sort of music I did and I stumbled; I didn't want to say topless choruses, just not the right thing to do. He wrote back immediately saying would I consider writing a piece for him? The answer was: are you serious? The answer is yes. I applied for a grant from the government when they were still giving them in those days: 73, 74, something like that. So I got six months' rent to write this piece for Marion Brown.

I was happy to do it, and I must say I had the time of my life, too. I was so passionate about the project in front of me; I think my enthusiasm was so infectious in a way that Marion fell right into it. At the time he was teaching for his living. He arranged to have the piece premiered at a concert at his university in Connecticut. God, I was just fucking thrilled. In the audience there was like Reggie Workman and Stanley Cowell, a really large, nice audience, really enthusiastic. I gave a tape of the concert to a friend of mine in California. He sent it off without my knowing to Gavin Bryars and Michael Nyman and they eventually gave it to Eno, who I didn't know anything about. Brian just called me up one day and said, 'I've just heard this tape of yours. Is this what you do? Why don't you come to London and record it?'

I have very fond memories of Marion Brown. I was an academic at the time, I was teaching at university, and he told me that it was actually possible to make a living as a serious artist in American society, but you really have to fucking work hard at it, and get started now before you're very much older, which I did.

ARTIST
Labradford

TITLE
Banco

SOURCE
A Stable Reference

LABEL
Flying Nun

Hauntingly lovely piece. I like that spoken voice that's completely unintelligible, it's just perfect. To some extent, and I'm probably way off the track, it sounds like some of those pattern pieces that Bill Nelson does every now and then.

It's actually a group from Virginia called Labradford.

I'm totally in the dark about them but this is lovely. I'm very impressed. This could go on forever. Well, they certainly have my attention. It's a great mood. It's not a threatening mood, it's not even sombre, but it's like that beautiful statue called *Religion* that's right next to Christina Rossetti's grave in Highgate Cemetery. It has a ghostly something about it that's pretty at the same time as being not quite of the real world somehow.

Do you listen to much new music?

I'm afraid I don't keep up and I feel bad about it. I feel I really should be participating more in the culture that's happening at the moment. I think it's due to inertia, and it also has something to do with the fact that, every now and again, I have to admit to myself that there are long stretches of time where I'm not really a music fan. It's certainly nothing to do with the 'product' that's available. . . For example, the chaps up in Hull who do Pork Records have sent me three of their CDs, all of which I have liked very much. They do moody dance-type rhythms and to me it seems very captivating because it's not making a big splash: its sub rosa, based on patterns and rhythms but not whacking you over the side of the face with it.

How did your collaboration with The Cocteau Twins happen?

[Guitarist] Simon Raymonde called me out of the clear blue sky one day. Actually I was warned, if that's the right word, that he was going to call. I didn't know much about them and went to a friend of mine, who was a distributor, who made up an anthology cassette, and I thought it was wonderful music. I really loved it and I was embarrassed that I didn't know who they were. They were going to cover a piece, I think it was off *The Plateaux Of Mirror* [Budd's collaboration with Eno], one of those piano-based ones. It turned out they didn't do anything of the sort. Robin [Guthrie] called me back and asked if I'd want to collaborate on a full album [i.e. *The Moon And The Melodies*].

I have to tell you though, I've always had problems with that album, and the fault is entirely mine. I didn't quite understand what was happening, I didn't have it together. They did. I thank them for putting up with my not being quite as with it as they were. It was a good lesson for me.

The other good lesson was that Robin is absolutely masterful in the studio. The way they work – which is as a tight group, but not exactly rehearsing together, putting down things and agreeing if it's good or bad, and this interplay of personalities happening – was a revelation to me because I had been such an isolated person.

Every time I work with someone else I learn something new. With Andy Partridge, for example, I learned the importance of not just taking what you can get, but taking extra time to get it even a little bit better: it's worth the effort. It was good for me because I have an in-born laissez-faire attitude about things: it's good enough and let it go.

Jon Hassell &
Bluescreen

Dressing For Pleasure

Warner Brothers

Steppin' Thru Time

I keep expecting to hear William Burroughs's voice. What on earth is this going to be? Let me think about it. This isn't from [Miles Davis's] *Tutu* is it? From that time?

It was recorded in 94.

You've got me.

It's Jon Hassell, a track from *Dressing For Pleasure*.

[Budd looks at the CD] Sonofabitch! Wouldn't you know it? I have this damn CD. That's a particularly handsome piece. It's a great sound. This is a record that should have done a lot better commercially than it did. I think it had the bad fortune to be on a big label which means that no one cared. And people who would otherwise be attracted to this language are not going to Warner Brothers to find it. . . Good one.

You worked with similar rhythms to the ones Hassell is using here on *Glyph* with Hector Zazou.

That was Hector's idea. It seemed like a really good thing to do at the time and it was very much an experiment with me: let's see if there is anything that I can bring to it that makes any sense. I think it's a little iffy, myself. I can't say that I'm going to go up against a wall for it, but you know, what's life without risk, man?

When did you last play with Hassell?

Never have. We eat dinner a lot. If we did play it would probably be the end of our friendship.

Hassell's trumpet sound is still very distinctive.

He's obviously developed some way of getting a sound that's. . . It isn't about pressing the mouthpiece tight against your teeth the way Dizzy Gillespie would, or even Miles for that matter. It's more oblique: kind of a sideways embouchure that misses a lot. It's a nice sound but it must have taken a lifetime to develop. [Budd goes to the hotel bathroom and re-emerges] Jon Hassell has a subscription to *The Wire*. When he reads that I didn't recognise him, he's never going to talk to me again.

Rob Hann

John Cale

039 >

Born in Garnant, South Wales in 1942, John Cale established himself as a piano prodigy by the age of eight, performing pieces for the BBC. He studied musicology at Goldsmith's College in London between 1960–63 under Aaron Copland, and won a Leonard Bernstein scholarship to study with Iannis Xenakis in America. Drawn to the avant garde, he collaborated with John Cage and played viola, alongside Tony Conrad, in LaMonte Young's Dream Syndicate which specialised in just-intonation drone-based music. Cale met Lou Reed at a New York party in 1963 and began a working relationship that eventually led to the formation of The Velvet Underground. After recording *White Light/White Heat* Cale left in 1968. (The group briefly reformed in 1993.) Cale released his first solo album, *Vintage Violence*, in 1970, followed a year later by *Church Of Anthrax*, an instrumental collaboration with Terry Riley. In the 70s he signed to Island Records, joining an eclectic roster that also included Nick Drake, Kevin Ayers and Brian Eno. An idiosyncratic series of solo albums followed, including *Paris 1919* (1973) and *Music For A New Society* (1982). In 1990 Cale co-wrote and performed the Andy Warhol tribute *Songs For Drella* with Lou Reed and, later the same year, *Wrong Way Up* with Eno. Cale has also made his name as a producer, working most notably with Nico, The Stooges, Patti Smith, Jonathan Richman and Happy Mondays. He has also written extensively for film, theatre and ballet, and helped curate a John Cage tribute album, *Caged/Uncaged*.

It sounds like Tony. Is it Tony?

It is Tony, with brise glace: Jim O'Rourke and David Grubbs.

Nicely done. Very difficult to do.

What are the technical difficulties in doing this kind of drone-based music?

Well, I'll give you an idea. The Morton Feldman *String Quartet* is very similar in that it has long durations. It was supposed to be premiered again at the Lincoln Centre Festival. The Kronos Quartet, who performed the premiere of it in Japan, I think, withdrew because they said it was physically too taxing to do. There are physical things that happen when you play just – intonation. Things lock in because all the vibrations are related to each other and they fit together when they're in tune.

They resonate?

Exactly. They resonate down your arm and in your chin and the lower you play the more powerful that resonance is. [Referring to The Dream Syndicate's 60s performances] We'd hold it for an hour and a half, and the effect on the audience was usually psychedelic. People would come up to us afterwards and they'd say, 'Who was playing flute?' [There was no flute] You'd get lost.

Due to the clashing overtones?

Exactly. But that's very well recorded, that arrangement. It's nice.

Conrad seems uncompromising about keeping to his chosen path. This is a recent recording, but it doesn't sound that different from stuff he was doing 20 years ago with Faust, say, or even further back with you and LaMonte Young.

Yeah, well, it's good, because LaMonte refuses to acknowledge that we had any role in the music. He wants everything. He said, 'Well, I started off playing this, that and the other.' And I'd say, 'Yes, but when we started playing harmonics the whole system changed – not just the notes that you were playing, the whole system that you were involved with suddenly became adjusted because of the strings. The saxophone didn't do it for you, you were forced to give up the sax and start singing; and what you were singing was a system that was peculiar to strings, and therefore, we forced your hand into that.' He refuses to accept that when that happened we were into jazz and everyone was a collaborator.

I've heard rumours that the tapes of those sessions with you and Young and Conrad are finally going to be released.

[Young, who owns the tapes] has repeatedly said to me, 'Let's talk about it,' and then he doesn't talk about it. So I take everything with a grain of salt. There's a lot of it. There's over a year's worth of everyday work, these recordings we did, and I don't know what condition they're in. And destroying a library of effort no matter how abstract or arcane this sort of thing is, it represented for Tony and I at least, and I'm sure it did for LaMonte and Marian [Zazeela, Young's wife], a devoted effort and a labour of love really, because we didn't get paid anything for it.

Conrad has said that this formative era of his life has now been relegated to memory.

But that's all LaMonte. He doesn't care if the music comes out at all. He has his own system derived from that, that he is happy with. The power and majesty that was in that music is still on those tapes he's got and I don't know how to. . . What more we can hope for from him?

ARTIST
Nick Drake

TITLE
Black-Eyed Dog

SOURCE
Time Of No Reply

LABEL
Hannibal

[Listens intently] I've no idea who this is.
Nick Drake.
That was my first instinct, but I thought, 'No, he's too old sounding.' The only other guy with a voice like that was the fat guy from the blues band in San Francisco. [Canned Heat's Bob Hite]

In the 70s you played on some of Drake's records. Did you do so because you liked the music or was it just a session job?
No, I liked his stuff. It was also a question of how to make a grand.
When I met [Drake] I had a 12-string guitar and he'd never seen a D12 before, a Martin. And you know that very complicated picking that he had? He just picked up the guitar and it was just like this orchestral sound coming out. He went nuts. He was sitting there stunned by it.

What was Drake like to work with?
Very introverted. I hardly ever dealt with him.

What were your criteria for deciding which sessions to do and which production jobs to take? They cover an extremely wide range of music.
Well, who I knew. . . I knew Joe Boyd [then an executive at Island Records]. I was fresh out of The VU anyway, and I'd done Nico's *Marble Index* and I was interested in producing. And one other way of developing what I did with *Marble Index* was to do Nick Drake and The Incredible String Band and whatever came around. Joe seemed to appreciate what I was doing. Everything he showed me was very interesting.

Was he instrumental in you going on to produce on a more regular basis?
He was instrumental in introducing me to Warner Brothers where I got an A&R job in 71, when I recorded The Stooges.

And you went from producing The Stooges to groups as diverse as Silverhead and Squeeze.
Silverhead was a little stranger. Silverhead was a one-off. Squeeze was. . . I worked for Miles Copeland and started Illegal Records with him and worked with him for quite a while. There was Squeeze, The Police, Sham 69 and another one – I can't remember the name of the other one.

You were quite involved in the New York punk scene in the mid-70s.
Once I'd moved on from Illegal, I went to New York and produced Patti [Smith], went on tour with Patti and put my own band together again, and did all right in CBGB's. But what I left behind here was the [Chris] Spedding band, the leather and the chains and stuff. And when I came back with a band wearing rugby shirts and beards, they handed me my head on a platter.

041

John Cale

ARTIST

Eno & Snatch

TITLE   °

RAF

SOURCE

RAF 7"

LABEL

Polydor

[Referring to the spoken voices] Well, they're German news reports. *Actuelle.* German news reports?

I'm not sure.

That sounds like real. . . Don't understand what they're saying. If you like your rock political this is the place to be! [A woman's voice comes in] Yeah, I know this.

It's Eno with Snatch, Judy Nylon and Patti Palladin, from 1977.

It needs to be later than that: 1986. But it could be 1977, too, because those synth sounds are fairly old. [At the end of the track there is a chant of '*No sacrifice'*] Ah, of course. I know that record. Patti and Judy. It was a little while after I met them that Judy told me about the song *No Sacrifice*. It would be 77.

Doesn't Patti sing on your *Fear* album?

No, Judy, on *The Man Who Couldn't Afford To Orgy.* She was in my band for a while. She and two other girls. It was a strange band: Ian Oxendale, Davy O'List. . . It was fairly funny circumstances because the girls were very raw there up on stage. I wrote *Salome* and *Even Cowgirls Get The Blues* for Judy. They were like the pivotal things in the set. It was 78, even later maybe.

Out of all the people you have collaborated with, Eno seem to be the person you've done the most with.

In what way?

Well, you've worked with him on various projects from the Ayers/Cale/Nico/Eno album in 1974 through to *Wrong Way Up* in 1990.

Yeah, there's a very good working relationship, that's true. And he was very easy going. By the time I did *Caribbean Sunset* [1983] it was a case of just setting four tracks aside at the end of the board, then I'd bring the caviar and the champagne. He'd show up at 12 and I'd be back at six. When I got back everything would be finished.

What was the impetus behind *Wrong Way Up*? That was a whole album of collaborations.

Well, *Songs For Drella* happened between *Words For The Dying* and *Wrong Way Up.* [Eno] became the record company [i.e. Island], he was very much the record company at that point. And he figured that now was a good time to do a rock record because we could take advantage of it and I agreed with him. But we thought of doing it as a show. I said, 'What's really important is if we can put together a theatre piece around a record. We would have a show that we could put up and travel with, that would occupy maybe two days of a week for about five weeks in a year.' And that's all you'd need to do; put it up and perform it and it would be like a Robert Wilson piece.

The original playing card idea [a playing card appears on the *Wrong Way Up* sleeve] was what ended up as happening. That was the background for it. But [Eno] really didn't want to perform. I made it very clear when we were recording the album that I was not interested in doing an album that was going to sit on the shelf, but we would go out and perform it, because I'd been through that with

Drella, performed it three, four days and that was it. And if you're going to make a record you've got to commit to at least New York, San Francisco, Chicago, Boston and London, Berlin, Paris, whatever – the bare minimum, just go out and perform. It would be easy and [Eno] agreed to that. And he's maintained ever since that he's never agreed to it, especially from the minute that he decided not to do anything. I don't know why I believed him, I mean he's always recalcitrant to perform.

ARTIST
The Jesus And Mary Chain

SOURCE
Psychocandy
LABEL
Blanco Y Negro

TITLE
Never Understand

That's not a crowd in there, is it? No, it's a noise. It's like high violin harmonics. **It's feedback that was apparently sampled and then played back when the track was being recorded. It's The Jesus And Mary Chain from ten years ago. Were you aware of them?**
Yeah, I've just heard about a band called Lilacs which is made up of one of the guys from The Jesus And Mary Chain. . . This is The Jesus And Mary Chain.
They were one of countless groups who appeared in the 80s and made it clear that they were influenced by The. . .
VU.
How do you feel about groups still being influenced by something that you did so many years ago?
It may be there in the music but whether it's there in the mind is something else. I mean there are some very good qualities that I come across in other bands from other countries, useful commodities like the ability to annoy intensely. And that's a very useful thing to have.
Do they mean what they are doing or are they just doing it? Is it a matter of life and death to them that the music sounds like this? Are they doing it because this is what they are, or are they doing this because they think this might work? It doesn't matter because The Jesus And Mary Chain have been quite successful.
Do you think that The Velvet Underground's position at the time was relatively hard won?
You see I had no second thoughts about it. Once I knew that we'd done stuff like *Venus In Furs*, *Heroin*, *All Tomorrow's Parties*, I knew we'd done something that set us apart from everyone else and that it would always be the case. So I just went to sleep at that point and I just thought of more ideas.
When you toured The Velvet Underground reunion shows you were supported by Luna, who are probably the most bare-faced Velvets copyists of all. Was that a deliberate choice?
They were on Warner Brothers.
Are you particularly interested in rock music these days, or are you more interested in composition?

043

John Cale

No, not composition; what's being done rather than. . . Hands-on music and where it's all coming from.

Are there any musicians or groups that you particularly like?

Apart from Beck? There's a lively scene out there in LA. There's a little band I produced called Maids Of Gravity who are out there. They have the same sort of attitude, the same psychedelia in their toolbox, use tape delay, use samples, analogue Moogs.

ARTIST
Lou Reed

TITLE
Am-2

SOURCE
Metal Machine Music
LABEL
RCA

Sounds like Suicide. The guy from Suicide [Marty Rev]. When you listen to a Suicide concert it affects the way you talk. It actually affects the way your voice works because of the beats in the air.

It's not Suicide, it's actually *Metal Machine Music.*

Ah yeah. It sounded like radio. . . It's one way out of a contract.

What did you think of it as a piece of music?

I thought it was a ploy.

Do you think it has any qualities at all?

The quality to annoy. The quality to annoy intensely.

Reed claimed it was a classical piece, up there with Beethoven and Vivaldi.

He's good at that, though. What a wind-up.

It's been suggested that *Metal Machine Music* was influenced by your organ piece *Loop*, which was recorded when you were still in The Velvets, so Reed must have heard it in the late 6os.

I think he was influenced by his lawyer, who probably told him, 'You're never going to get out of this contract' [laughs] and he immediately took that down and said, 'Oh yeah? Watch this!' I think he remembered a few things that he'd picked up along the way in Ludlow Street and thought, 'This is my ticket to the big time.' [Ludlow Street was the mid-6os New York home of Cale, Reed and Angus MacLise, the original VU drummer and a participant on those early Young/Conrad/Cale sessions.]

When you compiled *Caged/Uncaged*, you included an excerpt from *Metal Machine Music.*

[Mishearing] What's *Caged/Uncaged*?

***Caged/Uncaged*. The John Cage tribute album that you compiled.**

No, it was one of the tracks that was offered by Lou. It wasn't decided by me, it was decided by the art director of the show at the Venice Biennale – that's what it was for. It was an exhibition of Cage's pieces at the Venice Biennale, and the CD to go with it. . .

Turn it off. Aah, pheww! I've been doing this all day. I'm going to go to bed in a minute. I gotta go talk to Patti. [Cale had a meeting scheduled with Patti Smith immediately following the interview.] Where was I? It was one of the pieces that they chose to be part of [the Cage tribute album]. They asked me to take care of it and I did. I mean I actually taught Joey Ramone to sing the *Wonderful Widow Of 18 Springs*, which was really funny. I had to teach Joey note-by-note and bar-by-bar. He was sitting next to me, getting taller by the minute.

ARTIST
Brian Wilson & Van Dyke Parks

TITLE
Lullaby

SOURCE
Orange Crate Art

LABEL
Warner Brothers

I'm waiting for The Three Tenors to come in here!

It's the closing instrumental from Brian Wilson and Van Dyke Parks's *Orange Crate Art*.

Ah, Fred Myrow. Van Dyke works with Fred Myrow a lot, who I think did this.

This is one of two tracks that Myrow orchestrated. Have you heard this record?

I've heard the 'new Van Dyke Parks': Rufus Wainwright. Do you know that song from Loudon Wainwright, *Rufus Is A Tit Man*? Well, Loudon had a boy with Kate McGarrigle. So Kate calls me up the other day, she says, 'I want you to hear my boy, he's down there, he's been signed by Mo Austin and Lenny Waronker to Dreamworks and I want to keep an eye on him, make sure he gets the right treatment, so go down and see what you think.' So I went down, I met him and it was uncanny. His songs were. . . He has a tremendous voice, and 20 years old. You're looking at a young Cole Porter writing acid songs, entirely in the Randy Newman, Van Dyke Parks vein. It was like they never forgot who was there at the old Warner Brothers. Now they have their new Van Dyke Parks.

Was Brian Wilson an influence?

Well, it's the harmony, it's so full-blooded and sweet. Lou and I both loved those songs. And *Pet Sounds* was a mindblower.

Wilson's singing on this album is really good, although on a TV appearance a few years ago it seemed like his voice was on its way out.

His voice. I don't know how he feels about his voice, because it was something his father had instilled in him. Have you seen that movie that Don Was made about him? If you saw that you'd get an idea of the abuse. That song *In My Room* – the background to that was he used to get beaten and he would retreat into his room and write these songs. His father was a real menace. Then you see his mother in the film and think, 'Where the hell were you when this was going on?'

I think Brian felt a little strange about it being Van Dyke's album. There's a long history. It goes back to internecine warfare in the band, how many people actually blamed Van Dyke for the collapse of The Beach Boys. They couldn't stand to sing his lyrics. And he writes the most literate lyrics – he's wonderful. This is All-American music, looking at it: the Great Plains, little Broadway.

'American Gothic' is one phrase that's been used to describe Parks.

Well, it's not Gothic, it's too melodic. You know, the Eastman School of Music and learning to sing in the choir with Toscanini conducting, that's all a part of Van Dyke's background. Very loquacious he is about it, too. He regales you with these stories in a stylish way. He's like a southern gentleman.

John Cale

One last question. I've always been interested in the fact that you often use the names of historical or fictional characters in song titles: 'Charlemagne', 'Milton', 'Hedda Gabler', 'Macbeth'.

Sometimes. Sometimes place names: 'Crazy Egypt', 'Andalucia'.

Occasionally the names seem to have a rather peripheral connection to the lyrics.

They have like a hypnotic thing about them when they happen. To me they have connotations that are kind of blinding. It depends on when they happen. I mean there's no rhyme or reason to it, it's like my attempt at hypnosis probably. They have a buzz in my head. I picked that up from trying to practise to be like Dylan Thomas. So that's kind of the background: if you're going to try and be like Dylan Thomas you don't really need to make sense all the time, but the noise will really get you through. A lot of thunder.

Neneh Cherry spent her youth split between schools in New York and Sweden, and touring with her step-father, the pioneering free jazz trumpeter and world musician Don Cherry. After leaving school she came to London, becoming enmeshed in the post-punk pageant, making her musical debut singing backing vocals with The Slits. After this she became a member of the Bristol's 80s avant garde bohemian punk-funk collective Rip Rig & Panic. In 1985 RR&P was briefly reborn as Float Up CP but Neneh never really hit payback until she cut *Buffalo Stance*, making her legendary appearance, pregnant, on *Top Of The Pops*. A string of hit singles followed and in 1989 the huge-selling LP *Raw Like Sushi*. At the time of the Jukebox she had just released *Homebrew*, recorded in her family home in Sweden, with her husband Cameron McVey, Johnny Dollar and (contributors) Gang Starr and REM's Michael Stipe.

ARTIST
Don Cherry

TITLE
Brown Rice

SOURCE
Brown Rice
LABEL
Horizon

This brings back memories. This is the first record when Don actually went more electric and kinda put funk into his music. The funk was always there, but this piece kinda travels ahead with it. He studied Indian music, he studied African music – he was bringing all these elements into what he was doing. See all these things in here? This is funny, it's like a whole jigsaw. That rhyme '*Chic-a-da*' was a family rhyme that Dad got from my grandmother and he always used to tell them to us when we were kids. Then there's all the food things – brown rice, miso – healthy living. That was all we used to eat at the time.

You would have been about 12 when this was made, how aware of it were you?

I think it was the first record where he actually had a proper recording budget to go and make the album that he wanted to make. Young people have always been into him and he always played with a lot of young people – people have sometimes just turned up here and he was always into that. This was recorded in New York and I think this Italian guy produced it. It's funny because the guy who did the sleeve photograph is now one of the presidents at Virgin America – it's a funny connection.

ARTIST
Gil Scott-Heron & Brian Jackson

TITLE
H2Ogate Blues

SOURCE
Winter In America
LABEL
Strata East

Is this Gil Scott-Heron? Good, thank God for that – I got it. Gil Scott-Heron and The Last Poets, they're the root of rap – real-life poetry, which is what rap is.
[Gil sings: '*If H-2-O is still water and G-A-T-E is still gate then what are we getting ready to deal on is the Watergate blues.*']
Yeah, wicked. Like speak the truth brothers. This makes complete sense to me – nothing's changed obviously. This is great because there's like a timelessness in his voice. We are still right up against the same problems. It's just a nice thing to hear someone speaking the truth.
['*America the international Jekyll and Hyde/The land of a thousand disguises/Sneaks up on you but rarely surprises.*']
Wicked. Poetry. There's a group from LA called The Watts Prophets who were around at the same time as The Last Poets. There's also someone called Nikki Giovanni, a female poet. She did an album with a gospel choir that is just so articulate – that's the thing about it – playing with the beat, using the beat to articulate things in a kinda concious way. I think what I get from hearing something like this is the heartfelt sense of pride in hearing something that really matters – you just wanna go tell it like it is.

ARTIST
Roxanne Shante

SOURCE
Big Mama 12"

LABEL
Livin' Large

TITLE
Big Mama

I love this song. We listen to this all the time. When I heard this I thought whatever happened to all the girl rappers, the female rappers with the real grit? Everyone just seems to be polishing their stuff down to fit into the pop charts. Even Latifah's last album was kinda sweet compared to the first one which had much more crust. The first time I heard Roxanne Shante was on the radio in New York and I couldn't figure out whether it was a young boy or girl. She's just got such a rhythm and timing in what she is doing. She disses everybody.

This is full of so much attitude, she means what she is saying. Rhythmically she's really good. She really plays around with her rhyming. She's done some really conscious stuff, like *Independent Woman*. Her voice cuts through, it's like a weapon – I love her. You could play this next to Gil Scott-Heron; this is poetry, too. Like in Gil Scott-Heron's time nothing the media was saying related to us, but rap does relate and it has got a place in the heart in the same sense that Gil Scott-Heron has a place in the heart. It's reality but it's still playful and expressive.

ARTIST
Ornette Coleman

SOURCE
The Shape Of Jazz To Come

LABEL
Atlantic

049

TITLE
Lonely Woman

Neneh Cherry

Mmmm. This is called *Lonely Woman*. Ornette Coleman is a genius – his sound. This is so weird because all his music was going on around me when I was growing up – it's like coming home when I hear these tunes because I know them so well. I used to hear them rehearsing them – we'd just be around, we weren't really listening, so the music would just become part of what you were feeling. This is one of the early records, but at the time this was militant. That's why I always connect things like bebop, HipHop, punk; all those things where people have kinda found themselves. And it's like a heart-rending cry sometimes. He's saying as much as Gil Scott-Heron was on the other track. Wicked.

What's it like listening to this now?

It's nice now being able to *really* listen to these tracks – really get something out of them and also knowing what they're about. When I was a kid sometimes we used to be at these gigs, but me and my brother would go to sleep completely unaffected by what was going on around us. Ornette was one of the first people to move to SoHo [in New York], he had a gallery on Prince Street, and I can remember he used to have a son [Denardo] playing with him who I was really fascinated with. You get a feeling of the classical, the African, the good, the bad, the ugly, the tender. Sometimes it'll be really angry then it's *ooooooaaaaaa* and let off steam. There's lyrics to this song – it would be a challenge.

ARTIST
John Coltrane

TITLE
India

SOURCE
Impressions

LABEL
Impulse!

Another thing about bebop is that it's real quirky, this has got a real sense of humour. It's really expressive but it's also quite. . . This sounds like Coltrane. It's kinda saying something but without the lyrics. You can feel the mood swing; sometimes it's really heart rendering but this feels quite amusing the way the first part started. Not humorous as in funny, but you could almost imagine. . . You could put a picture to the beginning of that track, something quite funny because there's like a playfulness there. It's not demented and tortured, it's moving though mood changes; you can get a feeling of real beauty, then the tempos change. What amazes me is how different people play the same instrument and it sounds completely different, it makes you think about voices; they can make it sound different because of who they are. This has gone into like *aahh! aahh!*, kinda let off steam, whereas the beginning was far more gentle. It's kinda like going through someone's life.

ARTIST
Buju Banton

TITLE
Boom By By

SOURCE
Boom By By 12"

LABEL
Shang Muzik

Ragga! Wicked! Yeah, that's got the grind. Who's that?

This is the most offensive ragga record I could find.

I didn't listen to the lyrics . . . Oh yeah, I've heard of this, right.

Basically it's about shooting up gays.

No, that's not cool. I jumped in too quick there. I just heard the beat. Now we know how he feels about it. You wanna wake up, man. It's weird the amount of homophobia around. This is just one person saying something you can't generalise.

This was a big hit on the reggae charts.

I bet people didn't buy this record because of the lyrical content. I don't think a whole bunch of people went out and thought: great, a record dissing gays. Quite often people ignore what's in there. I think the song has stupid lyrics but a lot of ragga tunes do – what I like about them is that they are playful and it's kinda warped. I love the way they throw in something like a Suzanne Vega song or a Frank Sinatra song, it's really like freeform.

ARTIST
Pharoah Sanders

TITLE
Thembi

SOURCE
Thembi

LABEL
Impulse!

I love this double bass. That's what's nice about A Tribe Called Quest's album with [double bassist] Ron Carter [*Low End Theories*]. Who's this? Eddie Harris? It's not Coltrane again?

Closer.

Pharoah Sanders? That's what I thought at first, because he always used those bells a lot. Do you know a singer called Leon Thomas? My favourite singer of all time. He sang *The Creator Has A Master Plan* with Pharoah Sanders. He like yodels and sings in African and the blues – he's just deep. This is just beautiful. This is really light and . . .

Joyous?

Yes, joyous, that's the word. What's wicked about it is that you might get someone going *weeaaahh weeaaahh* and just letting off yet still maintaining the beauty in there, you know? I've got Louis Armstrong and Leon Thomas singing *The Creator Has A Master Plan* – beautiful. This is a good feeling music. This is the kind of thing I'd put on if I was like cooking; evening music.

ARTIST

Ice T

TITLE

OG: Original Gangster

SOURCE

OG: Original Gangster

LABEL

Sire

I like Ice T. He's got a lot to say. I think he is a seriously intelligent guy. When I first heard his voice it really marked him out as being another speaker of the truth. I met him just the other day – my heart was in my throat. I just went up to him and said 'Hi'. He was a sweetheart, looked you right in the eye, really positive.

What do you think about the 'Cop Killer' debacle?

I'm on his side with the whole 'Cop Killer' scenario because he lived in something that he knows something about and he's just saying that. You've got to have the right to say what you think even if it's not necessarily the truth. I think he's got the right to say something coming from where he is coming from.

ARTIST

Miles Davis

TITLE

Pharoah's Dance

SOURCE

Bitches Brew

LABEL

CBS

Miles Davis? Miles Davis is like the king of the tripped-out scene. There's this really funny story where this drummer that we know went to audition for him one time and Miles turned round and said, 'Listen man I don't want no Jimi Hendrix – just drum.' He was one of those people who was a superstar before anything ever happened to him; he always believed that he was great – that was the sexiest thing about him. He definitely had sex appeal to the max.

I met him once when I was a kid, it was one of the most glamorous experiences I've ever had. I was about four and a half or five and we'd been driving up from Turkey, we'd been on the bus going through Yugoslavia and we pulled up in Paris where Miles was playing. We went backstage and I remember my mum getting me all dressed up. I wore this brown velvet dress with a kind of paisley lining, kneesocks. Before or after the show Don goes in and Miles was wearing a two- piece snakesuit and he put me up on his lap and it was like the first sexual kind of thing I'd had – I'll never forget the feeling of his snakeskin on my legs. He had this voice, he was one of those people who you knew was kinda dangerous because he was like a snake. He was one of those people who'll say what he thinks – he would spare no one mercy. Even at that age, feeling that he liked me was the most flattering thing ever.

I really like this stuff; Miles was someone who brought in the modern vibe, the funk, the electric thing into jazz in a really particular way. He was always kinda curious – searching, looking, seeking and he valued what was going on around him. He was like a vampire with a need for blood – he needed young blood around him to keep him going. He wouldn't want anyone in his band over 30 – he kept moving with the youth and that kept him alive. It was the challenge of having young kids who could really play that pushed him on. A lot of people settle into what becomes safe for them and end up imitating what they've done already.

053 >

Matt Black and Jonathan More formed Coldcut in 1986; their hit *Say, Kids, What Time Is It?* arrived as the final link in the chain connecting European collage-experiment with the dance-remix scratch edit. In 1988 their remix of Eric B & Rakim's *Paid In Full* laid the groundwork for HipHop's entry into the UK mainstream, following which they collaborated with James Brown, Junior Reed, Queen Latifah and The Fall, and wrote hits for Yazz and Lisa Stansfield. Dissatisfied with a long-term major record contract, they dropped out in 1991 to form their Ninja Tune label. As well as their own records, they have issued albums of 'DJ tools' and signed a diverse roster of artists who have defined the 90s 'TripHop' aesthetic: DJ Food, Funki Porcini, DJ Vadim, Neotropic, The Herbaliser, Amon Tobin and more, promoted via a highly successful London club night, *Stealth*. Fascinated by the latest developments in computer graphics and multimedia, they initiated Hex, under which guise they explore computer animation and interactive performance techniques. Their latest album, *Let Us Play*, which features an interactive CD-ROM, was released in 1997. For the Jukebox they were assisted by studio engineer Patrick Carpenter.

ARTIST
VIM

TITLE
Maggie's Last Party

SOURCE
Maggie's Last Party 12″
LABEL
BOZ white label

JM: I hate her voice! [The record consists entirely of Thatcher samples] It's quite well put together, I suppose, though it's full of every cliché in the book. It is good.

MB: I remember! I liked this one. I remember hearing it and thinking that although these are very obvious sources to sample, the bits that they sampled are very cleverly put together. I was really cracking up. I thought this was just a white label, though.

JM: The thing I really don't believe is that Maggie ever said, '*The bass goes on. . .*'

MB: No, but she could have said, '*The military base must be safeguarded*', and, '*So-and-so goes to Europe. . .*

JM: Then it's pretty good matching. It's just her voice that puts me off. I can't listen to it.

MB: But I wouldn't really want to dance to it. It was good. Good and stupid.

ARTIST
Meat Beat Manifesto

TITLE
DV8

SOURCE
Dog Star Man EP
LABEL
Play It Again Sam

JM: [After some time] Probably an indie band. What about Meat Beat Manifesto? **That's it.**

MB: Excellent! They're really good. There's only one of them left now. They're contemporaries of Stereo MCs, almost. They've been out there, British, on the fringes, and they've cracked it at last. It's nice. We played the new Meat Beat last week, didn't we? It's good.

This is DV8 from the *Dog Star Man* EP, on Play It Again Sam. I think it's the first thing they did.

MB: It was too punk for that time. It sounds all right now.

JM: It's still got that, you know. . .

MB: It's a bit kind of lumpen. How old did you say it was? Five or six years? Even using a break like this for that time was quite advanced.

JM: It's Kraftwerk, isn't it, that peeper?

ARTIST
Dr Alimantado

TITLE
Ride On

SOURCE
Best Dressed Chicken In Town
LABEL
Greensleeves

JM: Yabby YU, introducing himself?

MB: I don't know who it is, but I'd guess it isn't anyone very well known.

He's got a name which is sort of legendary.

MB: Yes, but only in reggae circles.

JM: It's that funk in there that's interesting.

MB: It sounds a bit like King Tubby. There are only about three possibilities for producer. It's very good. One of many unknown rarities.

It's Dr Alimantado. A Black Ark/Lee Perry production.

JM: Oh right! *Best Dressed Chicken!* I haven't listened to that for ages.

MB: I could have sworn I'd never heard that, man. He's not my main enthusiasm, though. Big Youth's my man from that period.

JM: It reminds me to dig it out.

ARTIST
Holger Czukay

TITLE
Persian Love

SOURCE
Movies

LABEL
EMI

JM: This is lovely, whatever it is. Cheb somebody or other!

The voice is taken off shortwave radio. I don't know if they knew who it was.

JM: The guitar's really nice.

MB: It's good stuff. If it was a bit more 'produced' I'd say it was Byrne and Eno.

PC: It's what's-his-face, Klaus what's-his-face.

JM: Barbie?

PC: Klaus Schulze?

MB: It's Can!

That's it: Holger Czukay.

JM: We nearly got to remix [Can's] *I Want More*, actually.

MB: Mixmaster Morris loves Can. [Long pause] It's very dreamy.

JM: Cheb Holger. It's wicked. I've not heard it before.

ARTIST
Davy D

TITLE
Keep Your Distance

SOURCE
Davy's Ride

LABEL
Def Jam

MB: I recognize that transform. It's *Keep Your Distance*, that break. This is Davy DMX. This was his comeback record, which I thought was pretty good. It's got a crap mix of *Funky Drummer* on it, which ruins it. Never delivered his early promise. Got some money out of Def Jam to make an album, took about three years to make it, and it wasn't very good. *One For The Treble* and the one after, *The DMX Will Rock*, though it's not so well known, that is *wicked*.

JM: Loose, Bruce!

MB: It's so loose! I don't like crashing beats, but I really like this looseness in scratching.

ARTIST
Bobby Konders

TITLE
Nervous Acid

SOURCE
Bobby Konders' House Rhythms

LABEL
NuGroove

PC: Tremendous bassline. Is it a 303?

MB: Could be. It's got that whingey tone to it.

PC: I like this a lot.

MB: This isn't older than 1987. There was that period when you experienced the joy of putting the snare drum in on every beat. *For quite a while.* Come on, guys, we can do this. Early House pioneer? American? Chicago? I can tell you who it isn't: it's not Marshall Jefferson, it's not Adonis, it's not Farley Jackmaster Funk, it's not Steve 'silk' Hurley. You know what it's like? It's like ESG meets *Acid Tracks*. The bassline's quite moody for Acid. But I'm afraid I'll have to pass.

JM: The bassline's the kind of thing Dee-Lite like to use.

MB: Are we going to kick ourselves? It's earlier than Joey Beltram, in between them and *Acid Tracks*.

JM: What's that geezer that did, er, oh, he's like the Prince of House music?

MB: Jamie Principle? It's got elements of *Baby Wants A Ride*, very much. But I think we're going to have to give up on this one.

Bobby Konders.

JM: Oh, right, of course!

MB: NuGroove, yes, of course.

ARTIST

Christian Marclay

TITLE

Frederic Chopin

SOURCE

More Encores

LABEL

No Man's Land

056

Coldcut

JM: This is probably some art record by some dada person, that plays like this because it's been specially designed, and sells for about £15,000 in a limited edition of two.

MB: Someone *highly* experimental, I'd say. John Cage?

It's Christian Marclay, from the New York art scene. He invented his own version of scratch-mixing. He puts records together, cuts them into pieces and makes collages with them, then plays them.

MB: Aaah! I'm sure you've told me about this geezer, or Morris told me.

JM: Anyway, I wasn't far off at all! A pretty good guess.

ARTIST

Dub Syndicate

TITLE

Fringe On Top Dub

SOURCE

Pounding System

LABEL

On-U Sound

JM: This is suitably out to lunch, as well.

MB: [Later] Did this start off incredibly weird? I've forgotten already.

JM: It sounds like that dub LP by Adrian.

MB: Adrian Sherwood, I was going to say that. On-U Sound, Creation Rebel. Or else Dennis Bovell.

It is Adrian; not Creation Rebel, though.

MB: But what's the difference? They're all the same band, his bands. He's been doing authentic experimental reggae with the best credibility for the longest. He's always had the right people, and a full understanding of reggae, but he's always put weirdness in as well. All these people like Style Scott, the people

from The Roots Radics, George Oban, you remember, we used to worship him! I wonder what happened to him? Of those early records I think to be honest some of them were pretty crap, but some of them were wildly excellent.
PC: Wicked.
MB: He always had a good collection of stupid noises.
It's called *Fringe On Top Dub*.
MB: I think you really have to be a hardcore fan to know the titles.

ARTIST
Miles Davis

SOURCE
Doo-Bop

LABEL
Warner Bros

TITLE
High Speed Chase

PC: [Instantly] Miles *The Chase*. Isn't that right? From *Doo-Bop*.
JM: It's posthumous.
MB: I think this is crap. What I do think is good, my idea of Miles playing an exciting mixture of contemporary stuff, is like *One Phone Call*. That is such a wicked track. This just sounds like someone's sampled him, and onto a bog-standard House track, as well.
He was actually dead when it was mixed, so I guess that's exactly what happened.
MB: That doesn't help, does it? That was a pretty evil thing, I think. Whoever was behind this, they weren't doing anyone any favours.
PC: Easy Moe Bee, wasn't it?
MB: Who the fuck's he?
JM: It's awfully politely produced.
MB: I don't know that much about Miles Davis, but he patently wasn't about very regimented music, which this is. He was right away from that. Anything with *The Chase* in the title has to have an excellent wah-wah guitarist, and that hasn't. A severe oversight on the part of Cool Moe Bee, or whatever he's called.

Coldcut

ARTIST
Lata Mangeshkar

SOURCE
Golden Voices From The Silver Screen Vol 3

TITLE
Satyam Shivam Sundaram

LABEL
Globestyle

MB: You've chosen all the hard ones.
JM: It's obviously the biggest hit from the biggest Indian film in the last year, or something.
MB: It's a nice piece to sample. That hasn't been gone into enough, that ullulation over heavy stupid beats. There's more there. Those guys with the monks, Enigma, they proved that when that went clear. A Soul II Soul beat and a bunch of monks wailing over it. But you're trying to trick us, aren't you? This is Ofra! [Haza, who Coldcut sampled for their remix of *Paid In Full*]
It isn't in fact. It does sound a bit like her.
MB: You expect us to have the command of ten Middle Eastern languages!
Maybe. This woman's recorded more songs than anyone else alive.
MB: That's a great statistic. We really ought to know who it is.

JM: She's definitely big in films. I saw a programme about her. She sounds like she's 15, and she's like 80, or something, isn't she? She's got a wicked little voice.

Lata Mangeshkar.

MB: Coldcut rating – sound.

ARTIST
King Sun-D Moët

TITLE
Hey Love

SOURCE
Hey Love 12″

LABEL
Rhythm King

MB: That's the *Moments In Love* riff. This is King Moe Sunny D, or something like that. *Moments In Love*, Art Of Noise, that ruled in New York for about a year, the first really heavy sounding record.

JM: It's really PM Dawn-ish, this, isn't it?

MB: *Hey Love*, it was called. It's almost proto-Soul-II-Soul-y, as well. That snare drum sound, that Art Of Noise/Def Jam snare drum sound, it ruled for about two years. It's completely out now. It was too big. It's that gated snare drum effect.

JM: It's time for the gate to come back, I think. He's got a really nice quality to his voice. [Later] He sounds bored now. Time he abdicated!

He didn't do anything else, did he?

MB: I think he was caught up in total litigation for the rest of his life [for sampling the AoN riff] from Moments In Love. He's probably still trying to pay them off.

JM: The backing track to that still sounds contemporary. It hasn't dated at all badly, unlike a lot of things from that period.

ARTIST
Testone

TITLE
Sweet Exorcist

SOURCE
Sweet Exorcist 12″

LABEL
Warp

JM/PC: [Simultaneously, but pronouncing it differently] Testone.

JM: On Warp. Absolutely. This is a good tune. Monster bleep!

MB: Bleep sampled from Yellow Magic Orchestra, mind you! I have it on authority!

JM: This is something to do with Cabaret Voltaire, isn't it? [It's by Cabaret Voltaire's Richard H Kirk]

MB: I mean, 'nuff respect to those Throbbing Gristle, Cabaret Voltaire, This Heat guys, etc, etc. A Certain Ratio. Remember seeing them? But they never delivered their early promise.

Amelia Stein

059 >

Elvis Costello was born Declan MacManus in West London in 1955. The son of a respected singer with Joe Loss's Orchestra, he seemed to arrive fully-formed in 1977 with his Nick Lowe-produced debut *My Aim Is True*. His 'revenge and guilt' songwriting period ended with a series of characteristically catholic records: *Get Happy!!* (1980), a soul/Stax/R&B tribute; *Almost Blue* (1981), recorded in Nashville by legendary country producer Billy Sherill; and *Imperial Bedroom* (1982), a pop record embellished by orchestral arrangements. Of his later output two albums stand tallest: *Spike* (1989), featuring contributions from Chrissie Hynde, Marc Ribot and The Dirty Dozen Brass Band, among others, and a collaboration with The Brodsky Quartet, *The Juliet Letters* (1993), a song sequence for voice and string quartet. Costello has also served time as a producer (The Specials, The Pogues), composed music for film and television, and worked with George Jones, Johnny Cash, Chet Baker and Hal Willner on the latter's Charlie Mingus tribute album *Weird Nightmare*. At the time of the Jukebox he was about to release *Brutal Youth*, featuring, for the first time since 1986's *Blood And Chocolate*, his 70s group The Attractions.

ARTIST

Dimitri Shostakovich

TITLE

Allegretto from String Quartet No 3 In F Major Op 73

SOURCE

Shostakovich String Quartets

LABEL

Teldec

It's the Brodskys. I haven't listened to the record we made for a while, but it's funny how different the timbre of the quartet sounds on that recording to when we recorded. It's just like a singer – it is a voice that is instantly recognisable. I went into a shop a couple of months ago and they were playing an old Beethoven string quartet recording by The Busch Quartet, and it was like somebody walking up to you and slapping you round the face. It wasn't like a modern digital recording; it had such a mood, it was very individual. So I immediately bought it, and I wondered how much of the way it sounded was the same as what I like about old blues records. It had an atmosphere. I usually prefer analogue recordings, even with classical music. I can stand the hiss because I grew up with vinyl.

Do you know what they are playing?

No. I recognise certain parts of it. That was Shostakovich? Oh, I'll get it in the neck from the Brodskys for not recognising that. But it didn't sound like him, it sounded Spanish. But I like the way he incorporated Spanish music, that might have been considered light or banal, and made it into something. Sometimes he did it ironically, and sometimes he did it just because he liked it, I'm fascinated by the Brodsky cycle because they play it from memory, and that's a daunting thing, to remember that amount of music.

[Shostakovich's] string quartets were probably less liable to interference than say the symphonies, because the symphonies were the big philosophical and political statements in praise of the collective farms or something, the ones that got big articles written about them in *Pravda* the next day, with the unseen hand of Stalin condemning him. Whereas, with that piece, it's as if it couldn't be more capricious and more personal.

The last time I read a decent interview with you, you were reading *Testimony*, Shostakovich's memoirs.

Yes, and I believed it then at face value. I didn't realise there was a controversy about it. And I've read other books about him since, and I think you have to pick intuitively what feels like the truth for the music, because even the things that he himself put his hand to are dubious. But there's still some very chilling and some very funny things in the book. But also nobody wants to believe that someone like Shostakovich, who could write music that good, could be so rubbery of will, that he was just a stooge of the state.

Elvis Costello

Hank Williams

The Wonderful World Of Hank Williams 1947–1950

I'll Be A Bachelor 'Til I Die

SPA

[After the first bar] That's Hank Williams. I don't know that song, but I don't really care so much for that kind of Hank Williams tune. That track's much more like pop music really, isn't it? And he *was* a pop star in a big way. It was instantly Hank Williams because of that scrapy fiddle sound. It's very distinctive. The atmosphere of the tune is better because it's [an] analogue [recording], and when it comes on there's this sort of air just before the voice all the time.

He's great with funny lyrics, but I prefer to hear him sing something really sad, really heart-rending, because then he really digs in. His voice is so great, it's wasted on a song like that. It's like I'd rather hear Billie Holiday sing *I Cover The Waterfront* or *Ghost Of Yesterday* than I would some blues thing where she's having fun, at that moment. It's just my personal disposition towards melancholia.

Is it the damage in the voice that attracts?
Well, it's partly that. I like that. Hank Williams had next to no voice, like Billie Holiday in a technical sense. He had very little range and a very one-dimensional tone. But even on that track you can't take your ear away from his voice. It's like a laser beam. Most of the Country records made in Nashville today sound like the theme tunes to bad daytime soap operas, and the actual exponents look like the actors in bad daytime soap operas. They have those stupid trimmed beards and creased jeans, and a lot of them won't even wear Western clothes. It's the 'I'm wind-surfing in a cowboy hat' look.

Do you think there is a Hank Williams legacy?
If there is, it's a cold place in the centre of the darker of today's songs. Inside his apparently limited technique as a singer and guitar player is real to-the-bone music. It would be daunting for anybody to try to get to the heart of the matter in quite the same way as he did. Hank Williams is the benchmark: he took from the tradition and made it his own. He's an artist. He's a true artist.

Count Basie

Count Basie Vol 11 1938–1940

Jazz Classics

Do You Wanna Jump, Children?

I guess it's American, from the sound of the brass more than anything. The woodwind had me foxed because it sounds like a kind of smoothie swing band, with the clarinet and everything. But it didn't sound like Ellington or anything like that. It's not as refined as that. It tended to sound more like an English dance band or someone doing Basie, but not as good as Basie. But I don't know who it is.

It's Basie actually.
Is it? Wow. Oh, so it's Jimmy Rushing singing. The thing that made me not think

061

Elvis Costello

it was Basie was that his piano solo sounded uncharacteristically busy, and that the woodwind sounded white. It sounded almost like a Miller-type band. I'm more an Ellington fan, but I like later Basie, like *The Atomic Basie*, the real driving sort of stuff. That's a much more powerhouse sound than on that track, which is slightly ingratiating.

Was there a lot of big band music at home when you were young?
No, it wasn't played so much in the house. Of course, the singers my mother and father listened to, particularly my mother, were accompanied by big bands. And when I used to go and see my dad play in the 60s, there used to be a big band playing on the same stage as the beat groups. But I do actually like that sound, that sweet, clarinet-heavy Miller-type sound, and the stiff alto playing. And I love the arrangements. I have this great recording of my dad, who was sometimes given incredible songs to cover, singing *See Emily Play* with the [Joe Loss] Orchestra, and it's phenomenal. The arrangement is mind-boggling.

ARTIST	SOURCE
PJ Harvey	**Peel Sessions**
	LABEL
TITLE	Strange Fruit
Water	

PJ Harvey. She fired that drummer [Rob Ellis] I heard, which is crazy. I haven't heard this particular version, but I actually like it better than the record, and better than the new album, where that [Steve] Albini guy does that sort of Nirvana trick all the time of playing the verse as quietly as possible so that when the chorus comes in it sounds like the voice of Armageddon. That's a great trick, but there's nothing so very new about it – it's about tension and release – and anybody who uses it too much is going to realise that it soon runs out of possibilities.

This has something real about it; there's an abandonment. Whatever it's about I have no idea, but I like the guitar sound very much. It's not a fake sound; it's just right, just right with her voice. I think there's quite a lot of Chrissie Hynde in her voice, more than people have ever mentioned, especially in the slight, occasional asides that she does. I like the sudden bursts of really good melody, or the little calm asides and pay-offs, in an otherwise screaming and shouting song. And I really like the drumming, he's wonderful. He [Ellis] may not be technically flawless, but that doesn't matter because his feel is amazing. It sounds as if the thing is turning around all the time, and that is very unsettling. But there's a lot more to the records, there's other sounds, there's quirkier instrumentation on some tracks, with the sudden appearance of cello or something, that's great.

You have returned to small group sound on *Brutal Youth*, haven't you?
Yes, but combo music is really only the same challenge as playing with a string quartet – except it's louder. When people thought it was a very radical thing for me to play with a string quartet, I couldn't really see it, because I have been in a quartet for most of my career. I'd been much more experimental on my previous two records where I was using the recording studio as if it were the score and trying to juxtapose different musical elements. Especially on *Spike*, in that each component part was its own section.

Is it fair to say that the new album is more a return to good ol' rock 'n' roll?

I've never been away from it. There was rock 'n' roll in *The Juliet Letters*.

What about a return to an idea of musical roots?

I don't see it as roots because nothing's roots to me. The first music I owned was by The Beatles, that's combo, so maybe you can draw it to that, but I'd heard lots of other music. I was buying records by the time I was eight or nine and I already knew a lot of music – folk music, jazz, big band music, ballad singers like Ella, Sinatra, Tony Bennett, and I'd been taken to classical concerts. It may be roots in terms of my professional career, but nothing is the natural thing I revert to. It's just whatever the songs dictate. I wrote all the songs for [Brutal Youth] on the guitar, so what other way am I going to do them? Whereas a lot of my previous songs, particularly on *Spike*, couldn't really go any other way because the component parts were written for certain sounds.

People get rather overheated about this. I remember after *Mighty Like A Rose* there was an hysterical piece, in *The Wire* I think it was, accusing me of trying to destroy pop music. Why in the world would I do that for my living? If you don't like something aesthetically, that's your prerogative, but no musician would ever dream of thinking like that. It's like saying, 'I've made a mistake by doing that.' But I haven't made any mistakes. I just made the record that I made then, and if you don't like it, then don't listen to it.

There's no such thing as a mistake in music. I really think that's true. It's like saying 'wrong harmonies'. That idiot Steve Martland went on television, or radio, and accused us of writing 'wrong harmonies' when we made *The Juliet Letters*. Wrong says who? Wrong says Bach? Wrong says Schoenberg? Wrong says Mingus? Wrong says me? Or him? Wrong harmony? Try telling that to Ornette Coleman or Charlie Parker. It's just different.

Everything is written consciously, deliberately. There's no mistakes in that sense. You can have bad intonation. You can sing out of tune. It's like that Bahamian guitar player, Joseph Spence, who Ry Cooder really admires. Well, his intonation would drive most people right out of the room, because it sounds berserk, but to him it's real. Or take Balinese music – it's all between the cracks.

But what about concepts of good and bad? There must be some critical benchmarks.

It's good and bad to you, though, in the moment that you hear it. And there's good and bad to me in the moment that I make it. So if I make something that doesn't appeal to people, then that's too bad, isn't it? I'm not making it at the whim of somebody else. I'm making it at my whim.

ARTIST
William S Burroughs

TITLE
Words Of Advice For Young People

SOURCE
Spare Ass Annie And Other Tales
LABEL
Island

William Burroughs? I don't know this album. Is this Willner's project with that rap band [The Disposable Heroes Of HipHoprisy]? I've been meaning to buy this. [Willner] came round to my house when we were talking about the Mingus record and he played me this version of Burroughs singing *Falling In Love Again* in German. Or maybe not; maybe I just heard it in German.

I like the groove, it sounded like a JBs groove. Great sound to the bass – it's so deep. But I've never read anything by William Burroughs. He's one of those people who were very fashionable when I started out – you had to have read Burroughs and Kerouac and listened to Kurt Weill and Jacques Brel. I've always been suspicious of bands who name themselves after book titles.

There are two things about Burroughs that have always put me off reading him. One is he shot his wife accidentally, by pretending to do a William Tell thing, which seemed to me to be enormously stupid. The second reason is that he took heroin, which also seemed enormously stupid. It's somehow become retrospectively hip that he survived it.

Maybe I should read the books and I would think of it differently, but heroin's never appealed to me. And I've always been a bit suspicious of the contrived bohemian; maybe he's the real item, I don't know. Perhaps the appeal is that people like to go and visit certain dark places and they want a guide. But if you have your own imagination, perhaps you don't need that help so much. Or there are more interesting places to go in other music and other books.

But, Burroughs is regarded fondly as being something of an agent provocateur. Doesn't that tally with people's idea of you being somewhat contrary or awkward by nature?

I don't think I'm particularly awkward. It just seems to me that everybody else is awkward.

How about artistically?

No, I think all that's bullshit as well. And the idea that I'm an outsider – for one thing that's an excuse for not being successful. I hate the words alternative rock. I was deeply offended by being nominated for an Alternative Grammy a couple of years back. As was Tom Waits, who I really, really admire. I know there are elements of the bohemian culture that go through his music, yet somehow, even though I know there's a contrivance to some of it, it has soul and humanity. There's a chilling thing in the Burroughs that doesn't appeal to me – but then again, I'd rather listen to that than to some rapper talking about how big his dick is.

ARTIST
Frank Sinatra & Bono

SOURCE
Duets

TITLE
I've Got You Under My Skin

LABEL
Capitol

[After a few bars] *I've Got You Under My Skin* – different one though. Is this from *Duets*? There's only two tracks on it worthwhile. That one, and the one with Tony Bennett. Sinatra sings great for a man of his age who's lived as hard as he has, but I think most others just embarrass themselves. He didn't need to do it. He's way hipper and more talented than any of the other singers – he makes all the others seem like amateurs.

You know the reason why Sinatra is hipper than Elvis? It's because Frank never sang anything about seafood. He made embarrassing records, I'm sure, but he never sang about clams. If he's having fun being back in the charts, then I think that's great, because he deserves all the respect for the music that he's done and

Bono at least has fun doing the thing. His performance is spectacular – I love the falsetto and it's bold. And it sounds like he's enjoying himself. He's saying, 'What the hell? This is not real; this is just like *Zoo TV*. This is plastic. Let's have fun.' But what's the fucking point of doing another version of this song? The original is one of the great pieces of music. And Sinatra's re-entry after the middle horn section – well, you can't notate that, there is no notation for that. That is genius in singing. Just that phrase. If someone asked me, 'What's great about Sinatra?', I'd say, 'That note.' That's what makes him better than anybody else.

ARTIST
Arnold Schoenberg

TITLE
Galgenlied and Enthauptung

SOURCE
Pierrot Lunaire

LABEL
Harmonia Mundi

Pierrot Lunaire. I tell you what, that's much better to go and see than listen to. I went to see Simon Rattle conduct it with the City of Birmingham Symphony Orchestra, their chamber ensemble, and there was a slight attempt at staging, and it was fantastic. They were really engaged in the music. But I think it's a little bit hard to listen to – the *Sprechgesang* is a bit hard to take. But you know, I went to hear the Monteverdi, *The Coronation Of Poppea*, a month or so back and there was real freedom in the singing there. Obviously it conformed to rules about harmony and form and everything, which Schoenberg broke up, but there's an argument for saying that that degree of free expression for the word and the emotion inside the structure is more of an achievement than just breaking all the rules, and just going anywhere. I went to see Schoenberg's *Pelleas And Melisande* at the Opera House and I was nearly asleep by the end of the first half. Not because it was bad; because it was so damn good. It was soporific in the most fantastic way. It was like a dream. The music was so beautiful it actually lulled you into complete calm. It was wonderful.

I think there's beautiful music in Schoenberg's work; I just don't think this is particularly it. But I'm glad this existed – like a lot of things that were terribly radical when they happened, they became a stepping stone to something else, like a freedom of expression. Without him doing this, certain other things wouldn't have been possible. It's like listening to the Vogue recordings of Stravinsky's early work, made in France just ten years or so after the premieres of things like *The Rite Of Spring*. They're absolutely unbelievable. Music critics will tell you they're badly played, but what I hear is the musicians struggling with the music, and that's what's thrilling. It's like going to a downtown club in New York and hearing somebody hammering out some new little corner of music – sure it isn't absolutely perfect, but it's a glimpse into some other possibility. And that's what this is.

ARTIST
Bobby Bland

TITLE
Fever

SOURCE
The Soul Of The Man

LABEL
MCA

[After the first few bars] *Fever*. Bobby Bland? I haven't heard that before. It's real music. It's the best. I like the kind of Shelly Manne/Chico Hamilton ensemble sound. It's very open, like a lot of 50s jazz recordings. It's really hip. *Really* hip. It's proper music. He's the greatest. There's something just so right about everything, about the way he sings. . . My favourite version of *Fever* has always been the Little Willie John version, just because his singing is so wild, like Little Richard on his ballads. I just love that melismatic singing – Little Willie John is just so fearless. But there's a moodier song to be had out of *Fever*; Bobby Bland tends to hit each song very hard. The Peggy Lee version is really great; and another one that often gets overlooked, that came out on that *Elvis Blues* album a few years ago, was Presley's version, which is tremendous. It's done similar to that, but even sparser, with just bongos and an upright bass, and it's one of those real tense Elvis performances. He was really a great blues singer, like intuitive, not like some guy singing in a choked-up kind of way, like some fake, I'm-really-soulful voice like Michael Bolton.

Bob Dylan & The Band

The Basement Tapes

Columbia

Tears Of Rage

Oh great. That's *Tears Of Rage*, isn't it? I didn't have this at the time – I never bought bootlegs so I didn't hear these songs until they were commercially released [in 1975], and I really love the record. It's one of the great records.

When he started, Dylan undoubtedly, and there's no secret to the fact, invented a persona, just like Woody Guthrie did, which became more and more credible as he went on because he was a naturally great artist. Plus he really liked rock 'n' roll; he wasn't one of those uptight folkies who couldn't deviate. What's interesting about this is that by the time he got here, I think he was trying to write songs that sounded like he'd just found them under a stone, as if they sound like real folk songs – because if you go back into the folk tradition you will find songs as dark and deep as these.

What I hear on this is something intangible, the sound is so carefree, and sombre as well, very serious. He's unbelievable. But I was never really that big a Dylan fan when I was a kid. I thought Bob Dylan was a pop singer because my dad used to bring home all the records he had to learn to cover in the band; they did *Subterranean Homesick Blues* and *Like A Rolling Stone* because they were in the charts – strange as it may seem to imagine The Joe Loss Orchestra playing those things. It was only later that I started buying the albums. I remember buying *Blonde On Blonde* in 1970 and really liking it.

Recently I recorded a demo tape of songs for George Jones, after we'd discussed the possibility of him making a more wide-ranging record of American songs that apparently fell outside Country music, but by just him singing them would be Country or George Jones songs. I recorded sketches of songs by Tom Waits, Ira Gershwin's *How Long Has This Been Going On?*, *Congratulations* by Paul Simon, Springsteen's *Brilliant Disguise*, and then I recorded Dylan's *I'm Going To Make You Lonesome Til You Go*, and the difference in the lyrics and the structure of Dylan's writing was amazing. Dylan's words blew everybody else right out of the water – even Ira Gershwin. No comparison.

Dean Belcher

Born in 1938 in Danzig, Germany, Holger Czukay studied music with the composer Karlheinz Stockhausen before forming Can in 1968 with Irmin Schmidt, Jaki Liebezeit and Michael Karoli. Over the next eight years Can became one of the most influential and infamous of all the so-called Krautrock groups, releasing a string of records which combined marathon improvisation jams, tape splicing, studio treatments, 'ethnic forgeries'. After Can folded in the late 70s (they briefly reformed in 1989 and released a new album, *Rite Time*), Czukay plunged into his own experiments with short-wave radio and sampling, which he'd been increasingly immersed in during the later stages of Can's career. On LPs like *Movies* (1979), he constructed music by improvising accompaniments to snippets of unknown, taped radio broadcasts, which were then rigorously edited and treated. He has been in demand as a collaborative musician ever since going solo, working with, among others, David Sylvian and Jah Wobble. At the time of the Jukebox he had just released the *Moving Pictures* album on Mute.

Holger Czukay

ARTIST
Karlheinz Stockhausen

SOURCE
Kontakte

LABEL
Sony

TITLE
Teil 2

[After a few seconds] Stockhausen, it's *Teil*.

Which members of Can studied under Stockhausen?

Irmin Schmidt and me.

Why did you both choose to work in the rock field subsequently?

Because we wanted to start something new. You have to remember we began in 1968, and 68 was a new beginning for most people, we wanted to forget everything we knew. Jaki Liebezeit, our drummer, said, 'The only chance to create something new is if we are going to reduce ourselves to a minimum of that which we can really do.' For example, play one note instead of three. I think Stockhausen is probably the last great classical composer, but the new style of composer will be very different. Classical musicians are now part of a sound museum. I know the problems Stockhausen had working with such people as a conductor. It was a horror! He always told me, 'You must know these people's psychology.' Do I want to be a psychologist for classical musicians? So I told him to go and play everything on his own: go and fire these people straight away. I think a new Beethoven will appear one of these days, attracted to the development of the present digital technique; he won't need to write it down.

ARTIST
Pink Floyd

SOURCE
Tonight Let's All Make Love In London

TITLE
Nick's Boogie

LABEL
See For Miles

I don't know what it is. It sounds a little bit like an unedited rehearsal by a live group.

It's from a soundtrack made in the late 60s; this song is by Pink Floyd.

That's what I thought, late 60s; in fact I thought of their first album. But I couldn't recognise the track.

Were they an early influence on Can?

Yes, of course, but I must say I was never personally so impressed by them; although I could see they were trying something different.

Did you consciously look around to see where you fitted in at that time?

Exactly, that's what we did. At that time we were very much trying to orientate ourselves. We were impressed by people who were instigators. The Pink Floyd were one such group and The Velvet Underground another. Something like *Sister Ray* seemed very wild and spontaneous.

Had you heard Pink Floyd or The Velvet Underground prior to Can's formation?

Before the band I was working as a music teacher. The pupils would play music to me; first The Beatles, then the hip pupils would bring something like The Velvet Underground. I met Michael Karoli, who was a pupil of mine, and decided to start a band.

So it was then you decided to start Can?

That came when the kids asked me to join them in the school band they had formed. It went so well, I thought why not do it professionally? Then I wrote to Karoli to suggest we start a band.

ARTIST
Herbie Hancock

TITLE
Hidden Shadows

SOURCE
Sextant

LABEL
Sony Japan

Strange rhythm. I don't know what it is, but it's live players and not sequenced. It sounds very 70s.

It's Herbie Hancock.

It's Hancock! I would never have guessed. It's a very strange complicated rhythm. It reminds me of *Aqualung* by Jethro Tull; they had completely crazy rhythms like this. What we're hearing would have fitted perfectly in to the German rock of the early 70s.

It's a group comprising Miles Davis acolytes from the late 60s/early 70s. Was that period of Miles an influence on Can?

Very much. *Bitches Brew* was a very big influence. That was when jazz became interesting and calculable. It became a thing where you could say yes or no, instead of becoming so free that you don't know what yes or no is. It became electric.

Were you aware of a free jazz movement at that time?

Yes, I was aware, but Jaki Liebezeit was actually a free jazz drummer, playing with a famous group led by Manfred Schoof. Then he felt it became too free; it was while playing in a modern jazz opera with four other drummers, he noticed that he could play what he wanted and the conductor wouldn't notice it or declare it right or wrong. Jaki wanted simplicity and to be able to tell right from wrong. So he said goodbye to that scene.

069

Holger Czukay

ARTIST
Ennio Morricone

TITLE
Humanity Part 2

SOURCE
The Thing: OST

LABEL
Varese Sarabande

It could be a track from a tragic sci-fi soundtrack.

Close. Do you have any idea which movie?

No, I only guessed by the sound of the piece.

It's Morricone's soundtrack for John Carpenter's version of *The Thing*.

Morricone! I would never have guessed it was him. You know I met him at a film festival. I was giving a lecture to the musicians attending, on how to make music that would lead to their own unemployment. I told them that the dilettante was of far more worth than all the experts on trumpets and violins. I saw Morricone in the audience and he was sitting there looking completely bored, thinking to himself what a hopeless case I was. Then I illustrated what I meant by playing them a recording of my music and accompanying video. I didn't see him again for a year. Then the day before Sergio Leone's funeral, I met him again and we went for a meal together. It was there that he said to me, 'When I saw you at that film festival, originally I thought you were completely nuts. I couldn't take you seriously at all. What you said sounded like complete nonsense. But then I heard the music and saw the video and thought: this man is even right.'

ARTIST
Brainticket

TITLE
Brainticket Part I

SOURCE
Brainticket

LABEL
Bellaphon

It sounds great. So far it sounds like the most modern song you've played me.
It's one of the oldest. It's from an obscure German band, released in 1971.
It's fantastic. I've never heard it before.
They're called Brainticket. It reminds me of a 70s funk/*musique concrète* crossover.
Yes, it is something like that. I had to wonder if it was a sample montage or some sort of jazz/rock mutation, but it was neither thankfully. The mix is very good with the organ so high in the mix. It could easily be a very early Phil Spector production. Spector's selection process, pushing the best instrument to drive a song, is fantastic. This is the way I choose to work now but obviously with a lot more editing involved, thousands of edits that you can't even hear. I no longer even use multitrack. I have a digital editing system.

ARTIST
David Sylvian

TITLE
Maria

SOURCE
Secrets Of The Beehive

LABEL
Virgin

Yes, of course this is obvious, not just from the voice but the music as well.
Are you very fond of Sylvian's music?
Yes, especially this album. I also really enjoy working with him. David is one of my favourite vocalists and musicians, particularly for making decisions on what sounds have to be used. He has great taste. He is a man who originates from the first sound onwards, in order to envelop the whole song.
Do you identify with his vision?
Yes, very much, he is one of the greatest Ambient musicians. This track is a piece of music I can always listen to.
Had you met Jon Hassell before sharing a recording date on Sylvian's *Brilliant Trees*?
We had both studied under Stockhausen, we became friends during that time. He, like myself, stepped out of the classical field and founded a strong identity since that decision. He also influenced me a lot as regards alien sounds and his method of playing an instrument; the idea of something requiring so little effort having so much effect.

Holger Czukay

ARTIST

AMM

TITLE

Ailantus Glandulosa

SOURCE

AMM Music 1966

LABEL

Matchless Recordings

A group of transit passengers passing by and then disappearing again. It could be a very early Can piece, we have done a lot of this type of chaotic recording, as well as live performances which incorporated this kind of technique. That was the principle of Can, you could say. To form a structure and then end up with chaos, and from that chaos start up again.

This is AMM from 1966. They're a group of British improvisors whose core is still working today.

This is, as regards our live recordings, one of the closest relatives I've heard to Can. Public Image of course were somehow influenced too, but this could easily be an old recording of Can. It's very, very interesting.

Keith Rowe, the guitarist, has also been a keen advocate of the abuse of short-wave radio.

The amount of chaos is very strongly related to free jazz but much more refreshing.

ARTIST

Public Image Limited

TITLE

Socialist

SOURCE

Metal Box

LABEL

Virgin

It could be Neu!. Certainly it's played live and very monotonous. Very cheap pure electronics on top; it could be an earlier influence on Techno, due to the monotony and bristling electronics. No refrains. Pure sound impact.

You've worked with one member of this group before.

Is it This Heat?

No, it's Public Image Ltd with Jah Wobble, from *Metal Box*.

That is very unusual for PiL, I mean it's instrumental. Jah Wobble told me about their recording sessions. He said they were a real adventure. They used similar techniques to Can's. They would play until they located and keep the mysterious parts; playing so long until you've got a track that retains a secret. They were one of my favourite bands, especially because of Wobble. I even liked *Flowers Of Romance*, although he had left the band by then. Jaki was especially fond of *Flowers*, because rhythmically it had been so reduced. This is where I find the power of their music and the quality. Now, of course, they are very uninteresting.

You made *Full Circle* with Wobble in 1980. How did that come about?

It's one of my favourite albums. We met through a mutual friend who had been working for *NME*. He set up a meeting and Wobble just drank beer after beer, which I didn't like very much. Then suddenly he stopped drinking and then I started to find him quite fascinating. Wobble then booked a very small studio in Soho, and we finished the recordings in about three hours, obviously excluding the editing and mixing.

So Jah Wobble was a fan of Can?

Yes, he and the others in PiL liked Can and demonstrated this by playing a 20 minute piece on Capital Radio to accompany an interview.

Holger Czukay

ARTIST
Brian Eno/David Byrne

TITLE
A Secret Life

SOURCE
My Life In The Bush Of Ghosts

LABEL
Editions EG

Is it *My Life In The Bush Of Ghosts*?

Yes, *A Secret Life*. How did you end up meeting Eno?
He was touring with Roxy Music and I went backstage and introduced myself. Later I played on two recording sessions with him. I played on *Music For Airports* but he didn't use the bassline in the end. He was right not to.

In 1968 you recorded a solo album, *Canaxis*, which featured a lot of ethnic music samples. Do you think it influenced an album like *Bush Of Ghosts*?
I spoke to Eno and he told me he was influenced more by my album *Movies*. Of course he made something different from ethnic samples, so he didn't copy me.

Do you feel guilty about the potentially exploitative aspects of sampling African tribes?
No, not at all. When Reebop [Kwaku Baah, percussionist on Can's *Saw Delight*, and an ex-Hendrix, Stones and Traffic session musician] came into Can with Rosko Gee, I had the radio set up and was listening out for possible signals from all over the world; the group was not fond of this idea, they wanted to become proper musicians. During a concert in Berlin, Reebop beat me up, because he felt I was stealing musicians' souls. I can assure you, other people may want to steal their souls, but not me. I wanted to create a new living being out of these sounds. The rest of the group remained passive while he hit me in the face. Then they unplugged me on stage. That was the end of Can. It was 1976 or 77.

ARTIST
Cheb Khaled

TITLE
Sidi Boumedienne

SOURCE
Raï Rebels

LABEL
Earthworks

Could it be one of the Afro/French things from Paris?

It's a raï recording by Cheb Khaled.
That is the type of music I meant. To tell you the truth, when I heard raï in the beginning I had thought to myself, if they had kept the music as natural as it once was it would have been much better than adding poor samples. The sampler on this recording sounds like shit. That these people are finding a new way of expressing themselves is fine by me. I find that positive. What I think is a horror is the thought or reality of 'cheap international' as I call it. Feeling at home in a hotel in Tokyo or London because they both look the same.

Do you think you can be accused of playing a part in introducing that kind of transglobal blandness, with a recording like *Canaxis*?
Yes, this is possible and could be an argument against my whole style of production. I have done that and played a part in starting it perhaps. But whether it was a good or bad idea only time will tell.

Lee Perry

Roast Fish & Cornbread

The Upsetter Presents Roast Fish & Cornbread

VP Records

Is that Lee Perry?

Yes, from the Black Ark period.

He is one of my greatest heroes. Brian Eno introduced me to Lee Perry's music. I think it was in 1973 or 75, at the Notting Hill Carnival. Reggae was completely new and exotic to me. The fact that they were playing so slow was something which fascinated me. Lee Perry felt like a brother to me in terms of musical relationships.

Kraftwerk

Ruckzuck

Kraftwerk

Philips

Laurie Anderson?

No, European.

It's one of Kraftwerk's first pieces. This song became very successful. It's now used as a theme tune for a TV news magazine.

At the time of this record they visited Can's studio nearly every second or third day. I respect them very much for what they have done because what they create is a type of mood picture. *Autobahn*, with its simple idea, gives such a strong identity. The bad side for me is that they are too clean and robotic now.

Did you feel that Can was part of some overall German movement or scene?

In a way, yet the feeling of wanting independence, especially from other groups, was dominant. It was a hippy time, when everyone wanted to be unified; then the experience of what that actually meant – you do the work and I take the benefits. So very quickly we decided not to be too brotherly.

Were you interested in Faust's experiments?

Faust seemed innovative to me, but to tell you the truth we didn't respect them very much. It seemed to us that they would be a one-day wonder and it happened exactly like that. Can at least developed.

How do you view groups like them and The Velvet Underground now that they have reformed?

Actually it's fine, musically it may not be such a good decision. I can understand Maureen Tucker wanting a new flat for her and her family.

What were the reasons for Can's reformation on the 1989 *Rite Time* album?

Because Malcolm Mooney [Can's first singer] suddenly wrote me a letter saying he would like to sing again, having only been working with sculpture. With the others I said it would have to be innovative in some way for it to be worthwhile.

So it was a musical decision and not an economical choice.

Yes, we got together for a test recording and it took me a week to decide to try again. The recording sessions lasted for three weeks and were very good. But then of course came the 95 per cent workload, with the mixing and editing. At the end the members of Can felt very differently about the results. It wasn't

073

Holger Czukay

a bad album [Rite Time] but I had to fight for *In The Distance Lies The Future*, the best track, to be included on the final CD.

Why?

Only God knows.

Will there be any further Can recordings?

I'm not so sure. I think that the time is over. I personally don't want to blame anyone but suddenly I felt surrounded by old people. I'm far more attracted to young people's ideas at the moment.

075>

A former star pupil at London's Royal College Of Music, Anne Dudley is one of the most prolific arrangers, composers and producers in British music. Her name is linked to some of the more notorious moments in the last 15 years of British pop music. Working with Trevor Horn, she had a major involvement in recordings by Frankie Goes To Hollywood, ABC, Malcolm McLaren and The Pet Shop Boys. Her 80s group The Art Of Noise, whose early use of digital sampling and editing has proved massively influential and prophetic, notched up hits like *Close (To The Edit)*, *Moments In Love* and a version of Prince's *Kiss*, which featured Tom Jones on vocals. Since then she has recorded *Songs From The Victorious City* (1990) with Killing Joke's Jaz Coleman, which sought ways to combine Eastern and Western tonalities. She has over 12 feature film soundtracks (including *The Crying Game* and *Buster*) to her credit, as well as numerous pieces of music for TV. In 1995 Dudley released her debut classical album of hymn settings, *Ancient And Modern* (Echo), to great acclaim. Now in her mid-thirties, she lives in the countryside outside London with her family.

ARTIST
John Adams

TITLE
Common Tones In Simple Time

SOURCE
The Chairman Dances

LABEL
Elektra Nonesuch

[Immediately] It's John Adams. . . Not *Harmonielehre*? No, it's *Common Tones*. I haven't heard this for ages. It's lovely. He's regained this wonderful passion for tonality, this ecstasy. He's so slick with his rhythms. I think it's amazing how performance has developed in the 20th century. I went to a series of Boulez concerts, and heard things like Webern's Opus 6, which I remember from college as a difficult and ugly thing. I think now that perhaps the recordings I'd previously heard weren't good enough. Boulez coaxed such a smooth, sensuous performance out of the musicians, who had no difficulty with the piece. It's interesting to see how something that's innovative is difficult for the musicians to understand, and then it becomes part of their everyday experience. I think this has happened with Adams. In his early days, musicians found these pulsing rhythms and the idea of a continuous beat quite alien. Now they're used to playing with click tracks, doing rock music, film music. It's second nature. It's easy. I'm sure that's what Adams wanted.

The title of your piece on *Ancient And Modern*, *Three Chorales In Common Time*, suggested an association with Adams.

Not many people noticed that. I remember hearing *Christian Zeal And Activity*, from this album, years ago, when we were doing the last Art Of Noise album. This was the track with the preacher on. I thought, 'this is such a brilliant idea!' I felt tremendously jealous that someone had got there first. Well, [Steve] Reich had really got there first, but this is less repetitive than *It's Gonna Rain*, a little more musical, much as I like Reich. Adams's idea of using hymn tunes – which are common to us all – started germinating in my mind at that time. I got myself a lot of Adams's music at this time. *The Wound Dresser* was wonderful, although I heard his *Violin Concerto* recently and was a bit disappointed. Fiendish violin part. There's a ghastly piece he did for synthesiser. What was it? *Hoodoo Zephyr*. But at his best, there's a sense of wonder in Adams which I really love. It's filmic in a way. It conjures up big landscapes.

ARTIST
Hussein El Masry

TITLE
Sydy Ya

SOURCE
Danses Orientales: Belly Dance In Cairo

LABEL
Playasound

I recognise the style. This reminds me of Jaz Coleman sitting here, about four years ago, playing Egyptian dance music. I don't know the artist here. This is commercial Egyptian music and I think it's this violin style that got Jaz going. The accordion player sounds like the chap we used on *Songs From The Victorious City*.

On that album, was it hard to work out a method in which you could combine Eastern and Western tonalities?

We didn't have such a purist approach. We approached it as Westerners taking on some of the exotic elements of Eastern music. The whole idea of the album was one of fusion with these melodies and decorations. It was difficult to get the balance right. The more you listen to this sort of music, the more normal it sounds. If you'd never heard it, it would sound extraordinarily exotic. Perhaps we lost the plot a bit; we made it too Eastern, I think, a bit too unapproachable. That doesn't mean to say it wasn't great fun to do. As we speak, that album is Number One in Lebanon. In the Middle East, that record is big news.

How many copies have you sold?

Oh, we don't sell any copies. It's all bootlegged on cassettes and there are no royalties off the radio either. But a friend told me that every second track on Turkish radio came from Jaz and mine's album, so we have made some impression, I suppose.

ARTIST
Japan

TITLE
Nightporter

SOURCE
Gentlemen Take Polaroids
LABEL
Virgin

Satie? No, it's a very conscious copy. I recognise this voice. David Sylvian, Japan. I haven't heard it before.

In the 80s, Japan seemed to be one of those very knowing bands who played about with various styles.

Japan were around at the time I was working with ABC and Spandau Ballet. I'm not sure that this music has aged very well. People say to me, 'What was it like being involved in such a classic album as ABC's *Lexicon Of Love*?' And I think, *classic*? Distance has lent some enchantment to that view. Fashion was tremendously important to New Romanticism, and one way that The Art Of Noise avoided being any part of that was by never having any photos circulated. We were very aloof. We used to release pictures of spanners in lieu of publicity shots. And those enigmatic press releases from Paul Morley that nobody understood. It wouldn't have done to appear on *Top Of The Pops* with eyeliner. . . Actually, we did do *Close (To The Edit)* on *TOTP* once. We were heavily disguised in masks, huge coats and hidden behind banks of synthesisers.

Anne Dudley

ARTIST
Henry Purcell

TITLE
I Was Glad When They Said Unto Me

SOURCE
The Complete Anthems And Services Volume Seven
LABEL
Hyperion

Is it Parry? Oh, Purcell? Well, Parry wrote *I Was Glad* as well. If it had not got to this stage, I'd have known that it wasn't 20th century, but there was an extraordinary chord change at the beginning that really got me.

There's something enduring about English hymnal music . . .

That it's sometimes difficult to spot which century it is? This choral tradition is so pervasive and the 20th century guys took it on wholeheartedly. This hasn't got the same smoothness of The Sixteen Choir.

What prompted your choral album?

Partially, it was hearing the sound of The Sixteen on one of those free CDs you get with classical magazines. I found it so beautiful. I felt that if I could just combine that sound with some of the ideas I had, everything would fall into place. . . I never had much involvement with this sort of music as I grew up. I wasn't a very good singer, and I never played the organ. It's always been there for me, but I come to it as an outsider. This is lovely. I'd rather listen to this than David Sylvian.

ARTIST
Bernard Herrmann

TITLE
Psycho

SOURCE
Bernard Herrmann Film Scores

LABEL
BMG

[Immediately] Bernard Herrmann. *Psycho*. I love it to death. Is this playing when Janet Leigh is driving? It is. If you see the sequence without music, it's just this woman driving. With music, it's tormenting. He's very economical in his score: he only uses strings and there are a lot of repeated figures. He's been so influential in the development of film music. He realised that it's not symphonic, it's something else. You're writing about emotion. It's a very different way to approach structure.

Do you think film composers have suffered in comparison with 'proper' composers? Is there an attitude that writing for commercial gain is less worthy than starving and writing concertos?

Yes, I think there is. [Composer] Elizabeth Lutyens, who wrote a lot of music for Hammer films, once said, 'I write two types of music. My own, and film music.' She obviously felt that her film music was not her real music and she disowned it. I think that's terrible.

She wrote a lot of her film music under a pseudonym.

There you have it. But to return to musicians playing avant garde music; if they do film scores, they have to play a lot of weird stuff. So when they come to play avant garde things, it is less alien to them. Also, audiences, without realising it, hear the most atonal and challenging stuff on soundtracks, which acclimatises them to avant garde sounds. Herrmann has been a major influence for me in my film writing. Also, John Williams at his best. Jerry Goldsmith – excellent. Morricone. Rota I like, but he's a lot more individual. Herrmann wanted to be taken seriously. He wrote some concert music. I haven't heard it; it goes to show you how he wasn't taken seriously. Maybe there won't be such a division in the future.

ARTIST
György Ligeti

TITLE
Lux Aeterna

SOURCE
Lux Aeterna

LABEL
Deutsche Grammophon

Ligeti. This was used on *2001* and I can't remember what it's called. . . *Eternal*

Light. You know that story about that film's score? They booked a composer to write it, and while he was writing, the editor started beavering away in his record collection. He pulled out a Strauss waltz, a bit of that, *Also Sprach [Zarathustra]*, the Ligeti. It seemed to be so right that they went with what we call a 'temp score', which is the music they put on just for screenings, before the dub's finished. So the poor old composer never got a look in. It was a bit like being the fifth Beatle.

When you're trying to score a film scene in which nothing much is happening, except, perhaps, mental processes or intense emotions or even just a pendulous atmosphere, how do you put that into sound?

It's so difficult to describe. Often you have to decide what it is that's going on inside that character. Whatever you write has to fit in with the style of the rest of the music; there has to be a unity. Each cue can't be different. It also depends on what stage of the film you're at. At the beginning you can't use the same intensity of expression that you can at the end. By the end, you've hopefully drawn the audience with you; at the start, the story is about to be revealed. There are so many factors involved. In the end, it has to be a direct response from yourself to what's going on.

ARTIST
Giya Kancheli

SOURCE
Abii Ne Viderem

LABEL
ECM

TITLE
Morning Prayers

It's lovely. Who is it?

A modern Georgian composer.

Not Pärt then, or Szymanowski or Schnittke. This one's a Holy Minimalist, isn't he? It's very filmic. I can see it, can't you? It's a big shot, very misty, a bit mysterious.

What do you make of the 'holiness' of some Minimalists and their popularity? Is it a *fin de siècle* phenomenon, with people trying to find something transcendental in a secular age?

Yes, but . . . I could happily listen to this without knowing what the text was. I could feel a sort of spirituality creeping across. But having said that, the texts are important. Anyone who thought that Górecki's Third was a dirge would have to revise their views once they realised how intense the words were. The more you know of it, the more spiritual it becomes.

ARTIST
The Orb

SOURCE
Orbvs Terrarvm

LABEL
Island

TITLE
Valley

Anne Dudley

Is it The Orb, or something like that? One review of *Ancient And Modern* said that it made everything The Orb had ever done redundant. We went out and bought two albums – I blame my husband for that – put them on and waited for something to happen. It's a bit like The Art Of Noise, it's that kind of genre, but we would have made one four minute track out of material that they extend for an hour. I guess I'm just not the sort of person who gets stoned. I want more stimulation than this. What this is lacking is wit. The Art Of Noise had a sense of humour. We used to throw in things that were a complete joke. But the idea of this lot doing anything funny – you'd tell them a joke and they'd laugh when they got home.

ARTIST
Prince

TITLE
Kiss

SOURCE
Parade

LABEL
Paisley Park

Well, yes, I think I know what this is. I love it. Prince writes great pop songs and then deconstructs them. We took *Kiss* and did a very direct, rock 'n' roll version of it. Nothing subtle. This is the opposite; so small sounding, a little bit introverted and he's singing in this ridiculously high voice. It's very explicit; he's singing about sex and yet the voice is *tiny*. On ours, Tom Jones sings it in full voice at about a fifth lower. Clare Fischer does some great arrangements on this album. The rumour is that Prince never meets Fischer, just sends her the tracks and lets her do her own thing. When Prince gets them back, he does odd things, like move the strings a bar behind the rhythm track or change the song. . . These string arrangements are, I think, tremendously influenced by The Beatles and George Martin. Their work was wonderful.

ARTIST
Marvin Gaye

TITLE
What's Goin' On

SOURCE
What's Goin' On

LABEL
Motown

Oh, W*hat's Goin' On*. Gaye. Keep this on. I still love this. There's a wonderful arrangement of this by Quincy Jones and nobody seems to know it, which is a pity because it anticipates all sorts of developments in funk and jazz funk. But this original is monstrous. What makes a great pop song? Voice, arrangements, songs. Great congas. This has got everything. Much more overtly sexy than Prince. I never saw Gaye perform. The closest I got was seeing Teddy Prendergast some place in Victoria. It was over the top enough to seem like a Lenny Henry piss take. You know, 'This is for all the ladies . . . yeah.' We sat there laughing. But this was the stuff I listened to most when I first got into pop music. The nice thing about Gaye is his extravagance. There are some nice ninths and elevenths. And the changes are really good, too: jazzy. It's a tragedy that he died. A real waste.

Andrea Giacobe

081 >

Garry Cobain and Brian Dougans, jointly Future Sound Of London, began making music together during the 80s as an obscure Industrial culture duo. They came to prominence in the early 90s, releasing a series of singles that plugged into the burgeoning Ambient/Techno/'Ardkore interface and which appeared under an array of pseudonyms: FSOL, Yage, Mental Cube, Indo Tribe, Semi Tribe, Smart Systems, Humanoid, etc. In 1993 the duo signed to Virgin following the success of their *Papua New Guinea* single and *Accelerator* album. At the time of the Jukebox they had released three Virgin albums – *Tales Of Ephidrina* (under the name Amorphous Androgynous), *Lifeforms* and the limited edition *ISDN* – as well as a number of singles and EPs, all combining the duo's interests in wayward electronics and sampladelia, and usually packaged in surreal digital montages. Cobain and Dougans disseminate their work via most of the vanguard technologies available to musicians in the 90s, most dramatically by transmitting real-time live performances down fibre optic cable (as documented on *ISDN*). Among other 'ultramedia' activities, they are also involved in an ongoing film project, *Yage*, and in producing a music-based TV programme, *Teachings From The Electronic Brain*. The jukebox took place at the duo's Earthbeat Studios in North West London. The lack of comments by Dougans was partly due to the fact that he spent most of the interview laying out text and artwork for FSOL's Internet pages. . .

ARTIST
Son'z Of A Loop Da Loop Era

TITLE
Peace And Lovism

SOURCE
Noise 3

LABEL
Jumpin' And Pumpin'

GC: That sounds like a harp pluck. [He stops the tape after 20 seconds and rewinds]
BD: That's Enya.
GC: Yeah. [He stops the tape again and starts fast forwarding]
BD: Does it change?
GC: You haven't got time to go through whole tracks these days. You have to contribute your kind of 'pornographic eye'. [He keeps fast forwarding] Martin Amis talks about the pornographic eye. If you like porn you learn to fast forward through the videos and catch the bits of porn. So us being samplers, we quickly learn just to forward through tracks to find what we like, and I can simply say, I don't like this.

Do you know who it is?
GC: Depends if it's new or old really. It sounds like it comes from that early XL camp – Prodigy, Liquid. If it came from 91 that would make it just about forgiveable. It wouldn't completely obliterate them from producing something good in the future. But if it's in the last two years, I'd say never listen to them again.

It's on XL from 92. It's Son'z Of A Loop Da Loop Era, aka Danny Breaks. He's now a big name in Jungle as Droppin' Science.
That was terrible. Deplorable era and a blind time. Anyone who managed to keep their head in that era and not do that sort of thing has benefited. I'm coming round to the point of thinking that being obvious can be really beautiful if you do it well. But that's a kind of obviousness I hate. It's a typical way of sampling that you get into in a certain period.

ARTIST
Brian Eno

TITLE
Brutal Ardour

SOURCE
Discreet Music

LABEL
Obscure

GC: From the council estate to The Lord's Chamber. We've been through our classical phase – we're not really in the mood now. There was a time five months ago when we were sucking on everything classical as maybe an inspiration. But I like to be quite shallow with music. I've been through the period of analysing music too heavily and now I'm just into a fix – how does it fix me on the spot? Certain aesthetics at certain times I just bypass and this isn't really giving me much. You think it's going to be very fulfilling, but it's not for me right now.

It's Brian Eno's version of Pachelbel's *Canon*, from *Discreet Music*, 1975. You used a version of this piece on *Lifeforms*.
GC: Did we, Brian?

BD: We did. It wasn't a sample though.

I'm wondering why you used it, as it's such a well-known piece.

GC: You'll have to ask Brian. That was Brian throwing something into the soup. [To BD] Why did you particularly recreate that piece?

BD: I really can't answer that.

GC: It was probably just a stoned night in Baker Street, so you'd have to go deep into Baker Street for that mythology.

BD: There's your answer.

GC: Our particular take was viewing everything as an electric soup and throwing anything and everything into it without any kind of theoretical analysis of why we were doing it. I guess the weird thing about being an artist is that you're taking all these influences and you are rejecting certain ones that you like, but you're rejecting them at a certain time. What I'm saying is, you've just caught me at a certain time. I know what I'm trying to create right now and I haven't done it; and I know my sources and what they are, and I'm rejecting sources that in the past have led me to creating bad work. And it was this kind of track particularly, and Eno specifically, that at a time three years ago, I was drawing on quite heavily, thinking that it would provide me with some answers. And generally I found that it pretended to give me the answers but didn't have them for me, so I learnt to go further afield, rejecting this kind of music. But it was extremely fulfilling for me a few years ago.

ARTIST
Material

TITLE
Disappearing

SOURCE
Memory Serves

LABEL
Celluloid

[Garry turns up the volume and he and Brian get out of their seats, face the speakers, and lurch back and forth in time to the rhythm]

GC: Yeah . . . scares me that one. I'm not sure who it is. I thought the key was with the trumpet player. The bass sound's awesome.

BD: George Clinton?

It's Material from 81.

GC: Brilliant. Really funky. I've not heard them before – it's a name I've seen mentioned, a re-emerging name. There's a new Bill Laswell band that I've been meaning to check out. It's quite A Certain Ratio in parts. We could sample that, which must mean it's quite good.

ARTIST
Sun Ra

TITLE
Journey To The Stars

SOURCE
My Brother The Wind Volume II

LABEL
Evidence

GC: Sounds like an EMS wired up to the cortex of the brain modulating and transmitting the brain waves.

BD [Looks at the sleeve] Sun Ra. Oh wow. Trippy.

Its a Sun Ra Mini-Moog solo from 1970.

GC: Is that what it's called?

No, It's called _Journey To The Stars_.

GC: If it was called _Mini-Moog Solo_ it would have a certain tongue-in-cheek quality that I like – bringing into question the whole solo thing of a musician, which would be quite cool. But called _Journey To The Stars_, he's just gone right up his own pipe. That was terrible.

I heard you were big fans of early Moog pieces like _Switched On Bach_. This is solo Moog but from a different tradition.

GC: Yeah, we've got loads of them. I like some of the Tomita versions of things, only because I like some of the Debussy things he's taken off: _The Girl With The Golden Hair_, or whatever it's called, which is beautiful. I went into a period where anything kitsch was brilliant. And there's also a lot of theoretical electronic shit from the early days, like Morton Subotnik. Just modulators producing amazing noises, but it doesn't ever evolve into a song or a track or a tune. We were into this phase of noise – fuck the tradition of songs and melodies, just pure 3D noise and freak-out of space. We did love it. But this is just modulating a sound that isn't that great. Not only that, but it's not even a tune. None of these things are bad. You don't have to write tunes, you don't have to use brilliant sounds, but it certainly helps.

Can you listen back to kitsch early synthesiser things like Tomita and think of them as good in their own right?

GC: Yeah . . . it takes a very, very good piece of music to be altered like that. It's quite hard to bend electronic sounds round some of the classical compositions like Tomita used to do. And in a lot of cases it sounds really grating and not very nice. Conversely, we had a piece scored for orchestra, a classical rendition of a track of ours [_Eggshell_] that was never released – because we suddenly realised what pompous assholes we were being by even trying to get a classical derivation of it done anyway. We realised how simple some of our melodies were and how they didn't transfer very well. Part of it was great and part of it was really bad – 24 tracks of classical meanderings.

ARTIST
King Tubby

SOURCE
Dub Gone Crazy

LABEL
Blood And Fire

TITLE
Satta Dread Dub

GC: Could be millions of people. Kneel to the powers of dub. Are you going to do it, Brian?

BD: No.

GC: What I don't understand is, if they love that echo machine so much and get so much pleasure fucking with echo machines, imagine how they'd like a sampler! What are you boys doing? Get yourself a fucking sampler, start fucking with the sound more. This is straight dub with no frills.

BD: This is 1972, though.

GC: Yeah, I don't care. Who is it, King Tubby?

Yes, from the mid-70s.

GC: That was a good bleep there. I think it's mundane.

Your music hits at dub at times.

GC: We do it in a more obscure way – without trying to sound too pompous.

We try to throw in everything in a shallow way. We do dub every day. I must say I prefer the Western slant where everything gets more fucked up – like Tackhead, Adrian Sherwood, African Head Charge, Dub Syndicate. I just find their use of sound much more interesting and find traditional dub just as bad as traditional anything.

ARTIST
Brian Eno & David Byrne

TITLE
Come With Us

SOURCE
My Life In The Bush Of Ghosts

LABEL
Editions EG

GC: [Immediately] This is Eno. This album has four really amazing tracks in a row and the rest is absolute cack. [Pauses] Ah . . . I think I understand. [To BD] You understand, of course, what's going on here?
BD: Oh yeah, I understand.
GC: It's amazing how embarrassed you are to say how much you hate things, because it reflects on you in a way. But I don't like too much optimism and 'everything's beautiful'. It is, but I really like getting to the root of the problem as well. That's a great track and I'm almost forced from my reaction to everything else to go completely over the top and say how great it was.
I assume that when you said you 'understand', you thought we'd picked this track because we thought it sounded similar to you, which we did.
GC: Are we influenced by that? As much as by Barbra Streisand. I always listen to those four tracks and I've discounted the rest of the album, rightly or wrongly. But those four tracks are the ones that I play a couple of times a month, which is quite a lot in a short life.
Do you think it stands up as an early use of sampling?
GC: Yeah, it's done in a way that I couldn't do right now, and that's what appeals to me.

ARTIST
Tangerine Dream

TITLE
Mysterious Semblance At The Strand Of Nightmares

SOURCE
Phaedra

LABEL
Virgin

GC: Where's the rock records, man? Where's the vocals?
BD: Tangerine Dream.
GC: It's that bubbling, that analogue bubbling. You wouldn't think that someone could achieve that sound so characteristically. We've got virtually all the albums, but I couldn't name more than two tracks off the whole lot.
This is *Mysterious Semblance At The Strand Of Nightmares*.
GC: From *Phaedra*. There's one track on that album that's still amazing. We are generally quite interested in Tangerine Dream. In fact they became a kind of yardstick for us. It's bizarre listening back to the albums. There are some tracks that

have really withstood time – but some of it does seem to be very lazy. There seems to have been a myth there and it's not totally justified. Maybe it's quite simple – if you do a couple of amazing tracks that sustain time, you're forgiven for all the rest of the crap.

It's strange how Tangerine Dream are being accepted and reappraised now after being vilified for so long.

GC: It's bizarre – how records change in the history of time and the way that people begin to look at the veneer of what's been created. It's weird when you listen to music like that and know the time it was written. You find yourself listening to it just to see if it still sounds modern. That's something, but it's then actually going beyond that and saying, 'Yes, it still sounds modern *and* it's a great track.'

ARTIST
Lonnie Liston Smith

SOURCE
Classic Jazz Funk Mastercuts Volume One

TITLE
Expansions

LABEL
Mastercuts

GC [Starts singing along with the bassline immediately] It's *Expansions*.
BD: Oh yes, yes, it's all coming back now!
GC: My first reaction as soon as I heard the intro was, Oh, they've sampled *Expansions*. Then the bassline came in and I thought, fuck, they've sampled a big chunk! And then I realised it was the original – so I guess that says that it's now become a bit of a classic. It's also become really hackneyed because every cheap-shit producer in danceland has had a go at this, and it's partly ruined it. I wish I could hear it without having had that discoloured experience – that's what sampling has done.

On *ISDN*, you started using a lot more jazz and fusion-based textures and beats.
BD: None from him, though, I'll quite quickly clarify.
GC: It's an interesting area and I'd like to produce a record that no one knows is being done on machines. We've been heavily into machines for eight years so, we do see a certain beauty in the way that a band would perform. We always have a problem: we like instrumentalists, but they've always got such an ego and want to play their instrument over the entire track. A lot of instrumentalists, they just blow, man, for fuckin' hours on end. And they lose some of the ability to hear the beauty of what they're doing. It takes editors like me and him to come along and give objective distance. We get in double bass players, saxophone players, trumpeters or whatever, and get them to blast and do their thing in the studio, and we come and edit it together. That's where a lot of *ISDN* comes from.

ARTIST
Afrika Bambaataa &
The Soul Sonic Force

SOURCE
Street Jams: Electric Funk Part One
LABEL
Skanless/Rhino

TITLE
Planet Rock

GC [Immediately] Brilliant! . . . This changes hands for 50 quid. I can't remember the artist. It's *Planet Rock*.

BD: Soul Sonic Force?

GC: Not Soul Sonic Force, is it?

Yes, with Afrika Bambaataa from 1982.

GC: Awesome instrumental. The vocal was of a particular time and I think that's aged really badly. I can't really get into the top layer, but underneath – awesome. There was a special sound you got from those old 606s through the desk in those days. We're putting the same machines through the desk and we're not getting quite that sound. There's something we haven't quite managed to pin down yet, about that old Electro, early House sound, which is weird.

ARTIST
Anonymous Solomon Island Musicians

TITLE
Water Play

SOURCE
Solomon Islands: 'Are 'Are Intimate And Ritual Music

LABEL
Le Chant Du Monde

GC: Sounds like that water drums album. [To BD] What's that called? I think we nicked this bit, didn't we, Brian? Got me thinking. Good one. It's throwing me into a nice area here, whether to criticise it musically. . . Obviously this has been a huge part of our music, environmental recordings and going out recording. Part of me wants to say, yes it's very good fun. It's a great laugh doing environmental recordings. But do we just present sound like that? In part, I think, but not for 90 minutes. Which leads me onto the question, why not? Because some of the sounds we've gathered are very interesting, with good histories and stories. I guess it's another area of electronic music that's very quickly been abused and even we abused it. Wow, weird stories on how you get these sounds: This is when I shot a fuckin' pigeon out of the sky. We've been everywhere getting environmental sounds and not only that, sitting at home with the DAT, taking digital sound from everything around the world. Big question is, which one is most fulfilling? History would have you believe that going there and having the story – 'I mingled with the vibes, took their drugs and then recorded their drums' – is a lot more interesting than saying, I sat at home and nicked it from TV.

So you've made your own field recordings in exotic locations?

I've surfed the waves, the continent beyond. You get beautiful sounds not just in exotic locations – you've just put yourself in it there. Lovely idea, but with a microphone, Peckham is exotic. That's the beauty of environmental recordings. I'm very suspicious in a way of this niche that has cropped up: packaging tribes, Westernised for loads of middle-class Ambient heads. Nice idea, but. . . Peckham schoolkids, man!

ARTIST
The Young Gods

TITLE
L'Eau Rouge

SOURCE
L'Eau Rouge

LABEL
Play It Again Sam

GC [Turns up the volume and wanders around occasionally punching the air] Fuckin' vocal's bollocks but the backing's great. Like it, Brian?

BD: Yeah, who's that?

GC: He's singing in French, which throws me a bit. It's probably Nitzer Ebb, or Laibach or something.

BD: Front 242.

They're from Switzerland.

GC: What?!

It's The Young Gods.

GC: Oh, is it? We're supposed to do a Young Gods remix. So what's this track called?

It's *L'Eau Rouge* from 89.

GC [Writes down name] We could mince this up, Brian, don't you think?

BD: Oh, yeah.

GC: Great! Well you just saved them, because we were just about to turn them down on a mix, because the new track's not good, but there's some great samples in this, and if they consent to us having these, we'll do a mix. That's the way we approach mixes – either they bung us a whole album full of sounds or we don't bother. I listen to this in a different way now. As a track it's got something, but I just hear it on a purely 'use' basis – you'll have to excuse me. It's completely selfish. I'd really like to get these sounds into my sampler. It's electronic, it's clean and it's got energy. The guitars – awesome. I could hear five guitar samples.

The singing's just like small-boys-behind-big-menacing-attitude. We've been through it, so we know. Back in the 80s we were there – building electric chairs! We did heavy Industrial shit! [Garry goes over to the telephone and dials a number] Martin, it's Garry. Can I just ask you a quick question? You were supposed to be getting the sounds from The Young Gods, yeah? Right. . . Well, I'm quite interested. I've heard a couple of tracks which I thought were quite interesting, but someone's just played me something which is really fuckin' good. . .

Paula Court

089 >

'My voice was given to me as an instrument of inspiration for my friends and a tool of torture and destruction to my enemies' is Diamanda Galás's most famous appraisal of her own voice. Born in San Diego, California and raised by Greek Orthodox parents, Galás initially played piano in her father's New Orleans-style jazz band and gospel group and went on to play in more eclectic jazz and improvising ensembles, as well as to study music, visual art and performance at the University of California. Galás's individual and uncompromising approach began with early solo works like *Wild Women With Steak Knives* and *Song From The Blood Of The Murdered*. Her first recorded work was *The Litanies Of Satan* in 82. The *Masque Of The Red Death* trilogy followed, Galás expanding her themes to encompass commentaries and critiques on the reaction to AIDS. Personal tragedy struck in 1989 when her brother Philip died of AIDS-related illnesses. This trilogy was later reworked as *Plague Mass,* which was first performed at Cathedral of St John The Divine, New York in 1990. A subsequent performance at Festival delle Colline in Italy resulted in Galás being denounced as blasphemous by members of the Italian government. Outside this central thrust of Galás's work lie *The Singer* (1993), a collection of blues songs and spirituals, and a collaboration with ex-Led Zeppelin bass player John Paul Jones, *The Sporting Life* (1994). Galás's first book of lyrics and texts, *The Shit Of God*, was published in 1996 by Serpent's Tail.

Skip James

The Roots Of Robert Johnson

Yazoo

The Devil Got My Woman

[Listens intently for two minutes] It's either Robert Johnson or Son House. It's not, is it?

It's not, but it is taken from a compilation album called *The Roots Of Robert Johnson*, recordings from 1927–35. It's Skip James.

I recognised the proximity of Robert Johnson, definitely. It's gorgeous. The guitar work is a little more conventional than I would expect from Son House, but it still has that country blues vibe.

What do you think about his high quavering voice?

I love that, it's an emotional thing, it just throws itself out, because that's where the emotion is: just throws itself up there and throws itself down there. It's not a technical thing, it's just a question of the sound. I like that with certain male singers. I hear that from Al Green and Marvin Gaye, pitching the voice up real high, what people call falsetto, but it isn't really – it is, but it's more than that.

When did you start listening to blues?

Oh, God, from the very beginning, since I was way high. My father had Fats Waller going and blues guys going and he really liked Art Tatum for piano. Certainly that's all blues-based, although New Orleans, taking it to another place, you know? But I always played blues piano as well, because in the band that he had, the New Orleans band [Jim And The Flames], we had to play everything from Kansas City Blues to Tony Orlando and Dawn. Jesus! We had to play everything and we didn't have charts. He didn't need charts and said, 'You don't need charts either.'

I used to teach guitar when I was 20. That was a very curious thing. I was asked to do that and I said, 'I can't even play guitar, how do you expect me to teach it?' So I used to tell all my students, 'Listen, I'm so advanced with this instrument, I think at this point you should play for me. You don't want to hear me play, you might get discouraged,' which was certainly true. So all these students of mine were playing *Stairway To Heaven* and I said, 'Let's try some rhythm shit, let's get some rhythm stuff.' I remember I thought, man, the only way I'm going to be able to teach this instrument is to sing real loud over it so people won't realise. So I was doing a lot of rhythm guitar things and singing over it.

It's kind of related to the way I play piano, really. The piano, especially in the low registers, is like the drums in a way, in pitch, especially if you're using a Bösendorfer, but even a Steinway, if you've got it EQed in a certain way, it can really be kind of the bass and the drums. That's how I perceive it, because my father was a bass player.

Cecil Taylor Ensemble

Always A Pleasure

FMP

Second

[Immediately] Cecil, bam! Oh keep it on, I like it. Oh I love this. Isn't this the 70s?

Diamanda Galás

No, it's recent.

You're kidding me.

It was recorded live three years ago, but it's only just been released.

Wow, really reminds me of the 70s. [Whispers, mock-conspiratorially] Hold it between us, don't tell anyone. I didn't say that. I saw him play recently in a restaurant in New York. It was really funny. It was a really polite restaurant. Someone one day is going to have to ask him about Henry Cowell, because it seems very, very clear to me that there's a Henry Cowell influence in Cecil's playing. I'm sure that he would have come across him at the Conservatory of Music. I think it would have been unavoidable. I just hear a lot of that. [At a particularly formidable piano run] I love that, it's just a bad riff, that's all there is to it. [At a lull in the music] I love it when he gets into this pensive shit, that's when he gets real refined. That was nice, that was beautiful.

Cecil was such a huge influence on my piano playing, my God, especially in the late 70s. Inescapably. *Unit Structures*, all that stuff. I love Cecil Taylor, just love him. It's so emotional, that sort of playing, it's so powerful. Going from the Bud Powell thing, suddenly going to Cecil Taylor, it's such an interesting stretch. I think of Cecil Taylor and I think of the way Duke Ellington played the piano, the importance of that bass, or that Art Tatum kind of thing, I see them as being very related in that orchestral sense. That's why my father always said to me, 'Please don't be a singer, I want you to play the piano then you'll learn about music, you learn about the orchestra. Then if you decide you want to do a hornline or whatever afterwards – which is the singing – then you can do that, but most singers are tone deaf, have no sense of time and can't read music.' He should know, because he had to accompany so many fucking drunk singers.

ARTIST
Sister Lilly Mae Littlefield

SOURCE
20 More Gospel Greats

LABEL
Cascade

TITLE
Dark Hours of Distress

Sounds like a very young Mahalia Jackson. It's not her, the voice is too high. Sounds very influenced by Mahalia but different. But I could be completely wrong.

It's Sister Lilly Mae Littlefield.

Never heard of her. Is she after Mahalia?

This was recorded in 1950.

She sounds so much stylistically like Mahalia, it's unbelievable. Gorgeous, gorgeous. I'm stealing this record. You just tell them I stole the fucking record from you! Can I buy it from you? I'd like to have it because it's great.

Yeah, fine.

A lot of this gospel music is like military music. What I meant by it is it's the thing you ride on, it's the shield, the armour, but also the way it's sung diaphragmatically, the power is like. . . [Diamanda gets up from the hotel bed] I don't mean to get personal, but if you feel my diaphragm, just punch it. . . [Embarrassed, I deliver a feeble punch to Galás's rock-hard diaphragm] See what

I'm saying? It's like a shield. A martial artist said, 'If anyone hits you you'll be just fine, but you've got to be in the right breathing position at the time.' And I said, 'Thank you, I hope you don't volunteer.' But do you know what I'm saying? It's like being surrounded by protective energy. I like that.

That was a very polite hit, but it's the first time I've ever hit anyone during an interview.

ARTIST
Sainkho

SOURCE
Out Of Tuva

LABEL
Cramworld

TITLE
Ritual Song

[At the end of the song] Oh, whoever she is, I love her tremendously. Now I'm just going to guess because I don't know who this is. Is it Iva Bittova, because I haven't heard Iva either? It sounds like she would be Slavic. [She looks at the CD] Oh, I've heard about her. Sainkho. OK, has she worked with Bill Laswell?

Quite possibly. She's worked with Hector Zazou.

I really love her sound. I've heard some older [Tuvan] guys singing, but this is different than that. This sounds influenced much more by Eastern European singing. That's why I was thinking that maybe it's Bittova, because I heard that she's a wonderful singer, but this sounds Slavic. Just the other day, I heard some of the Tuvanese singers, the guys, and I heard some stuff I couldn't believe. I thought it was wonderful, this really low. . . I think I liked it because they were all singing together and it was very, very thick timbrally and very beautiful. This didn't remind me of that.

I read somewhere, I'm not sure if it's true, that in Tuvan throat singing the very deep notes and the very high overtones resonate the skull so much that they can do some damage to the singer's brain.

Well, I'll tell you, it could be; maybe that's why I've had to take sleeping pills all these years. That's one of my favourite things to do, albeit in my own tradition, whatever that is: getting the low note, although in my case I'm getting the high note first and then the multiphonic sound underneath comes. I think for me I need to get this very pointed resonance with the note and then relax the note and allow it to resonate within all the bones of the skull and the chest, and then suddenly the more it relaxes then you get the lower pitch. I think the way that we end up EQing it makes it certainly abrasive to other people, because you're EQing not only the initial sound, but the sounds that come out of that sound, and it can become very, very. . .

It would seem that it could saw its way through a wall.

Yeah. That's how I like to think about it, like it's real razor sharp. This reminded me also of Yma, Yma Sumac. She was an improvisor although she wasn't like a really sophisticated improvisor, she'd go [does Yma Sumac impression, going from very low to very high notes]. You know what I mean? Sort of vaguely campy. Yma, oh, goddess!

I was going to play you some Yma Sumac . . .

But you knew I'd recognise it, so you played me something else.

Diamanda Galás

Yoko Ono

Walking On Thin Ice

LABEL

Rykodisc

TITLE

Woman Power

Is this Yoko? This sounds like her. Is it a remix?

It's actually from 1973, but the intro does sound like it could be a contemporary remix.

[At the entrance of the guitar] Oh, obviously. You can hear that with the guitars. I heard Yoko in the middle of my career. Someone played me *Plastic Ono Band* and I said, 'This is fantastic.' I hadn't heard her before. I think that has to do with being from San Diego, California. She's someone I was not influenced by. I mean obviously Yoko predates me by far because she was doing this when I was three years old or whatever, and yet at the same time I never heard her, so she wasn't an influence. [Distracted by the record] I hate it when she actually tries to sing. This shit, I think, is what pissed John's audiences off, when she would do this 'peace' shit, and she'd try to be 'with it', a 'with it dame'. I think she should have just not tried to do that, although I want to say that nicely, because her son comes to all my shows and stuff, and I don't want to insult her, she's universal. I think that – how can I say this? – lyrically she's the corniest woman alive, but I do love the stuff that she did with Plastic Ono [Band].

What kind of singers do you think had an influence on you?

I would say the Middle Eastern singers for me have been a huge influence, the Rembetikan singers and Oum Kolsoum and Maria Ewing. And then at the same time Albert Ayler and Ornette [Coleman] and that approach, the athletic performance of those instruments, that made me develop an athletic stamina on the voice just to compete with singing with a soprano saxophone, for example, that was doing Ornette's music. That's when I decided to study really seriously breathing because of those guys; so those guys are more direct influences I would say.

That's also why I studied bel canto, because I was interested in doing the long, long phrasing like Mozart. Singers don't really have circular breathing; we can do it, but it's not the same [as for saxophone players] you hear the ingressive breathing. You've really got to know how to use that diaphragm, do long breaths and then make decisions on the basis of that, otherwise you end up doing sort of what I hear in this, not to be denigrating Yoko, but you hear a person trying the lower part of the voice, then taking a break, then the higher part of the voice, then doing a little of this and then taking a break. You hear a lot of breaks; not breaks that necessarily have to do with what they hear, but what they're capable of doing. If I listen to Coltrane I never hear that. I mean those are the boys who played what they heard. They are like my teachers in a sense.

Yoko came to my concert, she came backstage, she said, 'You're like me, sister.' She was so gracious and sweet and generous.

ARTIST	SOURCE
Laurie Anderson	**The Ugly One With The Jewels**
	LABEL
TITLE	WEA
The Ugly One With The Jewels	

Oh God, now I know why they put those bags in aircraft. [Anderson begins her recitation] Aggh, oh no. [Diamanda hides her face behind a pillow] Is this who I think it is?

It's Laurie Anderson.

I told you that I'd end up insulting people who I know. I should. . . No, fuck it, I'll say what I think. This is too twee. I think she's sort of every American boy's dream. This is too Disneyland for me. You know Le Petomane? He was a real performance artist.

I think it was the hundredth anniversary of his death a few years ago. There was a newspaper article which featured a photo of him hunched up in the 'operating' position.

In full tuxedo? That's great. Have you seen the film that they made of his life?

I saw the one starring Leonard Rossiter.

I'm so jealous. I have to see that. We had the Hollywood equivalent, *Virginia And Her Singing Vagina*. This woman could sing all sorts of material but from below the waist. She came onstage to do a show, but the microphone was at half mast. [Diamanda notices my confused expression] It was a porn film.

ARTIST	SOURCE
Krzysztof Penderecki	**Complete Sacred Works For Chorus A Cappella 1962–92**
TITLE	LABEL
Miserere	Finlandia

I know this, I've sung this. . . Is it Ligeti?

No, it's Penderecki.

It's wonderful. Is it from *The Devils of Loudon*?

It's *Miserere*.

Beautiful, beautiful. You saw *2001*? You heard the Ligeti soundtrack to that?

Yes, *Lux Aeterna*, eternal light.

Most astonishing vocal writing I've ever heard.

One of the reasons that we played this is. . .

It's part of a mass.

Some of your own work has a strong sense of spirituality but it's delivered in an extreme way, which seems to alienate a lot of people. There were the blasphemy charges in Italy, for example.

They don't get it. The thing is that people like Penderecki and Lutoslawski and Ligeti and Mozart, these people are writing masses, requiems for the dead, requiems for people who were tortured, people in Auschwitz. This is like a tradition in classical music to write these kind of masses, very serious, and to incorporate texts from, let's say, the Old Testament. People from outside of the classical world don't really understand that tradition, so they just think of it as morbid and they don't understand death, dying, suffering, all these things as part of life. It doesn't mean that a person is preoccupied with passive morbid subjects, like lace tablecloths and things, it's just a part of life and if you see a lot going on around you, then you respond in different ways. I think I have a certain fraternity with these guys, definitely.

Can you envisage a time when your way of addressing AIDS, which obviously forms a great motivating factor in your work, will be accepted more readily by people at large, or do you think the climate of hypocrisy and double standards will continue?

People that are in the AIDS, quote, 'underground', people who are trying to stay alive in it, they can't be waiting around for anybody. They have their own networks and they have to do as much reading as they can. And a lot of people who I know, they know as much as a lot of medical doctors, much more, because they have to fight for their lives, and if nobody's going to sit there and really help them they have to do it themselves, and they know a hell of a lot. So it's kind of the same thing, you choose what you're interested in for whatever reason and you just do it and all the other shit, it just goes on forever. I've always addressed these subjects in my work anyway, these subjects of isolation and claustrophobia and outsider status and that kind of thing. . . Someone used to say [in jaunty voice], 'When are you going to write about something light?' I said, 'Well, as an artist you have to learn to embrace your limitations – embrace your limitations and make the most of 'em!'

095

Gautier de Blonde

097>

Bruce Gilbert's career has followed two parallel paths – as guitarist with Wire and as sonic experimenter. Wire formed in 1976 and quickly established themselves as one of the most inventive groups of the era, combining oblique, art house strategies and pop accessibility. Placing Wire on hold in the early 80s, Gilbert collaborated with Graham Lewis in Dome, P'o and Duet Emmo. Wire reformed in 1985, and until their demise in 1991 (by which time they were called Wir), Gilbert continued his role as experimentalist and collaborator in performance events – the support act on Wire's 'comeback' show was dancer Michael Clark performing Angela Conway's *Shivering Man* to music by Gilbert. He received more commissions for sound scores, notably from The Royal Ballet and The Paris Opera Ballet (again with Clark). He has also worked with animators and designed stage sets and installations. In 1994 he became the resident DJ at London's Disobey Club under the name The Beekeeper, where he delighted clubgoers with soundscapes and drone-based *musique concrète*.

ARTIST
Einheit Brötzmann

TITLE
Das 5 Federn Fuckhouse

SOURCE
Merry Christmas

LABEL
Blast First

We've started with an easy one. It's Einheit Brötzmann. It works well. There's a lot of life in it. Their approach is at times humorous as well. Every second counts. The physicality of Einheit. . . it's almost visual listening to it, and as a visual spectacle it's marvellous as well. With the tools he uses the only way that the sound can be created is by being physical – with the bricks and the metal sheets. It sounds very good slowed down, this section, and also looped with the CD player.

I thought the whole point of being a DJ – in quotation marks – was that you play other people's material and manipulate it – without any shame! I don't approve of sampling other people's work except if it's an amusing system of reference or if it's part of a conceptual approach to making a piece of work – when you make it clear you're sampling other people and that's the concept. So [DJing is] an ideal opportunity to learn what people are doing. I don't have a record player or a CD player, I don't consume music at all: it's Radio Four, or I'm working or it's television. I certainly wouldn't sit down in the evening and listen to something and haven't done since the early 70s.

I can't imagine many DJs who don't listen to music at home.
Well, I'm not really a DJ, let's face it. At the end of this year [1996] that will be the end of it. It's an opportunity to manipulate other people's sounds; it's a very complex journey of discovery.

Why are you opposed to sampling other people's pieces?
I think it's unnecessary. I know it can give a richer amount of references, etc, if that's the nature of the piece you're making, but I think it's more fun to make one's own samples. I have used samples – I've sampled Wire for instance – but that was a conceptual step rather than I'd run out of ideas for sounds. It's not a moral thing; I think it's a bit tedious to simply sample other people's things. It's more fun to create one's own.

ARTIST
Aphex Twin

TITLE
Disc One, Track One

SOURCE
Selected Ambient Works Volume II

LABEL
Warp

I haven't heard this before. It sounds like a remix, something newish. I keep thinking Kate Bush. I'm just trying to summon up people's names from the area. . . It's not Aphex, is it? As I said, I don't listen to music, I've heard about 30 seconds of [recorded] Aphex music.

It was a pretty good guess then.
It's probably the use of delays, actually, and that he does good recordings. I do like his attitude towards technology – that it's a means to an end that could be discarded, interfered with and destroyed if necessary to create something unexpected. Obviously he's extremely technically proficient and has a good ear, whatever that means.

You must have been at Disobey when he did his infamous sandpaper and food mixer routine. What did you think of it?

It was good. I thoroughly enjoyed it. I like his attitude. He recognised that the space was being offered to present things which, while they represent his general attitude to things, don't necessarily fit into his commercial activities. It's all context and Aphex Twin playing a food mixer means that some of his audience would say that has to be taken seriously because it's him – or not take it seriously as the case may be. It was an unusual idea from his context, but not from other contexts. But the fact that he's doing it is extremely interesting and important, I think, in terms of moving the audience on slightly. I know certainly he wouldn't make a career out of using food mixers and sandpaper, but it certainly bodes well.

ARTIST
Pink Floyd

TITLE
Astronomy Domine

SOURCE
Piper At The Gates Of Dawn
LABEL
Harvest

I was going to say this sounds like a pastiche of Pink Floyd. [Laughs] Is it Pink Floyd? I'm not terribly familiar with them. I went to see them once: in London, a kind of experimental place . . . with Liquid Len.

The UFO Club?

Yeah. I don't remember very much about it – not because of chemical alteration. It's curious how quaint it sounds, slightly tinny, but at the time it was extremely heavy and interesting.

A lot of people suggested that Wire were influenced by this area and period.

'New Psychedelia'. We never understood this comment at all really. They were certainly not an influence to me, but might have been to Graham Lewis or Colin [Newman], I'm not sure. But it would have been more to do with seepage-type influence rather than direct influence. Syd Barrett, perhaps. . . Colin definitely was a child of the 60s, so it was the perfect time frame for him – he was quite young. Pink Floyd, I should imagine, was a topic of conversation in the playground.

Would you agree that Wire had a distinct sense of Englishness about it?

Yeah. I think it was a combination of playing and thinking. . . The group did play some covers, some American covers, but with a certain amount of irony.

And irreverence?

Well, irreverence is a funny word; not so much irreverence towards the music as irreverence towards people who consume that kind of music. The word 'assassination' comes to mind! So really the Englishness or the European way of looking at it comes from something as simple and physical as the fact that we were making it up as we went along quite often, in terms of creating pieces, and the tools we were using were of our own devising. American groups didn't as a rule – perhaps with the exception of Captain Beefheart – have a song and say, 'It's kind of all right, but I wonder what it would sound like backwards?'

Bruce Gilbert

ARTIST

Oval

TITLE

The Politics Of Digital Audio

SOURCE

Systemisch

LABEL

Mille Plateaux

Is it German? Oval? On a personal level I could have done without the music. Obviously on a lot of tracks, they've dispensed with the music, which I find a bit more stimulating.

When they started, Oval claimed to deface CDs and misuse CD players as a form of subversion, in 'disobedience' to the manufacturer's specifications.

It's a good approach. I thoroughly approve. The shuttling CD is an interesting way of creating sounds. What's nice in using a CD is obviously that when you're not tempted to play a particular track it almost becomes a random experience, which I'm very keen on. I spray what CDs I have amassed recently – spraying one side black in order not to know what I'm playing. Having decided that I want to do 'DJing', I've got to sidestep my habits, and introducing a random element as often as possible is one way of doing that – and building from a random approach.

Do you think that this DJing experience as The Beekeeper will influence your own music making?

I've been working for about four years on something using a lot of methods I've been using for the last ten years. But with this DJing thing I've obviously been tainted, having been exposed to a lot of this stuff; it's informed me somehow and I found that the material I made in the last four years practically had no interest for me, so I had to start again, basically. I'm taking a very minimalist approach and really getting inside some of the sounds and chasing them to destruction. It's done mostly with effects, guitar pedals pushed to the absolute limit.

ARTIST

Morton Feldman

TITLE

Excerpt from Crippled Symmetry

SOURCE

Crippled Symmetry

LABEL

Hat Hut

Ligeti? Schaeffer? Parmegiani? He has done stuff with acoustic instruments. It's not Cage, is it? I thought there was a random system going there for a bit.

It's Morton Feldman from 1983, a five minute chunk out of a piece that lasts 90 minutes. He was interested in Persian rug designs as inspiration for music, with particular interest in the occasional flaws in the repeated patterns.

I like the sound of the length of it, because obviously after an extended period it becomes extremely hypnotic and the variations become almost the whole thing. I do like the idea of distressed systems.

Graham [Lewis] and I, in our Dome capacity, did a performance in Rotterdam many years ago: we used three proper musicians and we attempted to turn them into human loops where each one had a taped-out square, which made it obvious to that audience that they were three separate entities in their own right. I was going out and putting a piece of paper with an alphabetical note on it –

Bruce Gilbert

natural, high or low – and they had to keep repeating that as a loop. I added other notes over a period of time so that they were all looping in their own world against each other. [The idea was to] record this and overlay it over the previous simpler loops to build up to what we thought would be a rushing sound, somehow. But [laughs] our logic failed because we didn't take enough tape recorders.

ARTIST
György Ligeti

TITLE
Artikulation

SOURCE
Artikulation
LABEL
Wergo

You'll have to tell me.

Ligeti from 1958, with Gottfried Koenig and Cornelius Cardew playing on it.
[Looks at CD] I think I've got some of these on a compilation. Yes, I've got a faulty CD that skips about three tracks in about 30 seconds – it's quite nice. I enjoyed that very much. It's the complexity of it that I really enjoy; obviously the surprise element. The Beekeeper would slow that down or speed it up. It's quite exciting.

It's not a primitive piece, as you say it's quite complicated, but in terms of electronics it's an early piece. Do you think the sounds date it?
I have no problem with it. To me it didn't sound dated at all. It sounds like an interesting piece of noise. These recordings are unmapped territory and that is exciting. It can, if you listen to it in a certain way, sound quaint, but it's also terribly interesting. It's the sort of thing that people in the dance world naturally progress to, innocently anyway, once they've abandoned rhythm, the beat.

Ligeti must have felt out on a limb with this, as it was a step away from the more familiar sounds of orchestral instruments that he'd been trained to deploy.
People who have been classlcally trained do rely on formal structures, but using electronic sources, tape splicing, etc, you can create your own formal structure, internal structure, which comes from the sounds themselves, not some analogue of the world. If I did play music, this is the sort of thing I'd put on as a stimulating background. Most of the things I've got in my DJing bag are 50s and 60s electronic music, apart from 'bad taste' things and one or two newer things. It's a kind of conscious decision to use that as source material, because I knew very little about it, but what I had heard of it I instinctively knew would be ideal material for manipulation and mixing together, because there are interesting gaps; quite often the textures will be fairly similar so there is a cohesiveness of textures, which is not really what I'm looking for but adds to the confusion of 'what is it?'.

ARTIST
Pierre Henry

TITLE
Teen Tonic

SOURCE
Messe Pour Le Temps Présent
LABEL
Philips

Sounds like Booker T meets Pere Ubu. Is it someone well known?
Maybe not so well known for this kind of stuff. It's Pierre Henry, who mainly did *musique concrète*. That's part of a longer piece, a section called *Teen Tonic*.
For obvious reasons. [Looks at record] Hmm. . . Pierre Henry. I must get some of

101

this stuff. Not this particular piece, but the *musique concrète*. I could certainly have done without the organ. The electronic noises were very exciting. Some of his concepts were probably cultural cross-matching things that seemed like a really good idea – I can imagine that especially in the 1960s. It should marry up somehow: this is modern rock, this is teen music, and this is academic electronic music, but there must be a connection – it's as modern as you can get, these two things together, and surely they must work. The trouble is there are no compromises at all. It's so French, that jazzy rock organ.

There used to be whole sections of 'Electronic Music' in music shops, I seem to remember, and especially in classical shops. But now they have sections of 'World Music' or 'Modern Classical' and material like this is harder and harder to find.

Someone found, in a New Age or World Music section. a really nice CD of four Japanese firework displays which are absolutely beautiful. Being Japanese it's fantastically recorded and also there aren't 'oohs' and 'aahs', just [mimes polite applause] so no interference with the actual sounds. I got some wonderful loops with the CD machine. Some of them are quite embarrassing – they sound like heavy slow rock kind of things. A couple of starbursts going off in quick succession – when they're looped it creates some really hackneyed rhythms!

ARTIST	SOURCE
Elastica	**Elastica**
	LABEL
TITLE	Deceptive
Connection	

[The opening riff is a direct steal from Wire's *Three Girl Rhumba*: Bruce grins throughout] The infamous. . . No, I think it's really good actually, it's really impressive. It's short, clean and amusing. When I first heard it, my first thought was that I was really envious that they had sequencers, which we didn't when we did *Three Girl Rhumba*. It's well phrased, it's crisp and nice. However much you try to be crisp with a guitar, it's not the same. If you sequence it, it's really cold, precise and jerky.

You seem to have had a dual career of playing pop music and extremely rigorous experimental music. Are you still a pop fan or have you moved on from that now?
I'm moving back to absurdity. Obviously various kinds of melodic devices have their absurdity value and can put a piece into a different space, flavour, attitude, mood. If you do create a sequence of notes that do have an uncanny beauty, it's like a joke, a slightly surrealist joke, where you know it's funny but you don't know why. On one level you can say, 'Oh, that's really pretty,' but on another level you can tell that it's not the real thing, it's not going anywhere really. It's a pretty static musical device. These things have their uses in order to confound oneself as well as a potential audience.

ARTIST	SOURCE
Joy Division	**Unknown Pleasures**
	LABEL
TITLE	Factory
Wilderness	

Is this new?
No, it's quite old.

Joy Division? I've never heard this before. The voice of course is very distinctive, but I haven't heard much Joy Division. But the giveaway was the quality and tone of the text. . . We actually played with them once in Manchester. I liked the simplicity and the tone of the text. It has a nice cold quality. I suppose it does sound of its time, but only with hindsight. I think Ian Curtis was clearly a poet with his sights set on a higher plane, shall we say, of activity within music, but using music as a commercial avenue to do what he wanted to do, and I suspect that the others did as well, but I know very little about them. I think inescapably the album was significant. This is music done with intent. This is not messing around, it's not fun. Though one assumes they had a lot of fun doing it from time to time.

Did you know we had [ex-Factory Records boss] Anthony Wilson at Disobey? He came to read a section of Curtis's wife's book where he was quoted or misquoted or whichever is appropriate. His actual reading was rather good because he looped a phrase pertaining to a comment, pre-suicide, where he said, 'The best thing that could possibly happen to me is if Ian Curtis killed himself.' He just repeated it over and over again, which I think is a very good device and rather clever. I thought it was a very elegant answer.

ARTIST
Lee Ranaldo

TITLE
Fuzz/Locusts/To Mary x2/Lathe Speaks

SOURCE
East Jesus
LABEL
Blast First

Bruce Gilbert

Is this Earth? I haven't heard it. Could it be Main?
No, it's American. Lee Ranaldo.
I was going to say Sonic Youth.
What do you think of this kind of guitar manipulation?
I thoroughly approve. Actually I've done a project with [Main's] Robert Hampson – it's all manipulated guitar and, where possible, played. I think it's an instrument which still offers a lot of possibilities, especially if you simplify your approach to it and really listen to what it can do as a noise source. I have played guitar – I've never been a virtuoso – but I've always been more interested in its sonic qualities than its melodic qualities. It's still got possibilities, especially with new ways of manipulating, but then again it becomes irrelevant what the sound source is now, especially with ProTools software – it's almost an instrument in itself. But one should never ban the tape loop or the non-functioning guitar pedal where your one does something slightly different to someone else's.

Jack Mitchell

Alongside Steve Reich, Terry Riley and LaMonte Young, Philip Glass was one of the 'Big four' composers who defined a new strand of classical music in the 1960s that later became known as Minimalism. Born in 1937, Glass began studying flute at the Peabody Conservatory in his home town of Baltimore while in his teens. From there he studied composition at the Juilliard School in New York. Further studies under Nadia Boulanger and Darius Milhaud followed. A meeting with Ravi Shankar in 1965 caused a radical change in his music, where standard Western harmonic methods were rejected in favour of rhythmic cycles: it was a pivotal moment in defining Glass's ideas of Minimalism. In 1968 he formed The Philip Glass Ensemble to perform his music. He has continued to write concert music, but since his first opera *Einstein On The Beach* – a collaboration with Robert Wilson from 1975 – he has won wider audiences with music that accompanies other media: operas, film music scores (most famously *Koyaanisqatsi* and *Powaqqatsi*), dance pieces and theatre pieces – even a pop album, *Songs For Liquid Days*, with David Byrne, Laurie Anderson and others. Glass's return to tonality since *Einstein* has reached its apogee in the large-scale orchestral works: the programmatic *Itaipu*, and the *Low* and *Heroes* Symphonies, both based on the music of David Bowie and Brian Eno. In 1992 Glass formed his own Point label. On another level, in 1995 he collaborated with Aphex Twin on *Donkey Rhubarb*. The Jukebox took place in London. Glass took to the test with formidable enthusiasm.

Ravi Shankar

Sound Of The Sitar

BGO

Pakhari Dhun

Yeah, Ravi, I know who it is. Of course he was an enormously important person in my life and still is. I met him in 65 in Paris when I was hired to be his assistant in a film [*Chappaqua*] and it changed my life.

He was at that time a man of about 45, I was about 25. He was at the height – not of his fame, because his fame came a few years later; it took George Harrison to discover him and bring him to the West. He had been playing in the West for years but playing in small halls for people who were devotees of Oriental music. There weren't that many in those days. Once The Beatles went to India, that changed everything.

[WIth Ravi] the composer and performer become one person. In 1965 I was trying to figure out how was I going to make my way in the music world and it was inspiring seeing that there were people who were performers and composers in the same person. I had to separate the activities – I would write the music and then I would I play it. But Ravi did both.

I could talk about Ravi all morning because he was such an important person for me. After that I went to India, I went through North Africa, Central Asia and I began to look at the traditions of Western music in a much more critical way. I was in my late 20s at the time. I had what was considered by Western standards a complete education, I had all the degrees I needed and all the years of training I needed, and this guy comes along and plays this music and turned me completely upside down. You have to remember [World Music] wasn't around [in 1965]. You didn't go into record stores and find Indian music except if they had a section on Ethnic Music or Ethnomusicology. In the music schools you would find it under Ethnomusicology. It wasn't generally considered concert music. Incredible, isn't it? Can you believe that?

It sounds like it was seen more as anthropological research rather than music.

That's the way it was seen. When I studied Western music it was simply never considered that any 'serious' music could come from another source. So when I heard this in 65, it was like a bombshell. I'd say that it is virtually impossible for that to happen to a young musician today. I think there's so much around, the concept of World Music and the idea that there's a kind of equivalency or parity between the great traditions of classical music, whether they be Indonesian or Indian or African, Turkish. We understand now that there's music of quality, of precision of expression, of tradition. Sometimes it's not notated the way we do it, but the transmission from teacher to student is just as exact as it was for us. I went to India about that time. I came back and using what I knew I began to use that as a basis of reforming the language of music that I had been writing and the language of modern music to put it on a wider thing. And not just myself, a lot of other people did it too. My own personal journey was started through Ravi – other people did it in their own ways.

It seems to me that the interest in World Music has also brought its dangers and pitfalls: it's sometimes been misappropriated both in formally composed music and in the sampling of source material in electronic music.

One of the big problems, to put it technically, has been tuning. I remember in the 60s we used to put together things called World Bands. New York is a great place to do this, because you get musicians from all over the world living in New York. You can find Rastafarians, you can find people from Brazil, Iran, Turkey, Africa, Balinese gamelan players. We put all these people together and there would be these great improvising sessions. The problem was that all the tunings were slightly different and it sounded terrible. So these bands never lasted very long. We couldn't figure out how to play together.

What happened with the film *Powaqqatsi* was that we used a lot of these instruments and wanted to combine them in that film. There was a balafon from Africa, I remember Foday Suso was playing it, and in order to integrate it with the orchestra we were playing with, we sampled it and then retuned it. And we found an interesting thing. If we retuned it too much it lost its African-ness, it started to sound like a xylophone rather than a balafon. We found a compromise tuning of a lot of instruments through sampling technology, which you never could have done 20 years before. I've always liked that piece of music particularly, because it solved a problem that we had all been working on for years. What are the pitfalls? The pitfall is that you can end up with a piece of Esperanto garbage [laughs] that doesn't sound like anything. It's not something we particularly want to do.

How did the collaboration with Shankar work?

Ravi and I got together for two weeks in Los Angeles [sessions which produced the *Passages* album] and talked about how we could do music together. We started by saying, 'Let's get together. If we get an idea of what to do let's do it and if we don't we'll drop it.' What we didn't want to do was a chinoiserie of music where we put a gloss of Asian music on top of my music or Western music on top of his music. We wanted to find a way that the music could proceed from roots that were common to us and that would contribute mutually to what we were doing. We found a way to make something authentic. I've done three fairly extensive experiments with World Music integrating with my music and I'm not unhappy with them. You don't want to be lost in a New Age cosmopolitan thing when you don't know what anything is, where all the roots have been lost and all you've got are the least interesting aspects. There's no definite way to do it, but if you start with musicians of integrity and some kind of idealism about the music to begin with – I think that they have to have confidence in their ability to see through this tangle of possibilities and to find a true path that can work for them.

Philip Glass

ARTIST

Aphex Twin

TITLE

Come On You Slags!

SOURCE

I Care Because You Do

LABEL

Warp

Can you turn it up a little bit? [Long pause] Interesting. Part of it sounds like me, part of it sounds like somebody else. [Laughs] But it's a nice piece of music. I don't know who wrote it but I would say it was written in the last 18 months. I would say it was English. It's an older composer, it's not a young composer. And someone who's listened to me.

It's actually Richard James, Aphex Twin.

I thought it might be Richard. I like his music. That's why I said written in the last 18 months and English. The reason that I didn't say Richard was there are a lot of composers I don't know that are around now. But that would fit him. I said a little bit older because of the part that sounded like me. I like him. He has an interesting way of hearing. You can hear that. He listens to music, he can hear music. Not everybody can hear music. Painting is about looking, writing is about speaking, and music is about listening. That's obvious, isn't it? But it isn't obvious. It's obvious when you say it, but when you think about the fundamental activity of the composer, the first thing he has to be able to do is to listen. And Richard has that. His technical background or his music education is not important because he has that other quality of being able to hear critically, to hear intelligently, to hear creatively – he does all these things. Interesting guy, interesting piece of music. Very bright guy. I enjoyed my association with him. It was fun to work with him.

How did that association come about?
[Sounding puzzled] I don't really know. Somehow we got in touch with each other – I forget who called who. I got sent a piece of music by him [*Icct Hedral*]. It was a much denser piece than this. Very dense. I listened to it for a long period of time. I was given four or five pieces and I selected that piece as the one I wanted to work on because it intrigued me. The thing that interested me about it was that when I first heard it I couldn't hear it. I found myself having to learn to listen to it.

What does that mean?
What it means is that on my first hearing I couldn't hear all the parts separately and I couldn't hear the structure. It slowly revealed itself. I realised that I had to listen in a certain way. I listened to it until I could hear the parts and the structure, but the first hearing I didn't hear it at all.

Do you particularly like the repetitive aspects of Techno?
What do you think? [Laughs]

I was going to make a guess.
So many composers from my generation onwards have begun to develop that kind of hearing and that kind of writing so that repetitive structure is no longer something. . . I mean people don't throw tomatoes at me anymore. They did at one time.

You also did a remix of *Hey Music Lover* for S'Express.
[S'Express's Mark Moore] said, 'Do you want to do a remix?,' and I said 'Yes', without knowing what it was. I liked what he did. I've worked with Ravi, I've worked with Foday Suso. I like to work with other musicians and in a certain way I thought of these English composers as another form of ethnic music, if you will. [Laughs]

Are you interested in using the studio as an Instrument, rather than just a way of recording a performance of a composition?
We've done a lot of it. I have my own studio in New York; a group of people developed around the studio. It gave us access to the equipment and to the talents of these other people – sound designers, engineers, other composers who came in. We do all the Point Music stuff at this studio. There's a lot of activity around this workplace.
My home is three blocks from the studio. At home I have a piano, a desk and

an electric pencil sharpener – that's all that's there. Do I actually use [the studio] to compose? No, I don't. I'm a pencil and paper composer, basically.

My relationship to technology and the studio is a very positive one and yet I've kept the activity of writing separate from the activity of performing and playing. I haven't yet learnt to write with the equipment. And I think there's an age thing too. I've been a paper and pencil composer for over 40 years. I'm unlikely to change it. In three months I can write a whole piece of music. The question is, do I want to exchange a piece of music for that – for me – untried technique of writing? When it comes down to it, I end up writing the piece of music.

ARTIST
Steve Reich

TITLE
Extract from Music For 18 Musicians

SOURCE
Music For 18 Musicians
LABEL
ECM

Yeah, of course I know that. That's Steve. . . Very good composer, of course, very easy to identify. Which piece is it? *18 Musicians* maybe? I'm doing really well. I thought that defining Richard as a Brit of the last 18 months was actually pretty good. [Laughs] Location in time can tell you almost the whole story. This piece was written by Steve in the mid-70s, wasn't it?

It's a fairly obvious piece to play you, but the main reason I played it is that I read a copy of a review collected by Tom Johnson in his book *The Voice Of New Music: New York City 1972–1982*. It's about this piece. The reviewer says, 'I'm not questioning the actual merit of the music, I'm merely wondering whether I like the idea of going back to some kind of romanticism, and feeling a little sorry that the era of New York Minimalism has come to such an abrupt end.'

I think that was a premature judgement. This is a very good composer who is admired everywhere now. There's no question about the quality and integrity of the music. I suppose you could find some academic circles and some people that would still be alarmed by this, but I think that this is part of the language of our time now and one of the strongest voices around. If you look at Steve's work, I don't know *The Cave*, but what Steve offers you is a consistent quality and a consistent level of accomplishment. He doesn't write quickly in the sense that there is not a deluge of music. His pieces come at very measured intervals in a very regular way. And I think he also develops in a very regular way; I think that's one of the hallmarks of his work.

What was it like in the early days of Minimalism in New York? I heard that you and Steve Reich used to play in each other's ensembles. Was there a rivalry or mutual support in those days?

Back in the early 70s, this music wasn't recognised at all, so it was a very small community of people and there was a lot of mutual support in the groups so that people got together and did concerts together; if you needed players you'd just say, 'Look John, why don't you come and play? Are you free next week?' There was a lot of that going on. You'd be amazed at the people that walked through my [group]; people like Frederic Rzewski; [he] was in a group called Musica Elettronica Viva. Anthony Braxton played with me once, I think. They

Philip Glass

wanted to know what it was. It was a way to find out. It was a way for composers to learn about each other's music. At that time there weren't a lot of possibilities for performances and there wasn't a vast pool of players to draw from. It was a small community that all lived in the SoHo area of New York and worked in that area.

Do you look back on that period with special affection?
I do, because I enjoyed that, but I enjoy what I'm doing now, so it's not to say that I prefer it to the present at all. We got smaller audiences then by far. I gave weekly concerts at my loft in 10 Bleeker Street and there could often be 30 or 40 people at those concerts. When we went out into regular concert halls we would get three to four hundred people at the most. There was a sense that this was a defining moment – this may sound grandiose – for our music and for other people's music, as well. We were very aware that we were involved in a wholesale reform of the language of modern music. A very ambitious undertaking when you consider that our predecessors were men of enormous talent; people like Boulez, Xenakis, Ligeti, Berio and Stockhausen. These were formidable composers and basically we were a bunch of young guys coming along with our wrenches and crowbars and we were going to take apart this great edifice of 20th century music. And we took it apart. It's a rather nervy thing to do, and we did it with an unselfconsciousness that was part of the charm. When I said men, don't forget it was men and women: Meredith Monk was one of those early people.

ARTIST
Ornette Coleman & Howard Shore

SOURCE
Naked Lunch: OST
LABEL
Milan/BMG

TITLE
Naked Lunch Theme

Is that Ornette? I know that piece. It's a symphonic piece he did.
It's from the soundtrack to *Naked Lunch*.
He wrote the whole thing, didn't he? I would think so.
The music's actually composed by Howard Shore.
But that's Ornette. I didn't sit at his feet for all those years for nothing!
When I first came to New York in 57/58, I would go down to the Five Spot, [Thelonious] Monk was playing and on alternate sets Ornette Coleman was playing. Can you imagine that? They were there for months at a time and the place was virtually empty. It's hard to believe that now, but it wasn't packed with people at all. Then over at the Village Vanguard on the West Village you could hear John Coltrane playing. It wasn't packed either. I mean, Coltrane; everyone has the records now and all that, and people admire him, but he wasn't admired the way he is today. But he was a wonderful player.
[Ornette] had tremendous insights into music and he saw a path that no one else had seen. The whole free jazz movement comes from him. The origin is Ornette. And he's never had the recognition that I think he should have, as the innovator. People were very angry with him. Other jazz musicians were furious with him and they made statements like, 'Oh, he doesn't know how to play the saxophone.' That was the common statement that was made about him. I was

astonished. How could they say that? [But] he survived that. He persisted. He's still out playing.

In the years in the 70s when we got to be friendly, he had a studio on Prince Street and I often would go there and we hung out together. He gave me some advice from time to time. I've never forgotten one piece of advice he gave me because it was very helpful later on. He said, 'Remember, Philip, the music business and the music world are not the same thing.' Simple statement but very true. Let's not forget that.

He's just an outstanding personality and innovator, one of the most brilliant composers I've ever known. We've talked about doing a piece together. That would be a good project.

Have you had any ideas about how that collaboration might work?

Yeah, he told me. He said, 'Philip, there's only one way to do it. You get your band together, I get my band together and we start playing.' I don't know what that means. I have an idea for what we could do together. I would have to write my piece, but I would write a piece that would be an environment that he could write his piece in. I hope that we could do it sometime.

ARTIST
The Velvet Underground

SOURCE
The Velvet Underground And Nico
LABEL
Verve/Polydor

TITLE
Venus In Furs

What else have you got up your sleeve? I've done so splendidly on this I can't believe it. I've had some bullseyes. I'll probably miss this one by a mile. [Track starts] I know this piece. That's Lou Reed. You can't fool me, that's Lou Reed. I know him! [Laughs]

Lou is an interesting guy. The whole Velvet Underground was a very interesting thing. I know him pretty well. We see each other, I go to his shows, he goes to mine. He's a New Yorker. The New York community's quite small. We've even been on some odd kind of concerts together – there was one of those international TV hook-ups between Seoul, Korea and Tokyo and New York and we all were on that programme together. [This] makes me think of the Warhol years, that time when there was a very close connection between the world of abstract experimental art and popular music. And it made popular music more conscious to the possibilities of experimentation and maybe even – and this is a heavy word to use – of its responsibilities in that way. I think Lou was certainly part of that. On this side of the Atlantic, of course, there are David [Bowie] and Brian [Eno]. There are others, of course, but those are the ones that we knew in America. The idea that popular music could be an art music really comes from this generation. [That] links to people like Richard James – [the links] may seem tenuous, but in terms of ambition, in terms of that kind of self-possession, I think they are definitely there.

So did you attend any of the Warhol and Velvet Underground events in the 60s?

I did. I went to the shows, I went to the movies. Very interesting period. Yeah, I was around. I lived in New York. It was a very rich period. This is the constellation of things that were going on: The Living Theatre was performing on 7th Avenue and 14th Street; Allen Ginsberg and Gregory Corso were standing on tabletops in cafes screaming their poetry. . . I'm lumping this all together in a way to give you an idea that that stuff was really all happening at the same time. That started in 57, and things started moving through the next 10, 12, 15 years. The Warhol years really start in the late 60s and run through to the 70s, that's when that group was going. But that community of experimental people in art and in painting and in poetry, really the foundation was already there.

I used to go downtown and visit all these things, so I was very much involved with the theatre world, the music world and the art world as I am today. It's not new to me, it's what I've always done. I wasn't part of The Factory – I got to know Lou later on. I didn't hang out with that crowd – it was a wild bunch, you know. [Laughs]

But we all knew of each other and it was a powerful force in the art music world in the 70s.

ARTIST

David Bowie

TITLE

Sense Of Doubt

SOURCE

Heroes

LABEL

RCA

I've had 100 per cent today, I consider, and now I'm going to blow it on the last one! [Track starts] Oh, well, I just orchestrated this piece, [as part of the *Heroes* Symphony]. This is . . . *Doubt*.

Sense of Doubt.

Of the tracks on *Heroes*, I picked six, and this was one of the ones I was very attracted to. Some of them I did a lot of writing on. This one I did very little to. I considered this to be almost a completely finished piece.

This kind of music was what inspired me to do the piece. It's a highly sophisticated, very resolved piece of music. It's beautifully balanced and conceived.

I thought that *Low Symphony* was a very successful reworking of the original material, but when I first heard about it, I was a bit wary.

But why? The reason that composers do developments and covers and variations of other people's music is that we like it. It's like a homage in a way, and composers do it all the time for each other. People do it to my music, [laughs] sometimes unacknowledged.

And Eno and Bowie were also influenced by your music. The first time I heard about you was when they mentioned you in the rock music press.

Oh yes, they like my music. All through the 70s they talked about it and got people interested in it – and it was frankly helpful. I think it was generous on their part to do that. Although I think my music must have meant something to them. And clearly their music has meant something to me. I think these two symphonic pieces I've done say that in the best way that I can.

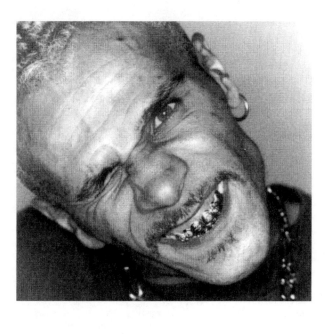

No face is more identified with drum 'n' bass than the shining, snarling visage of Goldie. Born in 1966 to a Scottish mother and Jamaican father, he spent his early years in Wolverhampton, being bounced in and out of care. His skills as a graffiti artist earned him a ticket to New York, where he starred alongside Afrika Bambaataa in *Bombin'*: a Channel 4 documentary about urban street culture. After a stint in Miami, he returned to London in 1988. Disillusioned with UK HipHop, he jumped headlong into the rave scene, regularly attending Heaven's seminal Rage Club and contributing artwork to the breakbeat label Reinforced. In 1992 he began producing his own tracks. A year later, under the pseudonym Metalheadz, he released *Terminator*, a prototype of Jungle that introduced the technique of timestretching, stretching a vocal sample over different bpm ranges without distorting its pitch. In 1994 came *Timeless*, a 21 minute single that fused dub, HipHop, jazz and Detroit Techno with processed breaks. His debut album of the same name was co-released by Londonffrr and his own Metalheadz label in September 1995. At the time of the Jukebox, Goldie was running a weekly drum 'n' bass club at London's Blue Note, and had begun work on a script and soundtrack for a film based on *Timeless*. Goldie's jukebox took place in Providence, Rhode Island, the penultimate stop on his 1996 US tour with Björk.

4 Hero

Mr Kirk's Nightmare

[Goldie starts reciting the opening piece of dialogue word for word] 4 Hero. Massive hit. I was in the Midlands [when it was released in 1991]. It was the stab that killed it, the stab that made it. It was marrying HipHop – break culture – with rave/Techno culture. It was a mixture of technology and street rawness. Good tune.

People forget that 4 Hero was there from day one. They are the pioneers. If you listen to them now, they've just gone so far, but they are so much the same. Mark and Dego never did drugs: you've got to understand that; they haven't experienced that. There is quite a message there as well; kind of along the thing that it's fucking too much, man: you're overboard. I remember hearing a story – I don't know if it was myth; there's a lot of mythology in breakbeat culture – there was a girl or a guy who died on an E at a rave, and the ambulance came and took him away and the music stopped. Then DJ Rap played '*Mr Kirk, your son is dead*' [the spoken refrain on *Mr Kirk's Nightmare*] straight after. That's how the story goes: whether it's true, you've got to ask Rap about it.

What influence did rave have on your music?

Oh, c'mon man, massive. You wouldn't have breakbeat culture if it wasn't for rave, and anybody who says different is so New School he's wearing diapers. [*Mr Kirk* is] a perfect example of something being raw and stepping out of being just rave. [It has] the basic break principle of loops and breaks. and the basic rave principle of stabs and analogue sound. Put the two together, and now they're both redefined.

A Guy Called Gerald

Automanikk

[After 30 seconds] This is Gerald, isn't it?

Yes, it's from 1990, when he was still making Detroit-styled Techno.

People forget that rave was the bastard child of Detroit Techno. Detroit Techno was the cutting edge. It was one of those genres of suppressed music that became a subculture. Detroit Techno has soul; soul that you can't get out of European Techno because it's four-to-the-floor. Detroit Techno even more so: it's the acceleration. I learned music backwards in that sense, where I had to learn what was Detroit Techno. I was given a manual, and then I had to read it. And it was like when you read the first few pages, you don't understand it all, and you have to read more of the book to understand that page, that first chapter: that's how I learned music.

People like Mark and Dego and Gerald grew up within that music: people like me, I'm a prototype of the products, if you like, of all these people. Being a prototype, it's like being programmed to make music with no holds barred, with no history, just going, 'Right. This is the program. I know that program.' I'm trying to be like them, yet something happens where it turns into more than that. If the strength of me is based on all these people, then I become stronger. And then, whoever I hand it down to, becomes even stronger. And who they hand it down to will be all-powerful.

That's why I am glad I was removed socially from the whole thing. Because I then had to go to America and miss out on a lot of things that were coming back on the rebound. I was in HipHop, New York, Miami – not in Detroit, not in Chicago – and a lot of these things were being created. Isn't that the same in any subculture? What happens is that you go back to go forward. You know what I mean?

Why did you call Gerald up and tell him he had to come down to London?

You're really informed, aren't you? I had a burning need to, man. It was my job to do that. It was a mission.

When I left the country, *Voodoo Ray* was massive. I didn't know who it was made by. Then I came back and people on the underground played me *28-Gun Badboy*. I was like, 'What the fuck is this?' There were a few Rebel MC things around, playing a spectrum of music: some Detroit Techno, Techno from Europe, the hybrid of rave and breakbeat, raw breakbeat. Before the word Jungle even came around, I remember a 10″ on Kickin' Records, an eight-track recording, and it went '*Jungle, Jungle duh duh duh duh*'. It was a tribal thing then. It was about urban jungle. It had fuck all to do with race. When it comes to Jungle, I can take you back to 10″s, a 10″ that Grooverider did. It went '*Grooverider, groove groove rider doo doo doodoodoodo.*' It was crusty as fuck, it was being played among high production European stuff, and it had an appeal because it was trash, it was street.

But I'm getting off the point. The reason I called Gerald was that Fabio was playing this stuff and Groove was playing this stuff, and I said, 'Who is this Guy Called Gerald?' I made all these connections that I had to make, but this one connection was outstanding. Where's this Guy Called Gerald? Well, he's a Northerner, so I'm a Northerner. It was a lot to do with that as well. I found a number and tracked him down, phoned him up, said, 'I don't think you know what you're doing. I don't think you know what your music's doing. Regardless of how overground things have become, people on the underground have a lot of respect for you, and you're doing a lot for me with the tunes you are doing right now.' Because I know what it's like to be in a bubble in the middle of nowhere, doing that kind of stuff. I didn't think he knew the impact. So I said, 'You've just got to come down. . .'

[It's] really important to make these connections. The technology became timeless. We used to look at things like this, and we'd see the spectrum. We could see things in perspective, and it was possible to make those connections. And if you made those connections, it squashes history. It makes people realise that you can reach your peers within a certain time. Think about screaming Beatles fans. We are products of our environments. We are disposable heroes, in that sense. And that was really important for me to make that connection with Gerald. I knew that the energy he had was no different than the energy that I had for the music.

We all listened to Gerald. We are all windows and mirrors, we reflect around each other: all catch the light at the right angle; keep spinning around. No one person can say they started Jungle, but everyone can say they contributed to it.

ARTIST
Can

TITLE
Yoo Doo Right

SOURCE
Monster Movie

LABEL
Spoon

When is this from?

1969.

What is it?

Can.

Did you get this from Gerald?

No. Why?

Because Gerald's a Can man. . . Can were mad, weren't they? They were eccentric. At the beginning they were really good, and then they went off into spacey stuff. But their early work is sensual, very drum and groove-oriented. But that's how it is – you go off, unless you make those connections.

I make my music for people who come home, worked hard. They sit down, play their Sega. They're not superheroes – well, they are; they come home, take their superhero suits off.

Can's Holger Czukay used to do extensive tape editing: he'd record hours of jams and assemble the final tracks from those tapes. It reminded me of what you do.

The whole thing with tape and reels – Gerald's a tape man. He puts everything on tape. The thing that made Gerald's stuff sound different was that it was fragmented. Things were out of time, but in time with the self. Fabio will tell you: mixing early Gerald tracks was hard. If you could roll them in a mix . . . you had to know them inside out, because the way the tape moves, the way its loops would move. . . When you're from the digital era of programming, you're sharper with it: the sounds become sharper.

ARTIST
Doc Scott

TITLE
Drums 96

SOURCE
Here Comes The Drumz Remix 12"

LABEL
Metalheadz

[Immediately] Where did you tape this from? Where did you tape this? You stole this from somewhere. . . I can't believe you got this on tape. . . You really got to understand something about this music. You just don't know, you don't know. [Pauses for about 15 seconds and begins again] So important to the curriculum, this one. Fucks me up, this one, fucks me up. Don't fuck with Doc Scotty. Doc was a roller, he was a king of rollers. You play four aces, he'd pull out five, know what I mean?

Let me show you something about Doc Scott. [He stops the track and rewinds it to a point where the drums suddenly fall out and there is a second of silence before they start up again] Space. It's space with Scotty. It's the track, but it's the space Scotty uses between the track. Style, man.

Scotty will drag you into the vortex and suck you in, man. And when Scotty made this track, the equipment wasn't there for him to do it. If you knew what Scotty worked on . . . Scotty is a bedroom boy, never had a mixing desk. When he made

Dark Angel it just came out, straight from the sampler. That's what people don't understand. He's walkin' the dog, man. When Scotty was making this, he was addressing people. I could go on for 10,000 words on this track.

It's a culture, man. It's just the way that we've learned from the DJ, because me and Scotty, that's all we made music for: for Grooverider's set, for Fabio's set, for Randall. We didn't make it for anybody else's set. They get bigger, play it on radio, and we can expand everything as they expand, which has been done.

What's really wicked is that we've all gone back to what we were. It's my fourth season. People forget I done an album in the summer. This is my season. It's going to get very dark this winter. It's a dark season now. Dark as in unnoticed: dark grooves, dark connotations. People are very, very angry. The music is making them angry, and they're out there going, 'Yeah, let's go.' It's a good anger. And I think a lot of people are angry as well because of the way Jungle has been taken out of rhetoric. They tried to step into all these different fashions, but let's not forget fashions, guys. We've been here for seasons; it's time to get back to the programme. It's about UK drum 'n' bass. It's not about ragga, it's not about soul, it's not about HipHop or any of those things. It's about the programme of British urban breakbeat culture. Nothing else deserves to come inside of this and rip it apart and make it something that it's not. You can't rise above the music. It took me a long time to get in this position where I am in now: I've walked a very straight path. Compilations? I didn't make any compilations to get my music out.

ARTIST
Afrika Bambaataa & Soul Sonic Force

TITLE
Planet Rock

SOURCE
Planet Rock 12"
LABEL
Tommy Boy

117

Goldie

[Starts singing along] The electronic era, man. . . This is huge. It had an impregnated influence. Really important. The Bambaataa thing obviously comes off the back of the HipHop thing and getting into the culture. I had already been to America and come back.

You appeared in a documentary with Bambaataa.
The deal with the film was learning about American subculture and history and getting into that. It made all these questions and doors open.

What kind of questions?
I wanted to know more about the history, because it concerned me and intrigued me. It made me want to do things. When I learned to break, it was like such a different thing: graffiti, the way they used it as a letter form. It just freaked me out, because it was like you were marrying into a culture that you liked but didn't understand, and I wanted more and more to understand. You're given things as fashion. When you're given them, they are on a TV screen no bigger than that on breakfast TV. You're given 20 guys in tracksuits, and you think, 'There's got to be more than that: it hasn't gone just because they've gone on to another subject the next day.' You want to pursue that, find out what it is, realise all of those things. And then when you go to that New York situation and realise that there are people busking on the sidewalk and spinning on their heads and it's mad and the graffiti and the textures and the layers, you started seeing the real side of it,

why it was socially provoked. And that connection was really important to me, to becoming a B-boy and not a wannabe. . .

At the point we were given HipHop, of course, we never understood it, because the social climate we were in wasn't at the decay where we are at now. That is why HipHop is so big in Europe, because of decay, because of the social climate. Because of the way integration and race is and has gone into that situation where . . . do you think these people knew what was in the third verse in *Wild Style*? They liked the energy they were giving off, but they didn't understand the words, the terminology. But within years of that, of knowing what they were talking about – that rap was talking about social events that were occurring – they thought, 'Fuck! They're singing about getting thrown out of the block and drugs and this and cops', and they realised it all because it was all there.

ARTIST
Public Enemy

TITLE
Night Of The Living Baseheads

SOURCE
It Takes A Nation Of Millions To Hold Us Back

LABEL
Def Jam

[Starts reciting the Malcolm X speech in the introducton] They smashed it all, man, smashed it. When they came in, I didn't know a lot of these issues, but look how they exploded it. They were an inspiration. The social aspect of what they said, it really hit people. So important I remember crashing my car to *Rebel Without A Pause* because I was so taken over by the music. It was so hardcore that I just lost control of my car. I was going around this curve, then whhhhap! I think its power has a lot to do with the way their producer, Hank Shocklee, stacks the samples so they hit you like a punch. He makes the music so dense.

And that was what this was: an album of production that could dominate. And that voice that you probably couldn't understand because it was the slang of New York. You finally had to hear all of those words and still be faced with the dark context of what he was dealing with in your face. It was production that was in your face. A lot of acts had to fix their program after that shit. If you removed the voice of the girl from that, and Chuck D's voice, you had beats and loops. And then, if you remove the voice from the music of Method Man, the music itself isn't just beats and loops now, it's dark as well. The music has a voice now. It has a mood.

That's what I find really interesting about those two. The production, the integration of the production, and the vocal lick, if you like. Drum 'n' bass is like this because it integrates the whole thing. You can't just talk all over it and lay it on. This isn't conventional, traditional music. It became faceless, it didn't need lyrics. We then provoked the mood, to revisit the lyric.

ARTIST
Nicolette

TITLE
Waking Up (Remix)

SOURCE
Now Is Late

LABEL
Shut Up And Dance

[As soon as Nicolette starts singing] Nicolette. Shut Up And Dance did Jungle years ago, before the word even came along. What's happening nowadays is urban breakbeat culture. I'm finding that I have to make these little word changes because. . . Let me find a good way to explain it. You can't help people listen to the vocabulary of this music. When you were saying 'dark' you thought 'demonic', but the word dark was used in dark grooves – dark as in not in the limelight. We'd all go, 'Did you hear that tune?' Everyone else was going, 'Nooooo.' And we're going, 'It's a dark tune, because it's in the shade, its back's against the wall.' That's where dark came from, having those dark aspects, tapping into the darker shade of your mind; which is always the part that's more productive if you can tap into it, know what I mean?

Back to Shut Up And Dance: I've never known them personally, but they were on the train before I ever got on it. Now I'm on the train and look back at these carriages. Very slow fuse burning. It was inevitable that it would explode.

Why?

The surge, man. You can never keep things down that are real. It's like oppression, isn't it? Walls are built to take down, are they not?

Do you mean musical or social oppression?

It's total class, man. I know it's class because people can't say Jungle's a black thing, they can't say it's a white thing. I could play you 20 tunes and ask you which colour person made it, and you wouldn't be able to tell me. . .

ARTIST
Sun Ra

TITLE
Everything Is Space

SOURCE
Somewhere Else

LABEL
Rounder

119

Goldie

Is this Miles?

Sun Ra.

Man, I think I have it on tape somewhere here. . .

Some people have started talking about a black sci-fi idea that threads through dub, George Clinton and Sun Ra, of finding another place, a place in outer space. Does it apply to you?

No, because the thing about it is we are the future now. People don't realise how far we are: we can travel through travel; to travel back to Sun Ra, to travel back to Miles. It's all been recorded and we can visit these places. I've come to terms with the fact that some of the most powerful things are things from the past. It's creating your future, right?

But don't you feel you need to find another place?

No, because that place is already there, and my mind dwells in it. Your mind is your future, it's your past; the energy in it is what will make you survive. I think the amount of energy I got from listening to those things . . . we're definitely in the future. What we can do with music is unreal. And technology is allowing me to make what's in my head – their riffs going round in there, all these things I want to do. And not only that, you can redefine things. There's five genres of history that have made world music and are part of my manual: Detroit Techno/Inner City, reggae/amplified music, HipHop, blues and jazz – they're all part of urban breakbeat culture. Out of those five, none of them knew when they were making it that what they were doing was going to be so influential. All have been revisited, all have gone overground, all still have the respect and integrity they had when they were begun. If you remember that, you're fine, because you can go between those things. And if all those things are powerful in themselves, if they're married together – well, they're already fused together, technology has bumped them up a bit. We've been allowed to take the live aspect of jazz, then the second generation of HipHop looped, and then they hook those loops to give you the break. Then came mixing the breaks with two decks. Detroit Techno then endeared itself to that, using the equipment to take it further. Then reggae, the amplification, the need to explore bass and that different rhythm. Breakbeat's got all of those things, and integrated technology and multiculturalism, if you like.

ARTIST
King Tubby

SOURCE
private tape

TITLE
Rebel Dance

Oh, it's my Dad's music. [After a few bars] This is not Shaka, is it?
No. King Tubby.
Massively influential, dub. All this stuff you've played me, it's all important. Because I'm a window. I'm an artist. And artists don't paint things without views. [A big echo crashes in] EQs, man. Reverbs and EQs. All these things have now been put in the digital age, which means we can do these things tenfold. Which is amazing. It's the same tradition: to distort, to corrupt music, to be off the wall, to have the fourth dimension of sound. That's what makes that haze. I'm completely inspired by it.

'He's done for the voice what Hendrix did for the guitar,' was Robert Fripp's opinion after Peter Hammill had guested on Fripp's 1979 album *Exposure*. As a teenager at the tail end of the 60s, Hammill formed Van Der Graaf Generator, who quickly established a reputation for extremity at odds with the safer climes of most of their contemporaries in the area of Progressive rock. Live performances were spontaneous and notoriously erratic and a contemporary source described *Pawn Hearts* as the most nihilistic album since The Velvet Underground's *White Light/White Heat*. With various line-ups the group recorded nine albums; Hammill's solo canon is currently standing at an intimidating 25 releases. Hammill always trod a challenging aesthetic path. Perhaps that's why, at the height of punk, he was one of the few of his contemporaries to escape vilification. Over the years his approach has expanded to encompass tape loop experiments, music for TV and ballet and an opera, *The Fall Of The House Of Usher* (which featured appearances by Lene Lovich and Erasure's Andy Bell). But what remains constant throughout is his singular take on the song. Hammill lives in Bath, recording in his own Terra Incognito studio, and running his Fie! label.

ARTIST	SOURCE
Todd Rundgren	**A Wizard, A True Star**

TITLE
LABEL
Bearsville

International Feel

Randy California? No, Rundgren. [He sings along] He was one of the only other people [in the early 70s] doing solo recording. He came from the angle of being a mega-producer and totally in control of things. This is the peak period: *A Wizard, A True Star* and *Todd*, the double one that's just after this. He had – I'm not sure that it remained much beyond this period – a self-deprecating sense of humour. I think on the cover of *Todd* there's a shot of him recording in a rented villa somewhere with an extremely expensive Neumann mic taped to a broom which was attached to a chair and that I thought was great. The true spirit of home recording! These two albums I thought were really fantastic. The Utopia stuff went completely barmy for me.

With all that, it's easy to overlook what a great white soul singer he is.
International Feel was complete rock stuff, but there is this Philly soul angle as well, and you can tell that all his enthusiasm's still there from when he was a teenager. Yeah, real good singer, great guitarist, too. He certainly made a big contribution. Prince wouldn't have been Prince if it hadn't been for Rundgren. *Purple Rain* could easily have been a Rundgren track on either of these two albums.

Was his self-contained solo approach an influence?
By the time I'd discovered him I was already underway with home recording. I started because Teac four-tracks came out – and it was simultaneously a defensive measure and a creative effort. The defensive measure was that even at this early stage, 72 or 73, I had an inkling that the music business might not wish to have me on its roster forever, and therefore I'd better get a means of production if I wanted to carry on doing music.
The creative part was that I thought a different music would turn out. It was much more wild and uncontrollable, now it's almost the norm. It's very hard now to be absolutely experimental in that self-recording role because there's so many possibilities, so many sound sources. When it was just a piano, guitar, harmonium and voice, it was in a way more challenging. And of course you can't unmake it – the culture now is a different thing.

ARTIST	SOURCE
William Byrd	**Choral Works**

TITLE
LABEL
Naxos

Lord Have Mercy Upon Me

Purcell? Sounds a bit too jolly for Dowland.
It's William Byrd.
My Byrd angle is usually the ecclesiastical one. I go for the masses because there's this wonderful secret musical aspect. He was a Catholic in the court of Elizabeth I and it was the time of priest holes and so on. Obviously he composed ecclesiastical music for the Church of England but being a Catholic he also wanted to compose masses, so he had to compose masses that could be sung by three

or four people because the maximum congregation would be about five. So he had this music which is devotional but is also secret. And because he's a Catholic he invests all his feeling into them and they're absolutely wonderful.

[I think] Byrd's stuff is great – without being an authority because they all drift past me, the Purcells, the Tallises, the Byrds, the Dowlands. But it's almost flotation tank music. The logic, without being that active Bachian or Mozartian logic, is very calm, rigid, very English. I don't know what it is about the Englishness of this music but it goes right through to Britten and Walton and so on. I do find that very attractive – without wanting to be nationalistic about it.

You say it's almost flotation tank music. Thinking of the packaging and success of the recent CDs of Spanish monks chanting, do you think this sort of ancient, spiritual music just becomes lifestyle Muzak today?

It's restful but it's very active at the same time. There's an uncertainty and a tension in there as well. I find it's very intense. My local classical CD shop has probably got three racks of Gregorian chants, and it's much the same as being a rock music punter in terms of which one you get – which cover you like, where it was recorded.

I know that I am in the wrong business. I should be releasing records with Gregorian chant, with a rhythm loop and the sea underneath. When all else fails, I'll be there with my sea tape.

ARTIST
Public Image Limited

SOURCE
John Peel Radio One session

LABEL
private tape

TITLE
Poptones

123

[Vocals come in] Ah, I suspected so. Is this Wobble-era bass? It's a very strange mix. Sounds like Wobble was there at the mix so the bass gets really shoved to the front. I always thought it was a great shame that PiL didn't have more success. It was a real effort to do something different but I think it was too difficult for people – this era and *Flowers Of Romance*. It was a real effort to advance something and it didn't really sell that much. These days it's hard to imagine someone coming out of a successful band [like The Sex Pistols] and going and doing something like this.

In 76/77, when your peers were getting pilloried, John Lydon was exhorting people to go out and buy your records.

Well, with him and with everyone else, I don't really know about being influential apart from a certain attitude; which might indeed be: if you've got a golden opportunity staring you in the face, the best thing to do is shoot yourself in the foot by doing something radically different or horrible – which I have had a certain tendency to do. Part of which is actually very good in terms of self-preservation and not losing it, I suppose. It was deeply dispiriting that [punk] was dissipated and swallowed up and made pastiche so quickly. My sympathies were with it, but obviously being a musician for eight or nine years there was no point in trying to pretend to be part of it. But noise remains a part of what I like about doing this. So a lack of politeness will always go down well, I think. Too much politeness in music – whatever style of music it is – is usually very bad news.

ARTIST
Soft Machine

TITLE
Lullaby Letters

SOURCE
Soft Machine
LABEL
Probe

The bass doesn't sound in tune.

No, we're in the 'questionable intonation of the bass' period. [Referring to the overdriven organ solo] It's not quite developed here: it just needs a little more nudge.

Well, Soft Machine were a great band, but the pop song, one felt, was never quite their forte. That's the unfair thing – in 67 those lyrics would not have seemed absurd. I've got deeply embarrassing things in my treasure chest as well. [Robert] Wyatt was obviously a great singer, but particularly once the organ sound was totally developed it was a really monumental experience. There was this strange cusp of time when Soft Machine were going, we started some time after, and we were technically known – Arthur Brown and King Crimson as well – as 'underground' bands. At that point it was a broad description for anything that didn't fit. In a way I don't know what audience we were aiming at, but we didn't think about that sort of thing.

Hugh [Banton, Van Der Graaf's keyboard player] was the only other organist with a sound remotely comparable to [Mike] Ratledge's. Again because both organs were so severely mangled, with fuzzboxes inserted and bits of Sellotape holding them together. He ended up designing one from scratch himself. Possibly they were the only two organists who were interested in making the organ go towards guitar and perhaps the fact that Soft Machine toured with Hendrix a few times in the States was influential. Both Hugh and I were very keen Hendrix fans and since the organs were the lead instruments in both bands maybe there was that temptation to go that way. Modern instruments have got much more capacity for lots of sounds but a Hammond being severely abused as Ratledge and Hugh did was a very full instrument which you can't synthesise successfully.

Did Van Der Graaf have any affinity with their contemporaries in the so-called Progressive scene?

Most Progressive bands at the time were going towards this thing where, 'The show is the show. We will play these bits, they are impressive, they go widdly-widdly at this point in the set, everyone is impressed and it is being "classical music", though it's rock music' – and so the shows would be the same. But with our shows – for better or worse – out of every five, two on average were completely appalling maelstroms of sound, organs and fuzzboxes akimbo, sheets of feedback from the sax, the vocalist's voice has gone because he's just been shouting for two days. And then one would be fantastic, where everything was great. This was not the way generally that the world of Progressive music was going. It was going down the line that to be fair to the audience, you have to present exactly this show everywhere you go and that isn't what we did. We were not trying to make it a shrine somehow.

Scott Walker

Tilt

Fontana

The Cockfighter

Not Scott Walker, is it? I've not heard any of his recent stuff. It's been hovering around the consciousness for years that he's somebody who does interesting stuff, and obviously I know all of the great pop stuff. I thought there was something about the voice immediately. Very interesting. What era is this from?

1995, *Tilt.*

I've been meaning to check this out and I'm not somebody who generally checks things out even as observation, but. . . [Track ends] I don't think he's trying to make the album with Gregorian chant and sea either – and good on him. I think it's fantastic that he's still making records. As I say, I haven't checked out all of the career. I'm not a massive Scott fan, but he's a great singer. And in a way it's a bit like the equivalent of PiL – a post-career – but even more so. There's no reason why he's doing this apart from what he wants to do with it. He's not doing it subject to any other agenda. And since there's so much subject to other agendas, I think that's great.

There might be a parallel here in the fact that you've both taken very singular and uncompromising paths – except he only comes up with an album every ten years.

It [Walker's music] requires attention. In terms of parallels, when I make records I don't make them to be just in the background, either. Even though I pump them out every year as opposed to ten years, I do listen to them and I do concentrate on them in an utterly unreasonable way. I think it can be a positive thing for some music to be background but that's not really what I think it's for. It should be concentrated on, and that makes it difficult exactly because you don't get it all straight away. I think if there's value it will take four or five times.

125

Peter Hammill

The Fall

The Infotainment Scan

Permanent

Paranoia Man In Cheap Shit Room

What era is this from? I think there should always be a place for Mark Smith. I didn't get it before the '*uh-ah*'s [imitates Smith]. He's certainly got a style which is all his own. Some of it is a bit of a rant, but some is really well written. And here's someone who pumps out records even more regularly than me. He used to be in touch with me and send me the vinyl as it came out, but I haven't heard from him for a while. He suggested that we did something – the area of sound that he was particularly interested in was [Hammill's] *The Future Now* [1978] which is a particularly difficult area to recreate.

So you were thinking of doing a collaboration?

Yes, with Scott on backing vocals! And of course the sea! It didn't happen in the end. I'm a bit of a control freak; with those of us generally that are survivors, there is a degree of control-freakery. For myself, I prefer to do instant collaborations. I'm not really interested spending six months labouring on something. And I'm not keen on the fabulous jam session.

ARTIST
Erasure

TITLE
Love To Hate You

SOURCE
The First 20 Hits
LABEL
Mute

He [Erasure's vocalist Andy Bell] was very good on *The Fall Of The House Of Usher* – I've guessed of course who it is. He worked incredibly hard and fast at it. It's not the easiest stuff to sing. He was great.

Were you aware of Bell's stuff prior to that?
Peripherally, in that peripheral pop world. I was aware of his voice. It's clear that not just in Erasure but going right through Vince Clarke's stuff there has been a constant thread – that's how he hears pop. So it falls into that category – yes, it's pop music, but it's honest and it's there.

How did you get to collaborate with him?
The connection at first was Lene Lovich who was involved from way, way back. She suggested us to him and him to us. So then he came down just to try and see how it was. And of course there was no written music involved in *Usher* at all. So all of the singers had to learn it. I sung all the parts and said, 'There you go – but this tune really *is* the tune and you can't scat around it.' He tried it out, was great at it and did it.

It seemed on paper an unlikely collaboration.
They were all unlikely. Lene would possibly seem to be the closest. I didn't and still don't want *Usher* to be viewed as just another album in the Peter Hammill endless flow – so the fact of having entirely disparate people involved was OK. Sarah Jane Morris wouldn't have seemed likely but I've worked with her before on a very good Japanese CD by Kazuo Isawa, who is a classical Japanese koto player. And Herbert [Grönemeyer] – people wouldn't know about him here but in Germany they certainly would – and it's as, if not even more, unlikely that he would be involved in something like this.

Even though we called it an opera we did not want operatic voices. We wanted to have singers who were used a) to singing neo-rock music, b) to articulating words. And within each given song there should be a degree of dramatic input – people who within the voice could act. So yeah, I think he did a fantastic job with minimal time and unfortunately minimal return in terms of visibility and event and so on. . .

ARTIST
John Coltrane

TITLE
Transition

SOURCE
Transition
LABEL
Impulse!

It was [David] Jackson [Van Der Graaf's sax player] who introduced me to Coltrane and [Archie] Shepp and all of this world, in the days of sharing bedsits and so on. We played [Coltrane's] *Ascension* fairly non-stop in the flat at the time. So again, a world of relaxed concentration. And again, I'm not a really authoritative buff: [it represents] a life and a time of life and an attitude to music that obviously I've never come remotely close to experiencing – the degree of commitment and belief to carry on doing this music, to invent this music in the first place, is mind boggling.

Certain aspects of Van Der Graaf seemed to draw on this era of jazz – the intensity and improvisation. . .

Well, both [Jackson] and Guy [Evans, drummer] came from the jazz world. In terms of a colour that would be so – because most of the time there wasn't a guitar and there certainly weren't that many horn players around in bands at the time. But what [Jackson] was playing on top of was not jazz. I love Coltrane and the sound and so on but I long for the band to hit something solid sometimes. Guy obviously would understand what the drums are doing – I just don't get that. I like the front end of things. . . Which is this from?

***Transition*, recorded in 1965.**

The real ones for me are *A Love Supreme* and *Ascension*: they are classic.

ARTIST
Edgard Varèse

TITLE
Intégrales

SOURCE
Passeport Pour Le XX Siècle

LABEL
Auvidis Montaigne

Is this the basis of some other tune trying to break out there, some traditional tune? Almost sounds like a bit of Ravel trying to break through.

It's Varèse.

Ah, right. Well, I wouldn't have known that because I don't know any Varèse apart from the immortal quote that, 'The duty of every modern day composer is not to die', or something, that Zappa constantly quoted. I've never heard any Varèse – Ligeti was more my man. I once went to a Ligeti concert where he gave a lecture. It was great because he was being very clear about saying, 'In the next piece there is this comic bit – a lot of people don't think there is any humour in my music but I think there are some very funny bits.' [With this] I really thought there was some traditional tune that was fractured and being reassembled.

According to the sleevenotes, the use of very high and low tones in this piece was seen as the origination of techniques later used in electronic music and *musique concrète*.

[Looks at CD insert] You only get it by reading. It says, 'Can be observed on the score.' So there one's into the land of music you listen to by reading. It either gets to somebody or doesn't get to somebody. If you have to read about it to have it happen, it's not happening.

ARTIST
John Lee Hooker

TITLE
Walking The Boogie

SOURCE
Chess Checkmate

LABEL
NME compilation tape

The important thing about John Lee Hooker is that he didn't play 12-bar blues. His riffs were always a little bit angular and chaotic. He was precisely in this land of not playing 4/4 but sounding like it was generally in fours. This slipping and sliding all the time was a great forte of his. He's hanging and pushing and pulling all the time rather than saying it's got to be [beats fist into palm] bang, bang, bang, straight on. [Referring to echoed stomp and double-tracked vocals] It's got that early studio experimentation. It's quite bizarre actually – like the Prog rock version!

So were you a young blues man?

I was a young blues man but it was obviously derived from British groups talking about the blues. This would be 63/64/65. So then it was Muddy Waters, John Lee Hooker, Sonny Boy Williamson, that urban stuff – even later than that, when it was really electric and the guitar sound is recognisable as the guitar sound now. And there was the form of – here are songs, you can write songs and they are simple and they have riffs. That's the way that I stumbled in and wrote this absolutely appalling collection of 15 year old's blues songs, lacking only that somewhat essential ingredient: a life that one has lived and experience that one has had. God, the mind cringes! But that's when I started to write, rather than trying to write pop songs. On the *other* other hand I was trying to get into the riff and particularly from John Lee Hooker this idea of riffs that go funny on you somewhere. A riff is still one of the central things for me. They're still hard to find, though. To get one that works you have to have a good day.

On the surface it seems an unusual connection between your music and Hooker's.

I realised I'm not going to be a blues writer because I'm a middle class 15 year old prat, so why try? But what I like about it is there's a riff happening, so I'll try to do something that's true to me. Actually it's not so strange. It's a direct parallel, I've just been doing things out of my own experience. Seriously, in all of those riffs, if there's been an origin, it's John Lee Hooker and Hendrix. But Hendrix also came through the same thing – he was the inheritor of all that tradition, especially the riff-world. So it's a straight line really.

Ice T, real name Tracy Marrow, emerged in the mid-80s as one of the pioneering and most controversial figures in West Coast gangsta rap, a scene where controversial figures weren't exactly in short supply. His first record, *The Coldest Rap* (1983), was heavily influenced by New York Electro and breakdancing. His 1986 single *Six In The Morning* shifted the mood, picking up on the violent, often misogynistic hardcore East Coast rap then being produced by Schooly D and Boogie Down Productions, slowing down the beats, introducing a more 'conversational' take on rap, and opening a gate through which would follow the likes of Ice Cube, Dr Dre, NWA, *et al.* Subsequent albums such as *Rhyme Pays* and *OG: Original Gangster* only sought to cement Ice's rep as the baddest gangsta in South Central LA. In 1991 he formed the rap/Metal group Body Count, performed on that year's Lollapalooza tour, and recorded the track *Cop Killer*, which caused an outcry in America and was eventually withdrawn from the *Body Count* album by Ice himself. Like fellow gangsta Ice Cube, Ice T has also moved into acting, appearing in *New Jack City* (1991), *Trespass* (1992) and *Johnny Mnemonic* (1996). In 1995 he published *The Ice Opinion*, a no-holds-barred collection of rants and opinion pieces. An irrepressible advocate of 'black-trash' culture, Ice T also fronted Channel 4's *Baadasss TV*. The Jukebox took place in London.

ARTIST
Cybotron

SOURCE
Interface: The Roots Of Techno

LABEL
Southbound

TITLE
Alleys Of Your Mind

I've never heard it before. It kind of reminds me of the stuff we used to do in the early days back in LA, and also some old Kraftwerk stuff, that *Trans-Europe Express* stuff and pre-Techno; the same instruments in it but it's not fast. I don't know what you would call it. It's cool. If it came on in a club I'd be dancing off of it. It's a cross of funk, electronics: computer-age funk. Who is this?

It's Cybotron, a pre-Techno Detroit duo consisting of Juan Atkins and Rick Davies. It was released in 1983, but actually recorded in 1981.

[Looks at CD] Oh, there it is – *The Roots Of Techno*. That's what I said. It reminds me of the older stuff: Egyptian Lover, Uncle Jam's Army, stuff like that. OK then, I was right.

Would you say that *The Coldest Rap* was in any way similar to this?

When I put my record out, all the records before then were on this level on the West Coast. I intentionally made my record sound different – it was the first record on the West Coast that didn't sound like this. I was closer to New York rap. Egyptian Lover and them were doing their own thing. I call it 'aerobic music' – everybody was breathing on it. [He breathes rhythmically] All those records, *Planet Rock*, were inspired by Kraftwerk, *Tour De France*. I knew about it, but I wasn't really sprung on it. I was into Run DMC and rap and so on.

Derrick May thought that Techno could have been a radical form of black music. He said [in *The Wire*]: 'Techno is not the future music it could have been. If black people had been there, we're talking about a revolution, truly. Rock 'n' roll would no longer exist.'

That's because he's a Techno artist and some people like to think that they could change things. Rock 'n' roll will always be around. Techno's just another form of music. I disagree with him. The closest thing you've got to black Techno now is Jungle. Jungle is Techno on steroids, with balls, and with Jamaican influences and rap influences. So for anyone who wants to know what black people would do with Techno, hear Jungle.

ARTIST
MC Det

SOURCE
Out Of Det

LABEL
SOUR

TITLE
Freeform Reality

Yeah, exactly, this is Jungle. I've been [coming] over here for three years trying to analyse this stuff. This shit is like off the hook, but it's extremely creative, a hybrid of all different forms. This stuff right here is still a little commercial compared to some of the stuff I've been listening to. I like the stuff that's got those real, real, super subs in it.

My favourite [Jungle] record right now is called *Super Sharp Shooter*. It goes from Jungle into like a rap record, like an Old School rap record. Then it does a break and the whole damn record just stops for a long time, longer than normal, and the whole crowd just has to stand there. And the DJ just lets this shit play and it comes back on: EEEOOOWWW! [Ice makes a sound like an approaching racing car]. And it's almost like the record itself does what the Jungle DJs do. It stops, it rewinds itself. It makes you sound like a good DJ. [Laughs] What's this one called? I've never heard this.

It's MC Det.

The MC part ain't the hard part, it's the damn snare drum!

How much is Jungle known over in Los Angeles?

Not at all. And I'm really out to break it in the States.

It could be huge.

It can be, but somebody's got to do it.

ARTIST

Porno For Pyros

TITLE

Porno For Pyros

SOURCE
Porno For Pyros
LABEL
WEA

I thought this sounded like Jane's Addiction but it's Porno For Pyros, right? We were out on tour with Jane's Addiction [Lollapalooza 1991] and I'd been introduced to [Perry Farrell] but I had to go out and watch this shit work. After a while you can really tell what it is. What they do is they got this kinda like rock but it's *always* got these African-like drums up under it. It keeps it funky in its own way. And he's got a really original voice. I like this. It's cool but it stands alone. It's not Grunge, it's not 'We're hard funk rock' like The Chilli Peppers. It's like that Jane's Addiction music they made, y'know?

How did you get to meet Farrell?

My guitar player hooked up with him somehow. Perry was trying to do that record *(Don't Call Me) Nigger, Whitey* and he was like, 'Ice T's the only person you can do it with.' So I met him and he was really cool and a fan of mine – he knew more about me. I had to review [Jane's Addiction's] first album for *Playboy* and I got off into them. To me that sounds like old Jane's Addiction. Perry was mad cool, always hanging out, a real hip cat, y'know? And prior to that you were seeing Perry in braids and dresses and stuff. And [at Lollapalooza] he got up on the stage, he had his big pants and his tank top and big hat and – this dude is different, definitely cool. We got down with them, it was fun. By the end of the tour we would always stay out there and watch the whole set.

I heard that you were down in the moshpit.

Oh yeah, most definitely. You don't want to just shout it, sometimes you've got to be about it. You want to make this music, you got to go into the audience, see what they're feeling. It helps you make it.

The lyrics on this track are about watching the LA riots and jacking off.

That's what Perry probably did. That's his style. I can see he could write a lyric like that. He's crazy but he's cool. I see him on the streets of LA walking around just tripping. He's cool, but the whole group was cool.

As you were playing on a largely white rock billing, half the set as Ice T and half of it as Body Count, Lollapalooza could have been an ideal time to put into practice the infiltration into the white audience that you showed on the cover of your *Home Invasion* album.

Well, *Home Invasion* was like a way of me saying it's already happened: you

131

Ice T

want to know why your kids are talking this way? You want to know why when you spoke on the riots negatively, your little daughter jumped up and said, 'No, mother, they're not niggers'? It's because these kids have been listening to this rap music, and you didn't notice that your daughter has this Public Enemy T-shirt on. There's a severe fear by some parents of their daughter pulling that Take That poster down and putting Ice T up over the Little Princess bedroom set. It's a problem, but I'm saying it's too late, this is what happened, it's home invasion, we're in your house – more black people than you could possibly imagine. Snoop Dogg's there, Eazy E's there, Too Short's there. And your kid is listening to us, so now what you going to do?

Were you surprised by the massive popularity of gangsta rap with white kids?
It's rock, [and] in order to be a rock 'n' roller you have to be a gangster. What is a gangster? A gangster is somebody who says, 'Fuck the rules.' In a black sense it's like, 'Fuck the police, fuck you, I do what I do,' y'know what I'm saying? 'I'm'a sell dope, I don't give a fuck.' What's a rock 'n' roll record about? 'I'm'a do dope. Fuck authority.' That's the essence of good rock. Anarchy damn near, that's the basis of all real rock: 'FUCK YOU!' That's what we say and [for] white kids it's like it's punk rock, the same exact thing.

It is also connected to Country music, because they sing about their neighbourhood and their dialogue, and if you don't like it you can kiss their ass. They don't care who buys the records, because they've got their own fans. And they wear jeans to the Grammies, they wear hats and everybody says, 'Who are they?' It's a cultural-based music – a music sung to the culture, just like Jungle, just like reggae. Rap is its own culture, it's a street culture. And there's white people who know every Buju Banton record, and y'know, it's voyeuristic.

ARTIST
Lightnin' Rod

TITLE
Sport

SOURCE
Hustler's Convention
LABEL
Polydor

I know this, this is *Hustler's Convention*. [He raps along with the record. At the line, '*By the time I was 11, I could pad-roll seven*'] Pad-roll is like rolling dice on a pad. OK, I know what that is. Give me that tape! Where d'you get that at? On CD? Or somebody dubbed it. I need to get hold of that album.

It's a tape I borrowed. It's the guy's only copy. I was told to make sure I brought it back.
That record was out before rap. That's pre-rap rap. There was some other people that were doing that type of rhyme over records, like Iceberg Slim, who wrote the book *Pimp* and all that stuff, who I got my name from – he had a record out called *Reflections* and it was done in that format. On the other side you had people like The Last Poets, The Watts Prophets, who were doing that form of rap but it was political.

Jalal from The Last Poets has been critical of gangsta rap in the past, saying it isn't political *enough*.
But that's just one area. I didn't start rapping because of them, I started rapping because of this record, people on this line. You see what this is? This is as apolitical as you can get: '*bitches*' and '*shootin'*' and '*snortin' scag*'. It's like,

'Hey, this is how I'm living.' There was a lot of stuff out before rap that had this attitude. When you go to like a Dolemite movie, or if you get into a Red Fox album, there were a lot of black people who were just being black and had attitude. Those were the people I admired. I wasn't really into people who really cared what somebody thought about. So this record is excellent.

I would document this as being the first gangsta rap album. It's like maybe ten years before rap actually hit the scene. And it's done by guys old enough to be my father. So that's one of the things I always tell people: you're putting a lot on us [gangsta rappers] but this is part of a legacy of the streets, y'know, talkin' shit. Really that's what it is, talkin' shit. And I think black people tend to talk a lot of shit because if you ain't got a car, you ain't got no money, you ain't got a good job, all you can do is stand on the corner and say 'Mo'fucker', 'Fuck that nigger', 'Fuck that bitch'. [Laughs] You just talk shit, y'know. This is part of our culture. My father did it, my father could talk crazy like that, too. Now my son can say, 'My daddy can talk crazy.'

That's a classic. Play the next part. Trip off a bit. You've got to understand that that shit is early, way before us. The music is by Kool And The Gang. I did a record like this called *Soul On Ice*, on the *Power* album, the exact same. I inflect my voice the same way they did it.

Can you identify a particular point when gangsta rap started off in the 80s?

I did a record called *The Coldest Rap*, which is another gangsta rap, but way back. I'm talking about cocaine, all kinds of stuff in it: *The Pimp, the player, the woman layer, the ho-house ruler. . . Pimp whores slam Cadillac doors. . . '* [At the time] nobody could check that because they weren't ready for it, they were like, 'Uh?' Only real players [got it]. Then I tried to rap like New York rappers, and my friends were like, 'Ice, man, talk that shit, man.' Then we did *Six In The Morning*. [People said] 'That's what people like, you talk that shit.' So I was like, 'OK, cool.'

At the same time in Philly, a record called *PSK* [by Schooly D] came out. *PSK* really influenced me – it was gangsta but it was vague. Schooly was saying, '*PSK's making that dream/People always say what the hell does that mean/P is for the people who can't understand how one homeboy became a man/S for the way you scream and shout/One by one we're knockin' you out*'. So that's like, 'I'm knockin you out.' My shit was, 'I got a gun, I'm blastin', beat the bitch down.' Then when NWA took what I did to another channel, it was like off the hook. So that was how it went, but I [credit] Schooly D with the origins of just *ill* raps.

ARTIST

2 Pac With Dr Dre And Roger Troutmann

SOURCE
California Lovin' single
LABEL
Virgin

TITLE

California Lovin'

Yeah, OK, it's like a hot rap record, man. Dr Dre and 2 Pac's on it. They're using a loop that Ultramagnetic MCs used before. And they also got Roger Troutmann on there, who really is a powerful influence in West Coast music. On the West Coast we like Roger, we like *Atomic Dog*, Bootsy. There are certain records that are really LA records. I don't know where it's from, the gang culture or wherever. They're just rapping about the West Coast, just talking about the different things that we do in LA. There's no real message on it, there's no intention – just talking about themselves. It's not intentionally offensive or anything but it's still hardcore, because they're playing the edge real good. Dre knows how to hit that little edge right here, and it's one of those records that you can just hear coming over a radio station.

The whole P-funk thing has had a massive influence on West Coast rap.
Oh yeah, most definitely. I mean Eric Surman has looped Roger 1500 times; Ice Cube too. [There's] a vibe that comes off of those records – moods and shit that sets this tone. West Coast shit really has a lot to do with getting a mood. We accept rap over orchestration, whereas New York would prefer to hear drum loops and sporadic music. They don't want to hear too much music, that's the New York style. LA is different. You got two different cultures because New York is a more static culture: you listen to your music in your Walkman, you catch the train. In LA you're riding down the street with a $20,000 system in your car. I always say a guy in New York, if he's mad at you, he'll catch the train over to your house and shoot you. An LA guy will say, 'I'll kill him if I see him. [Laughs] We'll get around to it.' More laidback vibe.

What did you think about the spate of arrests of rappers in the last year or so – Flavor Flav, Snoop Doggy Dogg, 2 Pac?
I just think it's people, y'know? Living this life anything can happen. I mean rock 'n' roll people have killed themselves, drugs, overdosed, beat their wives. When you're in the spotlight, shit you do is on the news, y'know what I'm saying? Per ratio, rappers, we're staying out of trouble as far as the music industry goes.

The media seize upon it like the bad guys have got their comeuppance.
Yeah, well, whatever. [Laughs] I just think it's part of this business, man. I'm so scared of getting in some trouble, man. It's like anytime you're out you meet a girl, you don't know what's going to happen. Y'know what I'm saying? You go out, some guy jumps in your face and starts talking crazy, so it's not easy. It's got nothing to do with the music.

ARTIST
Black Sabbath

TITLE
Sweet Leaf

SOURCE
Master Of Reality
LABEL
Vertigo

[Immediately] *Sweet Leaf*, Black Sabbath. '*You introduced me to my mind.*' Big power chords. [Ice sings along in high voice] When I got into rock 'n' roll that was the group that I really got into, because it was more evil and ill and dark and harder. And that record was double hard, because it wasn't about some devil shit, they were singing about weed. I never got high, but just the fact that you would make a record, press it and put it out about drugs, when drugs were illegal – that was like taboo shit.

You know what I like about that record? That first cough, that was some ill Old School looping shit. Or either they ran it through some sort of guitar machine that made it loop like that – but just that beginning sound was some deep shit.

ARTIST
Queen Latifa

TITLE
Unity

SOURCE
Black Reign

LABEL
Motown

[Immediately] Latifa. Cool. I know this record. *Unity*, I think it's a dope record. It's like her making comments back to brothers on the street calling girls bitches and hoes. But this is like female rap – this is their perception, their version. I mean the way rap is going, anybody who is behind that mic is going to take their position. So the way I look at it is: touché. But I'm not going to stop calling them bitches or hoes, not because Latifa said it. I can come back with, 'Who're you calling a dog? I ain't your dog, I ain't your *sucker*.' That's where we coming from. It's like verbal jousting, we're all trying to jockey for position. Also, in the black culture, those words are thrown around so loosely, it doesn't even hold water any more. A man could say, 'I love my bitch, man', y'know what I'm saying? It's street slang. If you break the word down, a bitch is a female dog. And they call us dogs all day and all night. 'All men are dogs': how many times have you heard women say that? Now if I said all women are bitches it's the same exact statement.

Everything is 'bitches' and 'hoes' at this point, you're rolling like that. You heard *Hustler's Convention*: '*Bitches*', that's the mental of the street. I don't know how to change and don't expect for it to change. But you know what? The rap audience aren't offended, it's outsiders. They don't understand the dialogue. They say, 'Why don't you change the dialogue?' We're like, 'Why don't you hang the phone up? The record ain't for you.'

135

Ice T

Mary Scanlon

Lydia Lunch emerged in the late 70s during New York's No Wave era, fronting the witheringly nihilistic Teenage Jesus And The Jerks. During the early 80s her words and music evolved through such projects as 8-Eyed Spy, Beirut Slump (both featured alongside Teenage Jesus on the CD *Hysterie*, released through Lunch's Widowspeak company), 13.13 and Harry Crews – the latter, a collaboration with Sonic Youth's Kim Gordon, being a Hardcore tribute to the American author of the same name. She has also regularly collaborated with, among others, ex-Birthday Party guitarist Roland S Howard, Foetus/Jim Thirlwell (in Stinkfist) and Berlin's Die Haut. Outside music she has scripted and acted in numerous underground movies, most notoriously Richard Kern's *Fingered* and *Right Side Of My Brain*. Her most constant – and perhaps effective – mode of address has turned out to be spoken word, which she approaches like a cross between a confessional and a blood sport. Her earlier spoken word pieces have been published in book form (*Incriminating Evidence*) and on CD, in particular, the triple album compilation *Crimes Against Nature*. Lydia responded to each Jukebox selection cogently and decisively, though she was never out of her most characteristic mode – sardonic amusement.

ARTIST
Allen Ginsberg

TITLE
Cleveland, The Flats

SOURCE
The Lion For Real

LABEL
Antilles

I have no idea who or what it is, but anything that bases itself round the illustrated word is certainly preferable to me to the next pop-schlock post-punk hardcore crap-rock. So I'd give it another listen definitely. The music was good because it was unobtrusive, yet it illustrated the words. Although the words were fairly nonsensical. I preferred it when he started singing in a foreign language – I thought he should have mixed that up a little more, so that people didn't have to pretend they knew what he was going on about.

It's Allen Ginsberg from the 60s, with people like Bill Frisell and Arto Lindsay doing the music much more recently.

It's pretty damn good for Allen Ginsberg, who I'm not a fan of whatsoever. He wrote one good poem and he's been living off it ever since. But let him go.

ARTIST
Snatch

TITLE
Amputee

SOURCE
Snatch

LABEL
Witch

Is it Ut? I thought it was amusing, but I wouldn't listen to it again. I thought the music was kind of flabby, but it's not really musical. I liked the sound of the voices, but it left me fairly cold, it didn't really do anything for me.

It's Snatch. Were they an influence?

Absolutely not. They didn't influence me, though I did like some of the things that Judy Nylon went on to do.

I was trying to find my copy of *Pal Judy*. It's one of my favourite records in fact.

Yeah, I think Judy Nylon cut a very sharp figure. I'm not that familiar with her material. I've seen her perform a few times, and I thought she did some interesting things, but that to me, it's a one-time only kind of recording. Like most records I'm forced to listen to.

ARTIST
Ute Lemper

TITLE
The Ballad Of Sexual Dependency

SOURCE
Die Dreigroschenoper

LABEL
Decca

Well, any kind of opera or operatic vocalisation makes me often feel that if I had an erection it would terrify it into submission for probably six months at a time, and I'd be totally useless as a sexual entity. That's what opera does to me even if it's Germanic, dramatic. It always sounds to me so desperate – which is the beauty of it – yet also so terrifying. I always imagine opera singers as oral castrators. It kind of scares me. It reminds me of church too much. I'm not fond of recalling those memories. Vibrato in a voice of that dimension just terrifies me.

ARTIST
The Slits

TITLE
A Boring Life

SOURCE
Lipstick Traces
LABEL
Rough Trade

It was improved when the drills were still on. Absolutely dreadful.
It's The Slits' first ever recording.
Was it released?
As an official bootleg.
Yeah, well, fucking around should be left to the rehearsal studio. It's a dreadful mess. It sounds like *Suffragette City* and it's not an improvement on the original version. It just sounds like a bunch of spoiled children wailing around in the garage. I myself moved out of the garage about 15 years ago. Well, this was probably done 17 years ago – so I'll allow it to exist, but not in my reality. The only thing I ever liked about The Slits was their mud suits.

ARTIST
NWA

TITLE
One Less Bitch

SOURCE
Efil4taggin
LABEL
4th & Broadway

Dr Dre? NWA? First of all rap music is the only music I listen to at all at this point. I'm not interested in any other format. No 'alternative' music does anything for me, it's not hard enough, it doesn't deal with reality. You can say that rap music is misogynist, but it's *misanthropic*, which is the beauty to me. It's the only form of music which hates the rest of the world as much as I do, and will at least verbally violate the entire rest of the planet. And they're right, because they have every reason to complain about men, women and the world, because they've been raped for 400 years in my country. That they're angry is no surprise to me. My favourite rap acts are Geto Boys, Scarface, 2-Pac, Insane Poetry, Lench Mob. I love NWA. I love Dr Dre's new album, too, I'm glad he's got a massive new single. It doesn't bother me that they do songs like this – I find them not only humorous, but quite real, considering their situation. If they're expressing feelings that so many people feel in that situation they have every right to do it. I think it's the only music that's *politically correct*, that's dealing with reality. It's the closest thing to Spoken Word. It's the closest thing to *my* Spoken Word! I'm not into Ice T, I'm totally into death-rap and that's it. I don't think they're exaggerating, and anyone that does hasn't lived in that situation. I'm just glad that there are bands like NWA, Geto Boys and Scarface to tell it like it really fuckin' is. Anyway, anyone that samples Barry White can't be all bad.

139

Lydia Lunch

Eartha Kitt

I Want To Be Evil

The Best Of Eartha Kitt

RCA

Eartha Kitt. My sentiments exactly. Late night penthouse cocktail music, to be played immediately before you throw your lover out of the 34th storey of your condo. I love Eartha Kitt: A sexual powerhouse. There's no one like that any more. They can't pull it off. I'm sorry, the MTV generation doesn't know what real raunch or real evil is, and I don't suppose they ever will. Come back Eartha! She still performs in New York, so . . .

I don't think there were *many* people like that then.

No. Or like Millie Jackson, another hero of mine I saw perform recently. One thing I really miss in modern music, which is probably why I'm attracted to rap, is that no one knows how to be raunchy, they don't know how to be nasty, they don't know how to be dirty. When we have only Madonna as a feminine icon of any kind of twisted feminine sexuality, well I'm afraid it's just too fucking lollipop for me.

The Fall

Crap Rap/Like To Blow

Live At The Witch Trials

Step Forward

The Fall. Glorious slop. I've always had a soft spot for Mark E Smith. Anyone that's more bitter and sarcastic than I am I've got to respect. I've never had many of their albums, I know they've done many, the music never really mattered, just the spunk of Mark E Smith. It brings a smile to my lips, I know that he is so brooding and bitter. I've tried to entice him occasionally into doing Spoken Word, because I know that the lyrics, which one can only vaguely decipher on any of their records, are just beautiful. More power to him. I think he's getting more bitter as he gets older, and that really impresses me. Oh, Mark E, keep *going*! I love him. They don't understand sarcasm very well in America.

Scott Walker

Montague Terrace In Blue

The Best Of Scott Walker

Philips

Scott Walker. Beautiful touch with the lyrics. Bit schmaltzy in parts for me. I know he was considered a saint in parts by many that tried to impersonate his unique style – most of them unsuccessfully. Julian Cope comes to mind. I do have a fondness for Julian somewhere deep inside me. Though that has nothing to do with his music necessarily. It's down to the fact that if you pretend or think you're insane long enough you eventually become insane, I guess, and that's the beautiful aspect to probably Scott Walker and Julian Cope. It's a little too schmaltz-flavoured for me, but that was nice. 'Suicide Sunday' type material.

Big Black

The Model

Songs About Fucking

Blast First

It's a cover, first of all, of Ultravox or Kraftwerk or something. Who's doing this version? Big Black? Well, I didn't recognise Big Black there, but what I did like is the fact that it sounds as if there was more sound than what the tape can actually withstand. That's a beautiful concept to me. I'll reserve my opinions of Steve Albini. I do love Big Black; I love the fact that the guitars are so brain-crushing and that everything is so layered that it really sounds as if it is jumping off the tape. I prefer their original material though. Why they covered this is beyond me.

You're not a Kraftwerk fan?

Fuck, no. Not then, and not now.

Ishmael Reed

Judas

Conjure: Music For The Texts Of Ishmael Reed

Pangaea

[Lydia chuckles a lot during this] Beautiful. Last Poets? Who is it?

Ishmael Reed. I don't think he does many readings. It's a collection of his work, on Kip Hanrahan's label. He only does two readings on it – other people do the rest. It's beautiful. He doesn't need any musical illustration. The sound of his voice is superb and the piece is so beautiful. I could easily listen to a whole album of that and not at all get bored. It doesn't need an illustration. I've not read that much of his writing or his poetry. I know a little bit about him. I've not heard any of his recordings, but as you said, maybe he hasn't made many. Beautiful.

Debbie Harry

Invocation To Papa Legba

Like A Girl I Want You To Keep Coming

John Giorno Poetry Services

I love it. It sounds like Industrial hi-life. I have no idea where it's from.

It's from New York, one of those John Giorno records. There's no reason why anyone would guess who it is singing, it's so unlikely. It's Debbie Harry, singing an invocation to Papa Legba.

Beautiful. Yeah, the best thing she's ever done. I saw her doing something on late night TV, when she was singing with Nana Vasconcelos, a Brazilian tune, it was absolutely fantastic. But this is gorgeous. It's like happy trance-induction music. It just makes you want to start stomping around the room, singing along. Of course, it's beautiful that you can't understand any of the words. Debbie! Why did you just release another pop single? Please, go back to your roots, and I don't mean the ones you bleach. She's completely capable of doing any variety of beautiful abstract music, but she never does unless someone comes along and drags her by the hair, and I wish they would more often, because it sounds so like Industrial traditional music. She should do a whole album like this. I'll tell her next time I see her.

ARTIST
Alice Cooper
TITLE
Is It My Body?

SOURCE
The Beast Of Alice Cooper
LABEL
Warner Bros

[Straight away] Ooh, yeah. What, your scratchy old Alice Cooper records! All-time heroes! I think he's so underrated. Every one of his albums up to and including *Billion Dollar Babies* has been a great influence on me. So great Rowland Howard and I had to cover *Black Juju* – but we didn't do it justice. Who could? And now there's an Alice Cooper cover-compilation on Triple X in the States. Absolutely fantastic song: especially Alice singing is it *his* body? He never had a spectacular body. Nonetheless, he used it so well, who cared? I think he's one of the finest lyricists, but such an underrated singer – he's so sexy! Especially for such an atrocious visage. It's so hot, it's so great. He was the original death-rocker, got to give him that. Too bad he recorded after *Billion Dollar Babies*, but I guess he has to drink and eat. Maybe he doesn't drink any more. No one in England touched Alice Cooper – even Alex Harvey in all his fucking perversion couldn't reach the glorious heights that Alice scaled. I love you, Alice! I like any man who wears more make-up than me. No, that's not true.

ARTIST
Sinéad O'Connor
TITLE
Où Est Le Roi Perdu?

SOURCE
Am I Not Your Girl?
LABEL
Ensign

Is that Sinéad? She should do more Spoken Word and give up the pop songs. I still have goose bumps, it was so beautiful. I've never listened to many of her records. She doesn't have that many. As an entity I think she's fantastic, and all the bullshit she's gone through because she's an honest, unusual female is an utter crock of shit. That she got booed off-stage in Madison Square Gardens and none of those middle-aged asshole alcoholic men came to her defence is an absolutely pathetic outrage – I mean instead of ripping the Pope's picture in half she should have shot him in the left temple. Then she'd really be part of the Conspiracy of Women. Stick to Spoken Word, sweety! Give up the pop-rock – and I know she wants to, so more power to her. We don't need more pop songs. We don't need more pop songs, we need more Spoken Word.

Marc Marnie

James MacMillan was born in Ayrshire, Scotland in 1959, and now lives and works in Glasgow. He is considered to be one of the leading young composers in Britain, and his work was the subject of a special retrospective (which also included several premieres) at the Edinburgh International Festival in 1993. His orchestral works have been particularly admired for their energy and expressive directness, and he has scored two major successes at The Proms with *The Confession Of Isobel Gowdie* and his percussion concerto *Veni, Veni Emmanuel*. He is a committed Roman Catholic, and his work often reflects spiritual themes. He also has a particular interest in music theatre, and at the time of the Jukebox was working on his first opera for Scottish Opera's 1996 season. Despite an initial apprehension, he identified most selections, usually within the opening two or three bars.

ARTIST
Igor Stravinsky

TITLE
Excerpts from The Rite Of Spring

SOURCE
The Rite of Spring

LABEL
Sony Classical

This is *The Rite Of Spring*. It is a real one-off, this piece, and Stravinsky was right not to try to repeat himself with a *Rite* Mark II – I think it would have been very easy to slot into a groove or work out a formula along these lines, and he probably saw the dangers of that. It maybe got that convulsiveness out of his system early on.

Was he an influence on you?
I think he left a strong impression on 20th century composers in general, and that includes me. I think the most direct influence was probably on *Tryst* – in fact, I think I quoted something by Stravinsky in there. That was 1989, and my work was just opening out into large, public gestures at that point – it is probably quite overt in *The Confession Of Isobel Gowdie*, too. It's keeping that influence at bay that is the real problem!

ARTIST
Talking Heads

TITLE
Life During Wartime

SOURCE
Remain In Light

LABEL
EMI

Talking Heads. My experience with rock is an odd one – I usually get into things much later than the time that they were fashionable. My initial interest in music as a kid of 11 or 12 was in Beethoven and Wagner. I had heard *The Ring* before I was 12, and I still remember the spine-tingling excitement of it, which seemed profound even then, although I didn't understand the adult motivations behind it. My own playing background on trumpet was different again. It was the brass band repertoire that formed my first experience of communal music-making and I played in a folk band after I left school as well. I did play around with some friends in a rock band at school, but it was just pre-punk, and we did heavier, more bluesy things. I had a bit of a second youth much later on, when I began rediscovering all kinds of things that were not current at that point, but were new to me.

What I responded to most in Talking Heads was the rhythmic tautness of the music. I tend to pick up on musical rather than textual interest in the first instance, and this didn't have either the emptiness of much pre-punk rock music, or the nihilism of punk, and it was well played by good musicians.

ARTIST
Kronos Quartet

TITLE
Mai Nozipo

SOURCE
Pieces Of Africa

LABEL
Elektra Nonesuch

This is The Kronos Quartet from their African album, but I can't remember the name of the African composer.

Dumisane Maraire.
My daughter loves this track. She dances around to it whenever I play it.
I think this is one of the most successful on the record.
I agree. This is the most effective for me. It's simple but not facile, and the combination of very different traditions works very well. They took a gamble in bringing together such disparate elements, but I think that what they try to do in broadening the repertoire is a marvellous idea.
Even if it doesn't always work, it's still worth trying.
Yes, and some of it will work.
How does this relate to your *Sowetan Spring*?
Very different. There is no real ethnic aura in that work – the African elements in there have been deconstructed and rendered very abstract. I was trying to catch something of the mood of excitement and defiance over Mandela's release, and it came out quite violently. And very loud. It's the only piece of mine that ever gave me a migraine in rehearsal.

ARTIST
Alan Hovhaness

TITLE
Spirit Lake

SOURCE
Symphony No 50, Mount St Helens
LABEL
Delos

I don't recognise this at all. There was a Russian feel to it, and at other times it was almost Japanese in its modality and instrumental timbres. It sounded a little 19th century, but there is no tension in the tonality, which may mean it's more recent. No, I've no idea.
It's an American composer called Alan Hovhaness.
I've never heard him before.
Some people see parallels with his music and that of the Górecki–Tavener–Pärt axis. I'm not sure how true that is.
I would have to say I much prefer Górecki, and especially Pärt. I think those two have a genuine spiritual authenticity in their different ways, whether you like the music or not. Górecki's *Third Symphony* was quite a cult piece in New Music circles until it suddenly became popular, and they all dropped it immediately. Like me, Górecki is a Roman Catholic, and I think his music has much more subjectivity and personal anguish than that of Pärt or Tavener, who are coming from a more detached Orthodox tradition. My own faith comes out very differently in my music, although a couple of new pieces I've written are a bit more reflective.

ARTIST
John Cage

TITLE
Sonata No 1

SOURCE
Sonatas And Interludes For Prepared Piano
LABEL
Tall Poppies

This is Cage, from the *Sonatas And Interludes*. I value these earlier pieces more than his later work. I can appreciate the importance of the aesthetic behind the later music, but I need a time context which he definitely has here in the shaping of these gorgeous sounds. There is a drama here that I miss in the more amorphous later works.

Was he an influence?
I think so, and especially this piece, although the only specific place you might find it in my music is probably in *Three Dawn Rituals* from 1983.

ARTIST

Steve Martland

TITLE

Re-Mix

SOURCE
Rif
LABEL
Hat Art

Steve Martland's *Re-Mix*. This was the first piece of Steve's music I ever heard.
Do you know who it is by?
If it's not Steve, it must be Maarten Altena. Steve was one of a group of young composers who achieved an amazing proficiency at a very early age – something like *Babi Yar* is an exceptionally profound piece for a 24 year old to have written, and it had a confidence, which you also hear in someone like Mark Anthony Turnage, which I could never have had at that age. It took much longer for me.
Do you see parallels with Steve in your work?
I think maybe superficial ones, in terms of an interest in tonality and use of sounds, especially brass. After *Babi Yar*, though, Steve hasn't really been interested in exploring the orchestral palette – in fact, he has rejected that route, while that is the very world I have been trying to get to grips with. He is also very interested in crossing over with baroque and jazz and rock, which has no real parallel in my own writing.

ARTIST

Fripp & Eno

TITLE

Evening Star

SOURCE
A Brief History Of Ambient Vol 1
LABEL
Virgin

That is an electric guitar, but the sonority is strange – it almost sounds as if it is being bowed. I think it might be Eno on keyboards, but I'm not sure about the guitarist.
It's Robert Fripp.
Right. I used to listen to King Crimson, actually. It's all a bit background music, isn't it?
I think you have to hear it in terms of creating moods or atmospheres.
It's quite unpretentious in that way. I suspect people do use it as a backdrop to something else most of the time, though, and I also fear that people listen to contemporary Minimalists, and even the music of Górecki, in the same way, which I find a bit more worrying.

ARTIST

Frank Zappa

TITLE

The Perfect Stranger

SOURCE
Boulez Conducts Zappa
LABEL
EMI

Frank Zappa. *The Perfect Stranger*. I would love to hear this music played in

Scotland by one of the contemporary music groups. All the works on this record are really strong pieces, and Zappa is such a talent. I was listening to them a lot when I was writing *Tryst*, which was the beginning of a very important shift for me, and they must have been an influence, with those open tonalities and that big, open, very American sound. Zappa's music in general interests me, although I don't claim to be familiar with anything like the full range of it, but everything I have heard has made an impact.

ARTIST
Mícheál Ó'Súilleábháin

TITLE
flowansionnamare

SOURCE
Gaiseadh/Flowing
LABEL
Virgin

This is probably the Irish composer from Cork, whose name I can't remember. There is a lot of interest in this kind of thing in Ireland, bringing together traditional and classical music. The problem is that it can get very overblown, but this track sounds good, as though he has really got to grips with it. The Irish composer I like best is Gerald Barry. He came from the avant garde to rediscovering tonality and then to rediscovering his traditional heritage, and there is no trace of any misty-eyed Celtic twilight sound in his music.

Scottish composers are attracted by exactly the same lure, and I have to say I am very pleased with the way that composers like Edward McGuire and William Sweeney have approached that heritage in their music. You have to create something new and vital out of it, not just genuflect to the past.

ARTIST
Gavin Bryars

TITLE
First Viennese Dance

SOURCE
Three Viennese Dancers
LABEL
ECM

So far this could either be a composed piece or an improvised jazz thing. It appeals in a big way. The palette is very stark although it is also quite colourful, and it's not at all self-indulgent. I don't know who it is, though.

You would have got him if I'd played you the original choice, which was *Jesus' Blood Never Failed Me Yet*. That seemed too easy, though.

They are very, very different. I am very interested in composers like Bryars and Howard Skempton, who came through the period of English experimentalism in the 1960s, and have never seemed to belong in the rather dull mainstream of English contemporary music. I'm glad they are now coming to the fore, and I'm very impressed by this piece.

ARTIST
Edward Vesala

TITLE
A Glimmer Of Sepal

SOURCE
Ode To The Death Of Jazz
LABEL
ECM

It sounds like a very sophisticated tango. I haven't a clue who it might be.
It's a Finnish musician called Edward Vesala.

Listening to this, I realise just how much jazz is a closed book to me. The only jazz musician I ever really got into was Stan Kenton, again when I was very young, and it related to my obsession with Wagner, because Kenton had made some arrangements of Wagner's music. I have to say this leaves me a linle bit cold. I hear an attraction to some elements drawn from the world of contemporary music in there, but I wonder if it is the right elements he is picking up on. He doesn't seem to be doing all that much with the material.

ARTIST
Richard Barrett

TITLE
Another Heavenly Day

SOURCE
Chamber Works
LABEL
Etcetera

I much prefer this, but again, I'm not sure yet whether this is composed or a free jazz piece. I can hear three instruments – clarinet, electric guitar and double bass – but there is an amazingly wide range of sound and colour, and nothing seems to be repeated. That was really good. Could it have been Benedict Mason, maybe?

It's an exact contemporary of yours, a young Welsh composer called. . .
Richard Barrett! He was on my mind. I heard him perform with Ensemble Exposé at an ECAT [Edinburgh Contemporary Arts Trust] concert we did a couple of years ago. This was not really like anything I have heard from him before, which is why I wasn't sure. It's verging on the 'New Complexity', but with a real sense of direction and structure.

Does New Complexity interest you?
Selectively. I've generally been put off by a lot of what I have heard. I have to admit I can't really be bothered with [Brian] Ferneyhough, for example. But on the other hand I am interested in the music of James Dillon, and I was very impressed by this piece.

ARTIST
Carl Orff

TITLE
Fortuna Imperatrix Mundi

SOURCE
Carmina Burana: the Piano Version
LABEL
Wergo

It's Orff, *Carmina Burana*.
It's a bizarre thing to want to transcribe for piano.
I assume the pianist wanted to create a showpiece to play, but it's too long for a recital piece. No, this is very odd, but it sounds well played. Who is the pianist?
Eric Chumachenco.
He's good.

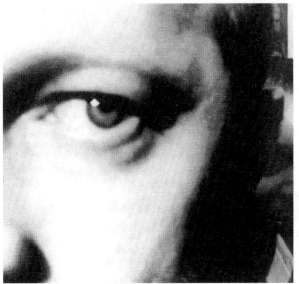

Graham Massey is a founder member of Manchester's 808 State. His early group, Biting Tongues, recorded for Factory Records during the mid-1980s. His work with Darren Partington and Andrew Barker in 808 State dates back to 1987. Despite scoring hits with singles like *Pacific State*, *In Yer Face*, and *Cubik*, their tangled collisions of studio technology and dance culture energy have given them a reputation for releasing uncommercial, uncompromising recordings. The fluidity gained through the group's history of collaborations – they've worked with A Guy Called Gerald, MC Tunes and Björk in the past – is mirrored by the trio's own ceaseless extra-curricular activities. As The Spinmasters, Partington and Barker DJ in clubs and on Manchester's Kiss 102 radio station, while Massey was involved in writing and producing Björk's *Post* LP. Their remix credits include work for Quincy Jones, REM, Jon Hassell, Primal Scream and David Bowie.

Cabaret Voltaire

Yashar 12"

Factory

Yashar

I've fallen at the first hurdle here; I've got no idea. It sounds like primitive sequencing, it's stumbling along.

It's Cabaret Voltaire when they'd started going funky, from 1983.

Yeah, right. 1983. It sounds alarmingly like New Order. It's completely un-Electro. It's super-white, Sheffield white. They're trying desperately to be funky, but there ain't an ounce of funk in it. I prefer Cabaret Voltaire when they were nasty and savage, doing *Nag Nag Nag* and things like that.

This is from that period when technology has come in and a whole lot of groups were trying to use it as a short-cut to funkiness. But there was a period of not quite managing it, and this is a classic example. It was an interesting period in the sense that people from Sheffield and Manchester were trying to assimilate New York influences, whereas people in New York and Chicago were probably trying to assimilate Joy Division, or even worse: Marshall Jefferson being completely into Led Zeppelin and Yes. He was into Prog rock in a big way. A lot of the Detroit Techno guys were into Prog rock.

This came out on Factory at the same time that Biting Tongues were signed to the label. Did you feel any connection between yourselves and other factory groups?

Not particularly. There was something very austere about it, and that was something that we never wanted to be. It was a period of raincoats and long fringes, and that's not really the way we wanted to be perceived. Factory had a strong label identity, but that was more to do with style, the design of the covers, rather than the music which was always pretty diverse. The reason we got signed to Factory was because of the soundtrack LP that we did.

Feverhouse?

Feverhouse, yeah. It was barely music.

But it was avant garde.

Yeah, and I think they liked the idea of that, and once we got our foot in the door we became ourselves more again, which was more in line with something like Can.

The things that were going on around that time that I liked were things like 23 Skidoo, and to a certain extent A Certain Ratio. Ratio live round that period; they had all the right elements, they were an influence.

And The Decoding Society, were they an influence?

It was more that James Blood Ulmer sound, which came from Ornette Coleman. Listening back to tapes of stuff we were doing at that time, we aspired to doing that kind of music, but it came out completely different. Again, it's that thing of looking at someone else's culture and trying to assimilate it and accidentally ending up in a completely new area.

Kraftwerk

François Kevorkian Remix 12″

EMI

Radioactivity

Kraftwerk. Is this a remix?

It is; by François Kevorkian.

Is it? We had conversations with him about being involved in the recording of our new album. Tommy Boy in New York put him in contact with us when we were in New York sussing studios out. He comes from the disco period, doesn't he? He was very interested in finding out what we were doing, but we convinced him that we weren't really interested in just doing the dance thing. I think he had perceived us as dance band.

Full-on and four-to-the-floor?

Yeah. And the way he's putting a four-to-the-floor with Kraftwerk on this is upsetting a little bit. With Kraftwerk it was the angles they used to throw in, on the drums particularly, which I liked, whereas this kind of treatment makes it sound like everything else.

Kevorkian was one of the first New York guys to get involved in remixing British stuff, wasn't he? He even did a mix of The Smiths' *This Charming Man* in 1983. Did he?

Yes, but that was back in the days when remixing meant something different. Now a remixer takes the song apart; then it was more a case of just beefing up the drums.

Or extending the middle eight. Remixing now is like a pool of money which record companies spend in order to promote something. You can get something that's just basically an indie rock record and they get incredibly diverse people to remix it. They don't even release an indie record without doing remixes, which is obviously great for people like me!

Graham Massey

Cachao

Descarga 77

Salsoul

La Trompete Y La Flauta

We've just done a tape for Matt Thompson's show on Kiss 102 and we actually included this track on it. I've got loads of Cachao. I've got one album he's on, *Ritmos Cubanos*, and I've been through about four copies of it, I've hammered it so much. The thing I like about it is that it's Cuban-based rather than Brazilian-based. There's a lot more dirt to the Cuban stuff: it's a lot more earthy. I certainly wouldn't call it Easy Listening. The *Ritmos Cubanos* record is by a group called Ecué, and it's just a bunch of session men, but you can tell they're not doing a tourist version of Cuban music, they're really doing it for themselves; it's them enjoying themselves.

How does this sort of stuff filter through to what you do?

Well, do you remember Inner Sense Percussion [a batucada drum troupe] from Manchester? They were often seen busking, doing sambas outside Marks & Spencer. The guy who ran Inner Sense Percussion was Colin Seddon from Biting

Tongues. He and I were in bands together when we were 14 and we learned a lot of music off each other. We've just recently been doing a little album together in Phil Kirby's studio in town, just me and Colin, doing percussion based stuff with electronics. We're trying to get the gutsy feeling of this kind of stuff.

It's an attempt also on my part to get away from being stuck to time-codes and things, so there's a lot of free electronics, and I've got a lot of old electric pianos and old organs which I've used in this project, and I've played a lot of wind instruments. Colin has played with 808 quite a lot, on things like *Bombadin*, and we've just done a remix of a track on the album, *Joyrider*, and that's very Cuban-based; he played on that.

There are all kinds of ways of twisting the beat up. Latin music has a lot of similarities with drum 'n' bass in that way, and the same kinds of feelings come out of it, of floating through things, and riding beats. It's not a military thing any more, it's about waves. In Latin music and drum 'n' bass there's the same twisting and turning, which is great for dancing.

ARTIST
T-Coy

TITLE
Carino

SOURCE
Carino 12"

LABEL
DeConstruction

It's T-Coy, isn't it? *Carino*. Again, it's extremely unfunky by today's standards. A lot of music from that era, when you hear it now, you wonder how people ever danced to it.

You must have danced to it a lot in your time.
I did, didn't I! Mike Pickering's Friday night at the Hacienda, where this was obviously a big track, because it was his record, was basically a Latin night first, before it became a House night: Simon Topping bongo-mania, and loads of dancing in spats. The Latin element in this record is so cod, cod Latin. There's a certain charm to it.

You can't imagine how there'd be 1200 people in the Hacienda going mad for it.
Yeah, because there's no madness in it.

And the BPMs are pretty low; this sounds so slow.
Definitely. Our body clocks have speeded up since those days.

Mike Pickering came out of the same scene as 808 State and a whole lot of other people. But he's gone in a very different direction from you, with all his chart-topping, arena-filling, award-winning stuff with M-People.
I guess we could have got a singer and gone the whole hog, but that wasn't what we were like. Even when we were on *Top Of The Pops* with our records, they were pretty uncompromising records: *Pacific State*, *In Yer Face*, *Cubik*, *The Only Rhyme That Bites*. It was just a fluke that because of timing and circumstances nobody knew what this new music was supposed to sound like – there were no rules – and it was accepted on Radio One and people got to hear it, and they liked it, it stuck in people's heads.

When we got *Pacific State* in the charts people kept telling us that it was the first instrumental in the charts since *Stranger On The Shore*, which is an exaggeration, but since that era there's been a lot of instrumentals. The only

Graham Massey

other time when instrumentals have been as popular was the early 60s, late 50s stuff, with Link Wray or whatever. Look how much that era of instrumentals has been used in films ever since to pin down a period of time much more than a vocal track. Instrumental music is undervalued in pop culture.

ARTIST
Eddie Henderson

TITLE
Moussaka

SOURCE
Inside Out

LABEL
Capricorn

Is it something from this year?
No, it's something from 1973!
Is it Herbie Hancock?
Yes, in all but name. The track was released under Eddie Henderson's name, but the personnel was the same as Herbie Hancock's group of the time.
The voicings and the gaps in it are very Herbie Hancock. It just shows you; I was very prepared to accept it was from this year, by Red Snapper or someone! It's well riffy, like sequencer music. I've got a tape of Herbie Hancock just doing sequencer based stuff, an early 70s thing, where it's just him on keyboards, sequencers, a Rhodes and things, and that sounds surprisingly modern as well. I love his textures. I love the *Headhunters* stuff, and the *Thrust* era. Sometimes he blands out completely, but there was a period when it had the right amount of colour for me.

I got into jazz through the jazz rock thing via Santana records when I was 14 or something. I didn't really get onto *Headhunters* until 1988 when I got lent some and I subsequently went through the complete Miles Davis thing. I love those colours, from the Rhodes and the bass clarinets; we still use a lot of those things in our music.

I really like the feeling of being able to listen to a record and not being able to absorb it completely. The information overload of that form of music is what's really attractive to me; that you have to surrender to it because you're getting fed so much information on so many different layers. Your brain grinds to a halt and it's doing what I like best about music; it's cleaning your head out.

The layered aspect has also been a big influence on what we do. I always think that if you can take it all in on one listening then you're not doing something right.
Which is why you're not in M-People.
That's right, exactly.

ARTIST
A Guy Called Gerald

TITLE
Voodoo Rage

SOURCE
Black Secret Technology

LABEL
Juice Box

[After about 15 seconds] It's Gerald. I win a fiver! I bet someone a fiver you'd play me a Gerald track! It's one of the tracks off *Black Secret Technology*. That album for me has got that thing I was talking about with Herbie Hancock, of not being able to absorb it, of being so multi-layered and drawn out and colourful.

It's funny what Gerald used to listen to. He used to go to Longsight library like myself and borrow the records. He used to come back with Chick Corea LPs, and we'd share things like Tania Maria LPs. So in the period when we first got together as a group, under the guise of dance music, we were listening to a lot of 70s stuff really.

The great thing about Gerald is that he's completely autonomous. He lives in Gerald world. No industry person could ever get near him or deal with him because it was too much hassle. You could do a great Jackson Five type cartoon of Gerald in Gerald world. Despite that dispute we had with Gerald when he filed for 100 per cent of the writing credits for *Pacific State* – which I still think is completely outrageous – I have a lot fondness for him. I should hate him.

The thing about music technology is that it has enabled people like Gerald or Aphex Twin to make music alone in their studios, whereas before they'd never have made music because they could never have functioned in a group.

Exactly. Gerald never felt comfortable about being in a group when we first did 808 State. God knows why we formed a group; I think it was largely to do with the fact that he had a drum machine and I had a keyboard that we got lumped in as a band.

This track's called *Voodoo Rage*.

What's he raging about now? There's bound to be some sort of story to do with someone's misdemeanour.

Drum 'n' bass covers a very wide territory now, with one version with obvious roots in Ambient music, and one which is much more raw, dark; real hard, booming stuff. Where do you think this sits?

You can go a lot rawer than Gerald. It's head music, really, it's got much more of a head element than a lot of Jungle. It has got authenticity about it, though, it's certainly not just pissing about with technology. He's transcended pissing about with technology and it's second nature to him now, the technology, so he is actually expressing himself.

To me it sounds like hours and hours of staying up all night in the studio, whereas a lot of Jungle records are made on limited budgets when there's a chance of a few hours' studio time and a borrowed sampler. That's a lot more like it was when we started working together. When me and Gerald were making records together if we had the chance of six hours of studio time we'd go in and do it. I've got tapes and tapes of me and Gerald that have never been put out. We used to hammer out a C90 and take it down to Jon Da Silva DJing at the Hacienda, and he used to play it off cassette to 1500 people E'd up. It's like you were saying about the T-Coy record, it was really primitive, one beat and a bassline, tweaking Acid stuff, but at that point it was completely acceptable. We used to churn it out like wallpaper.

ARTIST
Rhythm Device

TITLE
Acid Rock

SOURCE
Acid Rock 12"

LABEL
Music Man

It's *Acid Rock*. Top noises. There was a period of early Acid that was dead paranoid and strange, but there wasn't this kind of rock aggression.

Until the Belgians got hold of it.

But they had such sad beats, didn't they? They didn't have any good beats, although there were a handful of good records, this being one of them. This was a bit of a hit on the dancefloor, but again it's so slow, isn't it?

It's got a similar appeal to *Cubik*.

I don't know which came first, this or *Cubik*. This was a Frank de Wulf record, wasn't it? I remember he came over to the studio at one point while we were doing *EX-EL*.

This was the kind of record that The Spinmasters made their reputation playing, wasn't it?

The Hacienda always had a Handbag element, and even though it did get quite minimal, that thread was never broken. But there was a big split between the Hacienda and another club called the Thunderdome. The Thunderdome was in North Manchester, and it was a lot harder and a lot more aggressive, and Darren and Andy did the Friday and then the Saturday night there. It trod the darker path, away from what was essentially gay disco music.

It's the European influence, isn't it? You should play that next to the Cabaret Voltaire thing you opened up with.

How do you combine, The Spinmasters and you: how do you work it?

It's good to have more than one attitude in a band. Sometimes it has negative aspects, and sometimes positive ones, but at least you're always questioning what you're doing. You talk to them about a different aspect of music and they can talk the hind legs off a donkey about it, equally informed or whatever. They're very passionate about music. I grew up in an era when I was one person in a community of musicians and we all played together and learned from each other. They came into music in a period of Electro and HipHop and studio-based music. It's to do with an age gap, and taking different routes on the same journey.

They seem a lot more dancefloor-oriented than you. Is that a creative tension, or is it an upsetting split?

If it was that bad we wouldn't be seven years down the line. There's a lot more to being in a band than just making music, and our relationship waxes and wanes like a sort of marriage. But it means that people's perceptions of what 8o8 State is all about are invariably wrong if they only see it from either point of view. It makes us hard to pin down, but that's one of the reasons we've survived; we haven't been pinned down and buried. But that was a funny question.

No, it was a good question.

I found myself being very diplomatic. No, really; it balances itself out. It's like opposites attract.

155

Graham Massey

Mixmaster Morris was born in Lincolnshire in 1961. In the early 70s his interest in alternative culture was awakened by borrowing Timothy Leary's *The Politics Of Ecstacy* from the school library. In 1977 he formed a punk group and ran away from school to follow The Clash on tour. He worked for a year at the Lincolnshire indie label Company Records, and began giving electronic music performances as The Rhythm Method. While working as a systems analyst for the Greater London Council in 1985, he started presenting an eclectic radio show, *The Mongolian HipHop Show*, on the London pirate station Network 21. In the late 80s he started recording as The Irresistible Force, and began a DJ residency at the chillout room in London's Heaven club. In 1989 he was invited by The Shamen to DJ on their Synergy tour, staying with the group for two years. Since then Morris has been DJing worldwide, acting as a tireless proselytiser for Ambient music while zealously expanding standard definitions of the genre. In 1992 he released his first solo album, *Flying High*. Subsequent releases have included two volumes of *Dream Fish*, a collaboration with Pete Namlook, and 1994's *Global Chillage*. The Jukebox took place in Morris's flat in Camberwell, South London.

Coldcut

Journeys By DJ

JDJ

Extract from Journeys By DJ

It's the man Matt [Black]. Is this off the mix CD? You know how I'm connected with Coldcut – we used to be on the same pirate station [Network 21] in the mid-80s. As soon as I met them I found out what an amazing record collection they had. Matt and Jon [More] were the first people with perfect tempo I've ever met. Matt sat around here and I played him some tracks and he said, '114 [bpm], right?' That amazed me. I could do that now, but ten years ago I would have thought that was impossible.

In a lot of ways [Coldcut] are as responsible for the breakdown in law and order in music as anybody. They were the first British DJs to say, 'Well, let them arrest us, let's just do it.' They told me that when they went and did [their first sampling single] *Say Kids What Time Is It?*. They were sat outside in the car and thought, 'The police will be in there and we'll be arrested; they'll say, "This isn't your music; come along, Sonny."' The thing we had in common was that we were listening to all those Steinski records from New York and thinking, 'Hmm, this is very interesting.' I went to see them play at the Fridge in 85, when they played the test pressing of *Hey Kids*, and everyone went totally wild. I thought, 'That's it, that's the future of music.'

What kind of stuff were you doing on Network 21?

I used to do a show called *The Mongolian HipHop Show*. The first thing [I played] was an old Nonesuch Mongolian vocal record over a Run DMC B-side. Ten years later I'm still doing mixes like that. It's a parallel to the sampling aesthetic, because all music is data and it all has an equivalence. It's certainly of value to use the most eclectic source material.

How do you approach DJing now?

Put one record on, then you put another one on. Sometimes you put two on at the same time. [Laughs]

Yes, but I spoke to someone recently who tried it and made a mess of it.

He should go far. You see a lot of allegedly professional DJs, and the whole experience is so vacuous. Too many DJs have little choice over what they play. It's very bad for the thing of the DJ now that all the staff of all the major labels are trying to be DJs. It's their job to play all the label's releases and that's what's making the DJs so boring. I like DJs that go out and find records that you haven't heard before. There's still plenty of them; they're just being squeezed out by the industry-appointed ones. I'm also glad that DJs are going more left than I am, like Bruce Gilbert. It used to be my obsession to be leftmost goalpost and I'm happy to be relieved of that responsibility now.

Steve Reich

Chamber Works

Hungaroton

Music For Pieces Of Wood

[Immediately] It's great. *Music For Pieces Of Wood*. I love it. I can probably tell you which recording this is. I can't actually. It's not Nexus?

No. It's a Hungarian recording.

[He goes to his CD rack] I have this one as well, probably. Group 180?

No, it's by Amadinda Percussion Group.

Not even the same group; haven't got that one. You knew I'd know this one, because this was a piece that changed my life. I somehow get a feeling that Reich has lost the plot, because in these days he was playing music where all you needed to do was clap your hands and bang bits of wood together. And now you need four articulated trucks full of video screens and computers. Somehow Minimalism seems to have got lost along the way.

Obviously you're referring to *The Cave*. Did you go and see it performed?

No, I bailed out. Before that I bailed out around the time that he did this concert at the Proms [where Morris first heard this piece in 84]. He did his lecture and basically said, 'OK, I've done Minimalism, I want to do something else. If anyone wants to take it over, you're welcome to it. It's all yours.' And I must say at the time I felt that was a personal mandate. [Laughs]

At Heaven I used to play Reich's *Music For 18 Musicians*, and that takes an hour, which would give me time to set up all the rest of the kit. I would like to play [*Music For Pieces Of Wood*] one day with a group, because it must be a very exacting concentration that's needed. You can see the sweat on their foreheads when they think, 'I am coming in on three, aren't I?' It must be very satisfying to do it right. As soon as you play that sort of music you just go into a trance, suspend your normal consciousness. A part of the brain that you normally don't use seems to be in charge. It's like trance-dancing for your fingers.

Why did seeing this piece performed change your life? I heard it was because you saw that music could be made out of virtually nothing: just banging bits of wood together.

Well, I knew that, but you would usually expect electronics to do it. Lots of things around the time of 85 were showing that less is more in terms of equipment: the guys in Detroit didn't have a studio full of Fairlights, they had broken old 303s and 909s, and there was only one of each and they were doing the rounds.

You were once quoted as saying that the early Acid House rhythm patterns were similar to Reich's.

Er . . . probably; words to that effect. Some of the Acid records run three over four, or five over four; especially Larry Heard: running two different time signatures over each other, and you're just listening to where the downbeat is changing. The bassline is going on a different metre to the rest of the track. People do understand this as a Techno precursor now, even though it isn't electronic. The additive process, by which it's built up, is a parallel to the way people naturally write sequences, which is four bars, add in this four bars later, add in that. *Drumming* is the closest relative to that one.

I think you have to love [this] music to play it. That's why Nexus are so good, as most of them are in his [Reich's] band. They mix his stuff up with other stuff and put it in its historical context. They do Reich's stuff and then follow it with people like George Hamilton Green, who was a novelty xylophone player in the 30s. He was one of the top five recording artists in the world; he used to sell millions of 78s. But the whole concept of novelty xylophone has disappeared.

Instead of having Yngwie Malmsteen or John McLaughlin, they had people who played xylophones very fast.

ARTIST
The Shamen

TITLE
Move Any Mountain
(Live)

SOURCE
Heal (The Separation) CD single
LABEL
One Little Indian

[Immediately] Oh, no. I never wanted to hear that riff again in my life, actually! You're going to ask me to identify which mix this is, are you? Very live sounding piece. This is one of the hardest tracks to identify the mixes of, because there were 34 mixes or something. [The vocals come in] Good grief, is this live? Recently?

It was recorded at the Forum in December 1995.
I knew I wasn't in there, anyway. I used to come out and play this one on the live tours. By the end of the Synergy gigs there would always be seven people playing at once, total mayhem going on, which is what made those gigs very exciting. Always different every night, unpredictable. Then it just became a big pop show on the road, with no risks being taken, and I wasn't really interested in it.

When did you stop working with them?
When [the late] Will Sinnott stopped working with them. My attitude to The Shamen goes up and down depending on whether or not I've heard the music recently. I can't say I really love what they're doing, but I love what they were trying to do. It was a very important time for me, because it got me travelling around Britain. I think it blew a lot of people's minds, the Synergy show, in the remote places they went to. I did 120 gigs with The Shamen over two years and really got used to life in a mini-bus.

At the time of Synergy, The Shamen seemed like they were going to be in the vanguard of a rock/Techno crossover.
It was an important period and was exactly the same period that all the Manchester stuff was going on. When we were doing the Synergy gigs, there were always bands in the audience: Jesus Jones, EMF, Happy Mondays. We started a residency at the Town And Country Club and it was the hottest ticket in town for a few months, and then we took it all on the road. We tried to do some chillout rooms, but not many, because no one could understand why we needed another room with yet another sound system.

You seemed to share a common psychedelic vision with The Shamen, with an almost rigorous attitude to drug taking.
Rigorous? Vigorous, do you mean? I don't think you'd name a band The Shamen by accident. Colin [Angus] has always had such a single-minded psychedelic agenda; it's as single-minded as Sun Ra, and he kept plugging away at it, which I liked. I don't see where it is now. If they've diluted the music to get the message across, I don't know what the message is anymore.

Plug

Rebuilt Kev EP

Rising High

Cheesy (Pic 'N' Mix)

[Immediately starts singing along] Love that amplitude modulation. I know the track off by heart, but I'm buggered if I can remember the title.

It's *Cheesy* by Plug [Luke Vibert, aka Wagon Christ].

Cheesy listening. These records would have sold more if they'd actually been available, because Rising High went down between Plug 2 and Plug 3. To me those are the definitive 'Fungle' records, which to me is the bastard son of Jungle, sort of Jungle and mushrooms. And [Luke] is a fun guy to be with. Luke used to be a drummer – I mean, are you surprised? Jonah [Sharp] is a drummer. You can hear it in the programming.

One thing about Wagon Christ – I've never recognised a sample on one of his records, which is pretty rare because I usually recognise the samples. He must be sampling something so fucking obscure. *Throbbing Pouch* has been a huge album over the past year. One of the things that really warms me to the idea of TripHop . . . Ambient gives you an excuse for playing all sorts of weird music of one sort, TripHop does the same for a whole other file of music, where you don't have to justify it anymore. It's like World Music or Acid Jazz, everyone knows they're marketing terms, but they allow the sale of a lot of non-mainstream music, which I think is a good thing.

I've heard that your preference in drum 'n' bass is for 'non-scene' tracks.

Of course. The marginalia, that's always where all the interesting stuff is. Throughout the Techno period, 89/90/91/92, you were getting all these amazing records coming out and nobody playing them because the DJs were just looking for the hardest/fastest/loudest/stupidest at most parties. I was always looking for the strangest, weirdest, most original, most brilliant music, not just the most number of clichés you can pack into a record.

The Young Gods

The Young Gods Play Kurt Weill

Play It Again Sam

Salomon Song

Ah, *Salomon Song*, with different music. I used to sing this. I did a translation of this song. I was going to do a Brecht album and I still plan to do it. Rising High wanted me to do it. It never happened. I was a Brecht maniac, which is what started me going to Germany in the mid-80s, to buy Eisler records and get sheet music as well.

I suppose I should be able to work out who this is singing. I don't recognise it. Clue?

A group from Switzerland.

The Young Gods. I knew they did some of these songs, a couple of Kurt Weill songs. It's interesting to compare [Weill and Brecht's] fortunes: Kurt Weill did pretty good in America, Brecht did pretty terrible. He didn't do a lot of work when he was in America, he was too busy getting investigated by McCarthy. I have an LP of the trial. I have the most ridiculous collection of East German records and I got them just in time.

I have a whole box full of Ernst Busch 7"s called things like *Thank You Soviet Soldier*: great title. [Morris leaves the room and comes back with a stack of East German albums that he starts sorting through enthusiastically]

I have boxes and boxes of this stuff: Dessau children's songs, which is what you used to have to sing at East German schools. This one's got *The DDR Is Twenty Years Old, Hello Brother From Warsaw*. . . The thing with the songs is they're not written for bloody opera singers. I hate to hear Theresa Stratos or Rosa Witha-Trexler massacring these. . . [Morris starts pulling out more records] That's a fascinating East German album: 30 different versions of *The Internationale* including Robert Wyatt. . . That's the original 1928 *Threepenny Opera* with Brecht singing some of it. . .

How did you get into Brecht and Weill?

Two things. One was reading [Brecht's] poems, which are about the greatest poems ever written, really blew my head off; and another was hearing things like Henry Cow – it was obvious that they had a non-rock, non-jazz music source that I was not aware of at the time. I didn't identify it as Eisler, but when I heard Eisler's stuff I thought 'Yeah, this is where it's coming from.' Then when I got to study the Eisler songs, I found there were hundreds of songs of which there were no English translations. I won't say I had to learn to speak German, but for some of them I had to do my own translations. It was a pretty hard project to reconcile with the burgeoning Acid House movement, but I have continued it – I use Eisler themes in *Dream Fish*.

What did you reckon to The Young Gods' treatment of the material?

Well, I don't know what Brecht means to Swiss people; they are from the German end of Switzerland, aren't they? I was interested in The Young Gods because any band that was using samplers in the mid-80s was interesting to me, and they were finding their own context for sampling. I like the idea of appearing before a rock crowd and making guitar noise without having guitars on stage. But whereas dance music has taken [sampling] on, rock music really hasn't. At least [The Young Gods] aren't another Front 242 clone. I always hated them. I was on German radio and a guy said, 'Were you into electronic body music?' I said, 'No, I was always into electronic head music.'

ARTIST
This Heat

TITLE
Metal

SOURCE
Repeat

LABEL
These

This sounds like Bow Gamelan in London Docklands up to their necks in water. I have a tape of Bow Gamelan that sounds identical to this, but I guess one oil drum sounds pretty much like another. Is it some other prominent metal bashers? Actually it sounds like the place at the back of Cold Storage [a South London studio] where This Heat used to go and beat the shit out of metal. Is it the *Repeat* thing? In fact I've bashed these pieces of metal myself. [Laughs] I never saw This Heat record – I tried to. The studio was a real hotbed: Robert Wyatt was recording down there, and Chris Cutler and Tim Hodgkinson, all the Henry Cow people, and HipHop people and reggae people – all sorts of weird stuff going on, all fusing off each other.

This Heat were one of the most exciting live bands that ever existed – just totally brilliant. It doesn't really come across on their records how brilliant they were; maybe *Health And Efficiency* is the closest to it. They integrated tape and live music in a way that no one else ever did before. They were doing analogue sampling before digital sampling was available. I saw a very bizarre thing: This Heat supporting U2 at the Hammersmith Palais, and Charles Bullen riding around on a unicycle playing the guitar while people threw bottles at him.

In [the post-This Heat group] Camberwell Now, the third guy, Steve [Rickard], used to have a stack of tape recorders with loops on; 12 tape recorders or something, and he'd have them going through a bank of Morse code keys, so he'd punch them in and out. That was a really fantastic way of using pre-recorded music. I think Charles [Hayward]'s singing was a bit much for most people. I saw Charles playing at some squat thing a couple of years ago, where he spent his whole set crawling around on the floor playing with squeaky toys and pretending to be a baby.

It was through This Heat that I first heard Fela Kuti. They would never go on stage without playing [Fela] beforehand for at least an hour. If there was a DJ on, they would always get him off. Hearing Fela loud through a big PA, especially the really long pieces that go on for half an hour, was a really big influence. It was through Charles Hayward that I went to that *Music For Pieces Of Wood* concert. He was there, too. [Morris then disappears and comes back with a dozen This Heat live tapes]

ARTIST
Pete Namlook & Tetsu Inoue

SOURCE
2350 Broadway
LABEL
Fax

TITLE
Extract from The Invisible Landscape

This is nice but I don't know what it is.

It's Pete Namlook and Tetsu Inoue.

Tetsu introduced me to [Haruomi] Hosono from Yellow Magic Orchestra. Fax have just made their 200th album this month – they're not all by Peter but he's probably on half of them. [Looks at sleeve] Oh, this is *2350 Broadway*, Tetsu's address in New York, which is a cool title. Then when they made one in Peter's house they called it *62 Eulengasse*, which is Pete's address in Frankfurt. There is always a reason for things on Fax; there's a reason for the colour codings and stuff. If you've got nothing better to do, you can worry about it!

I guess I'm partly responsible for Peter being known in this country because I talked Rising High into releasing his albums, *Silence* particularly. At the time they were saying, 'Oh no, this has got such a limited market.' When it came out it was a huge seller; and it's still one of the best albums he did – it was obvious a lot more work had gone into that one.

[Namlook] used to be a jazz musician and he's going more and more towards using acoustic instruments and doing more work with classical and jazz musicians on Fax that hasn't been widely heard. I must say I indulged my Krautrock fantasies in *Dream Fish*, because I always wanted to pretend I was half of Cluster for a weekend. Who doesn't have such fantasies?

ARTIST
Can

TITLE
Mushroom

SOURCE
Tago Mago
LABEL
Spoon

[Immediately starts laughing] I actually saw Can on *Top Of The Pops* in 1976, when *I Want More* was in the Top 30. In the back of the mind I'm sure that I did. Somebody will probably write and say they weren't actually on.

I once did a set in Germany when I played no end of records that sampled Jaki Liebezeit breakbeats, because there were a lot of them. As far as the Germans are concerned, he was the original Funky Drummer. What's he up to?

He's playing in London in May.

Should be worth seeing. I quite fancy Jaki Liebezeit versus Charles Hayward, actually. Did you hear about the drum battle with Guigou Chenevier from the Recommended band Etron Fou Le Loublan? He had a drum battle at this festival in France, Rheims or somewhere. And the other guy beat him, so Guigou drew out a gun and shot him in the middle of his solo! Musician's jealousy. He didn't kill him. He was part of this band that Charles had in France, Les Batteries, with about four drummers. They did an album on a French label. It's got a Harry Partch cover version on it! [Morris laughs . . . then goes off to get his copy of the record]

Something that influenced me more than Can was *Cool In The Pool*, which Holger [Czukay] did in 79. EMI, in their wildest fantasies, thought it was going to be a hit single. When I heard that I thought, 'OK, this is how it's going to be', because there's thousands of edits; French horns, opera singers, all that stuff drops over it, complete anarchy, a *tour de force*.

I did a gig with Holger Czukay in the summer. He just showed his films and did a lecture, which was really funny. He's done a lot of home made videos, very home made, with him crawling around his garden on all fours and his wife with a camcorder. You know the *Blessed Easter* record, with the Pope singing? He's made a video of that and they've montaged him and the Pope. They kneel down and pray together and Holger's hand slips out from under his coat and pinches the Pope's wallet. If you're going to blaspheme then do it big.

You see, blasphemy and heresy have always been a natural proclivity for me. Something not a lot of people know – and you'll probably think I'm joking – but I'm a descendant of Copernicus. My family name used to be Copernicus, so heresy comes naturally to me. [Laughs]

ARTIST
Ornette Coleman

TITLE
Sleep Talk

SOURCE
Of Human Feelings
LABEL
Antilles

[Immediately] Oh, I love it. This is *Times Square*? No, the same album.

Yes. It's *Sleep Talk*.

This is one of the funkiest Ornette albums. I've just subscribed to the Harmolodics Mailing List on the Net; and I've just got [Coleman's new album] *Tone Dialing*. It's really interesting; it's got a rap track, and a Bach chorale arranged for guitars and drum machine. You'd never guess it was Ornette. I played it at some chillout room and said, 'Guess who this is?'

You once did a cut-up mix of *Times Square*: have you heard John Oswald's Grateful Dead cut-up on *Grayfolded*?

I haven't heard that one, I've got the *Plunderphonics* LP. Yeah, I was totally into Oswald, Negativland and all that sort of stuff. I thought Oswald's best piece was the Michael Jackson picture [on the cover of *Plunderphonics*]. [Laughs] Michael Jackson's head on a nude model; the sleeve of *Bad* cut with a porno shot; Michael Jackson with breasts and pudenda. It was a full page in *Mondo 2000*. They got some serious letters about that one: 'Our lawyers want to talk with you.'

ARTIST
The Master Musicians Of Jajouka

TITLE
Your Eyes Are Like A Cup Of Tea

SOURCE
Brian Jones Presents The Pipes Of Pan At Jajouka

LABEL
Point

It's very good, whatever it is. It's not The Master Musicians Of Jajouka? Is this the Brian Jones one?

Brian Jones produced the record with some very obtuse phasing.

[This is] brilliant – sounds like a loop from an Oval record. I haven't been to Morocco. I might be going to Egypt soon to do a party. Techno's spinning around that part of the world. Israel's got an active scene; a lot of the Goa scene's splitting to Israel, to Eilat. The Goa people are now setting up in Mozambique and Vietnam and Peru and that's helping to spread the germs.

Do you check out indigenous music when you're travelling around?

Well, I don't get to play in Third World countries that often; I guess it's coming more and more. But what's going to happen when serious music technology arrives in Africa? If it has happened I still haven't heard much output from it yet. Paris, I guess, is where it ought to be happening because that's where most of the African music gets recorded. Ten years ago they were starting to get really good production on King Sunny Ade's albums and things like that and it seemed something was happening there, but African music seemed to lose the plot at that point – or the Western marketing of African music lost the plot – so I don't really know what happened after that.

I thought raï was a very interesting music, and there are definitely House raï clubs in France. I'd love to do a remix of Cheb Khaled or somebody. They use the same instruments as Techno in a totally different way. To be honest, I'm more interested in Greek music because I lived in Greece for quite some time. Greek children will happily dance to 9/8: over here they have difficulty recognising 4/4. I did some tracks mixing Greek music with Techno that never came out. It's the sort of thing that Black Dog have done; they've expanded the media, done tracks in 7/8. I'd like to compile a Techno album with no 4/4 in it whatsoever.

Dean Belcher

167>

Alex Paterson's first brushes with the music industry were relatively inauspicious. A spell as a drum roadie for Killing Joke was followed by an A&R job at their label EG in the early 80s. In 1988 he formed The Orb with Jimmy Cauty, releasing *The Kiss* EP, a mash-up of samples culled from New York's Kiss FM radio station. The duo landed a DJ residency in the chillout room at Paul Oakenfold's Land Of Oz club and the eclectic, beatless collages that would greet exhausted club-goers effectively spawned a new genre, Ambient House. After the innovative sampladelia of *A Huge Ever Growing Pulsating Brain That Rules From The Centre Of The Ultraworld* in 1989, Cauty left to work with Bill Drummond in The KLF. The Orb then ostensibly became a collaborative unit based around Paterson. Youth, Paterson's former employer in Killing Joke, joined briefly for the third single *Little Fluffy Clouds* and the debut album *The Orb's Adventures Beyond The Ultraworld* (91), which also featured Kris 'Thrash' Weston, Thomas Fehlmann and two ex-members of Gong, Steve Hillage and Miquette Giraudy. Over the next few years The Orb released a series of albums and singles which managed to capture a huge rock/dance/Ambient crossover audience, but without compromising the kind of irreverant experimental spirit that characterised such side projects as the 1994 *FFWD* album, a collaboration with guitarist Robert Fripp. During the interview, Paterson was suffering from a mixture of jet-lag and party-lag which he attempted to rectify with a pre-Jukebox herbal livener.

Tonto's Expanding Head Band

Tonto Rides Again

Viceroy Vintage

Jetsex

It sounds like it's German, Kraftwerk influenced. Is it Neu!?

It's actually Tonto's Expanding Head Band from the early 70s. Have you heard them?

No. I was never into stuff like Tangerine Dream. People always think I was. The first record I ever bought was *Electric Warrior* by T Rex, then *In The Court Of The Crimson King* and then *Starless And Bible Black* [both by King Crimson]. I was only 11 or 12. I liked Alice Cooper as well. Then I got into dub, then punk, with The Pistols and The Clash, but when The Clash put out their second album [*Give 'Em Enough Rape*] I thought it was the biggest pile of shit I'd ever heard. I think one of the best albums that ever came out was *White Noise* [David Vorhaus's pre-sampling Electronica classic from 69].

Coincidentally, Malcolm Cecil, who was one half of Tonto, produced Steve Hillage's *Motivation Radio*.

Steve Hillage? Who's he? It's through working with Killing Joke and then going to work over in Conny Plank's studio in Düsseldorf that brought those connections together. And being a DJ. I DJed with Cluster recently. To be in your 50s and doing what they're doing still is something I can look up to and know that I could achieve stuff in 20 years' time.

King Tubby & The Aggrovators

Dub Gone Crazy

Blood And Fire

Dub Fi Gwan

Almost like *Jammin'* by Bob Marley, but I know it isn't. It's earlier than that for sure, but it's got the same intro. Do you want me to guess who this is then? [Alex claps his hands and rubs them together.] Who knows? It's a bit out of context after Tonto's Expanding Head Band. It's really obvious. I know this tune like the back of my hand. It's a toss-up between Scientist and King Tubby.

King Tubby, with The Aggrovators laying down the rhythms.

From 1977? It's not really got that 70s feel because it hasn't got enough brass on it. It sounded a lot like Culture without the vocals and that brass section – I think that's what's lacking on here. Because it's dub they've taken the brass out. But it's lovely bass, which could be the man himself, Robbie Shakespeare. It could be him or [Earl 'Flabba'] Holt. [It *is* Shakespeare] Holt came in 78 or 79. There's loads of vocal takes of this as well. [Looks at the CD] The track was produced by Bunny Lee. That would be those mad little drum scampering noises – he was a drummer.

You were saying that dub was an early influence. What did you particularly like about it?
The speed; the fact that the bass and drums were to the fore as opposed to the guitar and vocals. That shows very much in The Orb in that sense, even now. The rhythm; it's such a brilliant rhythm, reggae. And the space, probably. It's intuitive in that sense, it's not something you think about.

ARTIST
Fripp & Eno

SOURCE
The Essential Fripp And Eno

LABEL
EG

TITLE
Healthy Colours I–IV

This is annoying actually. I know it. *Pharrp!* Next. That's why I don't go on TV, actually – I'm too slow. When people ask me questions, I get them about three weeks later. Well you can put me out of misery, but I'll listen to it. It should be very obvious.

It's Fripp and Eno. I think it was recorded a bit before you worked at EG. It was on *The Essential Fripp & Eno* compilation.
I've got it, yeah. That's that guitar that was really annoying. It makes more sense now, because we've done a Fripp album, *FFWD*, and I knew the guitars he was doing are a lot better than those guitars there, that are just picking. I think I've listened to this once, actually. It's not as good as it should have been. *The Heavenly [Music] Corporation* from *No Pussyfooting* – this doesn't compare to that, I'm afraid to say.

I've only listened to it once or twice myself.
If you put that in the interview as well as what I said, that's fine, I'm happy with that, then you can take just as much of the brunt. When you first put it on I thought it was someone trying to copy Art Of Noise really badly and then it dawned on me that I knew it. It's a bit Talking Heads-ish. But Robert: Toppus Bananarus. It was like a dream working with him. I got to know him so well at EG anyway. I was the only one he could come and talk to about music, which I thought was quite a compliment. And he took it as far as to come and do a project with us. I'd like to do another album with him. [Adopts Fripp's Dorset burr] 'All roight, boy?' No, he's a lovely man.

How did he approach the *FFWD* project?
With a very open mind to what we were doing, whatever we were doing. He just gave us what went into his head and we turned various little loops into tracks. We actually started off with the idea of him doing it live and us putting noises and effects over things live. I've got over 70 minutes of these live outtakes we were doing in the studio in Devon – Dorset, sorry. We thought, 'This is really good', so we went into a big studio and did it, and the outcome was to me the best Orb-related album we've ever done, including Orb as well. *The Heavenly Music Corporation* is one of my favourite tracks ever for playing out in Ambient rooms. You can put so much underneath it or around it. It's a bit like [Steve Hillage's] *Rainbow Dome Music*, which was the connection between me and Steve. He heard me playing it out, I never knew who he was. I was a punk in 77. I decided then never to have any more heroes. [Referring to the track's juddering speeded-up voice] That! That's the sort of thing we used

when we used to do our Sunday afternoon experience at Trancentral when we'd been up all night. With our noses! [Alex rocks his head back activating an imaginary sampler.] I wonder if Brian Eno could DJ? That would be an interesting experience. It's interesting to do it. You're on one-to-one with people. They come and talk to you – if they don't like it they'll tell you. I've had that loads of times, especially in Ambient rooms, because people come in really rowdy from the dance rooms: 'Whheeeehhhh, Got anything we can dance to, mate!?' [Muttering] 'Fuck off. Get in the other room.'

ARTIST
Vivian Stanshall

SOURCE
John Peel radio session
LABEL

TITLE
Rawlinson End Part 37: An Entrance Of Trousers

[After a few chuckles] Well, I can say quite safely I haven't the faintest idea.
It's Vivian Stanshall from a 1978 John Peel session.
This is? Excellent. Have you ever read [Clive King's] *The Land Of Green Ginger*, the follow-on to *Aladdin's Lamp*? Have you got any kids? Well maybe you're a big kid anyway. Loads of mates of mine have got kids. I make them up little nursery songs, put music underneath. There are some very odd characters in there: Ben Nag Nag, Thud Thee Bonk or something. And magic carpets.
There's a lot of whimsical humour in The Orb, which is what made me play you some Vivian Stanshall. I thought you might have heard his stuff.
Probably round people's houses, other people's records, my brother more than anybody else. Anyway you thought you'd get me and you did. Well done! [Claps] I'm only good at reggae, you know that anyway, fuckin' hell. The only thing I listen to at home is reggae. Really. I've got stacks of it.
There are a lot of spoken word samples on *Orblivion*. Where do they come from?
I can't tell you where they come from or I'll get into trouble. You have to cover your tracks. It's where the voice doesn't sound like the original voice, or maybe cut the words up . . . just taking different words to become . . . there's all different ways round it, I suppose. It's just how much time you want to spend on the spoken word and what relevance it's going to have to the track.
How actively do you look out for speech samples for your records? There's one rant about barcodes and the apocalypse on *S.A.L.T.*.
That's taken directly from a film which we virtually had permission to use: [Mike Leigh's] *Naked*. That's David Thewlis. He's talking to a security guard about life and everything. I played that out on Saturday night. People were stunned by it because a lot of people hadn't heard it.

ARTIST
Bill Laswell

SOURCE
Oscillations
LABEL
Sub Rosa

TITLE
Wird

[Before the track starts] Are you going to put Killing Joke demos on? You've got something worse instead? I always used to come bottom of the class anyway, so there's no surprises here for me. [Track starts] Do you want a first impression? It's a bit like one of those North American Indian albums of flutes that come in gradually. I've got a few albums of North American Indian music. But this is synthetic as well. It's got all the Ambient noises and bird noises. But that's my first impression. I do like some of that stuff, natural Indian stuff. [At this point the breakbeats kick in. Alex laughs] Hmm, I was just thinking it was going to be someone really electronic doing an Ambient beginning. Yeah. Mad, brilliant.

The bass is played live, and it's the bass player's record, which might be a slight clue.

Slight clue? Don't like the bass part but I like the drums. [Laughs and rocks back in his chair] I'm not even going to say it, I'll keep my mouth well shut. The names that go through my head now are unbelievable.

It's Bill Laswell, a drum 'n' bass album that came out last year on Sub Rosa.

Sub Rosa? I've been trying to get all of Bill Laswell's records out of Island. It's weird because I'm being asked loads of things about music and to be honest, in the last year and a half all I've been doing has been thinking Orb. This is really nice, the loops are brilliant. I can see where they're coming from but the bass is in a completely different hole. It doesn't sit, it's not right in there for me. But that's unfortunate. That's just my feeling, and honesty is the best policy.

I see you've got a track on Laswell's new *Axiom* dub compilation.

We took it as a complete joke at the time. We called it *Cocksville USA*. He asked us if we had any spare tracks and that was a particular track that we'd done with Kris Needs, Simon Phillips, Nick Burton, Andy Hughes, myself and anyone else who happened to be in the studio. Anyway, we got loads of drink in and decided to do a vocal track. And Kris Needs was so pissed he was doing vocals. He was doing The Funky Cock [makes chicken noises] so that why it's called *Cocksville*. It was all done so tongue-in-cheek as usual. They're the best things that we can do as The Orb, there's a bit of humour in there. Alcohol used in the right way can be very invigorating.

Some of the tracks on *Orblivion* sound like they're influenced by drum 'n' bass.

A lot of these things were recorded a long time ago. We finished the album last May. It comes out in March, which will be almost a year since finishing it, when it should have been out two months after. So that in itself is a hint at what we were doing at the beginning of the year, and if we were doing the album now we would be hell for leather in there. But I think also that we would be taking it to another extreme. The intro was really beautiful. I can see Bill Laswell's influence in there.

When I was out in America a lot of people came up to me: 'Hey man, I hear David Bowie's doing Jungle, man.' He'd been working with A Guy Called Gerald, but no one's heard of A Guy Called Gerald, so everyone assumes that David Bowie's been in the studio doing Jungle tracks. Again, because Bill Laswell's associated with so many things, people assume he's doing them all, but other people are doing things and giving them for people to put out on his label. You've got to realise that it's not all him, but he's giving everyone the opportunity, that's what I think is so brilliant. . . I'm doing an 11 till 8.30 in the morning DJ spot on Saturday. If I'd brought all those records along, I'd only play things that were two months old. See how you got on with my record collection, you bugger! I've just woke up as well, that's the thing.

ARTIST
John Oswald

TITLE
Fault Forces

SOURCE
Grayfolded: Transitive Axis
LABEL
Swell/Artifact

This is a bit of a wild card.
Like the others weren't wild cards? Can't you just give me a normal card? [After a minute] Did you take any mushrooms before you came, or what? It's curious, that's all. I don't think it would go down very well with my reggae mates. It conjures up lots of things, but it's not something my mum would listen to. Probably someone really famous.

It is, but it's been reworked by someone else.
I can't stand that guitar. What is it?

It's John Oswald's reworking of The Grateful Dead's *Dark Star*. Obviously he got permission from the group to do this, but he got into trouble with all the uncleared samples on his Plunderphonics records. I interviewed Steve Reich recently and he apparently told his record company not to sue you for sampling his *Electric Counterpoint* on *Little Fluffy Clouds*.
[Laughs] That was done in our bedroom. We never even thought it would actually get anywhere. Those days we were selling 1000 records. With Rickie Lee Jones, at the end of the day it was a question of 5000 dollars just for using the vocal, because of the fact that we took it completely out of context. And she was just talking in an interview similar to this, but I haven't got a sexy voice like hers.

You used that Minnie Riperton sample from *Loving You* on *A Huge Ever Growing Pulsating Brain*, as well.
We're waiting for consequences. What Jimmy [Cauty] was doing with The Timelords and KLF, that kind of rubbed off on The Orb in that respect: Use it, abuse it and wait for the consequence. You'll get more news out of doing that than if you just do your own stuff.
I heard *Loving You* out in Manchester a couple of months ago, the dance version. Cor, dear oh dear. Have you ever heard of The Rotary Connection? That was the band she was originally in, Minnie Riperton.
They were like a fusion of jazz, disco, Heavy Metal. Really weird stuff.

So you don't like this track?
Never got into Grateful Dead. They're well respected in San Francisco but it doesn't float my boat. I never really was a West Coast hippy for a start. I had a manager once who wanted The Orb to become the new Grateful Dead, in terms of visuals and stuff, which was a bit weird. He kept showing us all these videos they'd done. I hate guitars like this. I'd probably get shot if I played that out.
We played three gigs in their gig hall in San Francisco; probably won't do any more gigs after this! We did a gig there in 1993 on my birthday, one of the best Orb gigs I ever remember. They let us use all their visuals. The visuals were

Alex Paterson

outstanding. It was like being in a time tunnel on stage. That's all I remember. It might be something else but it *was* my birthday; I was allowed to be like that!

Did you meet the group?
We might have done, but they were a bit 'san Francisco'. They talk really slow and you get bored after about three seconds. Go on, bung another one on, or is that enough torment?

ARTIST
Coldcut

TITLE
Atomic Moog 2000

SOURCE
Atomic Moog 2000
LABEL
Ninja Tune

[After a minute] Turn it up. This really reminds me of something from the 80s, but if it's really brand new as well, it's crap.

It's the new Coldcut single.
It's the vocal that's putting me off it. It's like the Reagan sample, the four minute warning. They're all right. That *Banana Walk* sample they did was brilliant, the reggae one that got to number one. But I was a bit disappointed with them when they did some *[Little] Fluffy Clouds* remixes for Big Life. It wasn't their fault. I was never entirely happy with those mixes and yet Big Life put them out. He [Matt Black] was doing stuff with Youth, but me and Youth just changed directions together.

Do you listen to their KISS FM sessions?
Been on and done the sessions with them. It was really good fun. As people they're really nice people, but. . . It's the first time I've heard this. I'd probably have to hear it really, really, really loud in a club in a different context. That's why I like DJing: listening to stuff at home then play it out at fucking maxi-level and it's like a different track. And that's how I work in the studio half the time as well.
[The interview is abruptly brought to a close earlier than planned. Paterson plays the next track on the Coldcut record at floor-shaking volume and turns the tape recorder back on] Is it on? OK. The second track [The Herbaliser's mix of *Post Nuclear Afterlife Lounge*] is a lot better. But it's only my humble opinion. You played something inadvertently, that I liked then. . .

173

Alex Paterson

John Peel was born in Heswell, Liverpool. He began his long career as a radio DJ after moving to America in the early 60s, working initially in Dallas, Texas for WRR. Over the next five years he worked for a variety of US radio stations, including KLMA in Oklahoma City and KMEN in Los Angeles. He returned to the UK in 1967 at the height of the Summer Of Love and joined Radio London to present *The Perfumed Garden*. The same year he joined the BBC's newly formed Radio One network where he presented the infamous *Top Gear* show. He has remained with the station ever since. His former producer John Walters has called Peel. 'The single most important figure in popular music over the last 25 years'. It's a fair if somewhat melodramatic assessment: more so than any other 'mainstream' DJ, Peel has consistently championed music's marginalised factions, from mid-60s psychedelia, through reggae, punk, rap, Jungle and so on, often in the face of concerted disapproval from his Radio One bosses. The Jukebox test took place at Peel's home in Stowmarket, Suffolk, where he lives with his wife and four children (who are all named in honour of Liverpool FC). The session lasted for around three hours before being brought to a premature halt when his children returned home from school and took over the house. The Jukebox selections which we didn't have time to play him included New Age Steppers, Huun-Huur-Tu, Little Richard, The Merseys and Fear Factory.

Bo Diddley

Signifying Blues: Charly Blues Masterworks Volume 43

Down Home Special

Charly R&B

I was very surprised when you did this to Steve Albini and you started with Bo Diddley's *Mumblin' Guitar* which he didn't recognise. For me it's one of the great records of all time.

So he's a particular favourite of yours?

Yeah. I never saw him live – which was always a mistake – until I went to see him at the University Of East Anglia about five or six years ago, and it was frankly terrible – it was going through the motions really. It was nice to see him, nice to be able to say that you've been in the same room as Bo Diddley, but he wasn't very good at all, alas. Some people said to me, about *Mumblin' Guitar*, 'Oh well, he's not actually that good a player, he keeps missing things or speeding up and slowing down.' But I don't care – it still sounds wonderful to me. . . And Jerome Green on maracas. His stuff is always very welcome. I always think any time you insert a Bo Diddley track into a programme it always seems to lift it – more so even than Chuck Berry. I must admit that although I love the Chuck Berry records, I can't separate out his rather unpleasant personal life from them. I keep thinking about some of his bizarre hobbies – alleged hobbies – when I'm listening to his records.

176

The West Coast Pop-Art Experimental Band

Transparent Day

Edsel

1906

John Peel

Sounds like The Shadows Of Knight.

I think they were around in the States when you were still there in 67 in the same sort of era.

Sounds a bit like Mark E Smith with that vaguely dissatisfied muttering in the background. Nice guitar sound. Is it Syndicate Of Sound? You're going to have to tell me.

It's The West Coast Pop-Art Experimental Band.

Is it? By God! I must admit I don't remember this track at all and I've actually got an LP by them. It's dead good – I shall dig it out and play it this weekend. I really like it. That guitar's really nice – it does remind me almost of Lonnie Mack at the end.

I actually saw them do a gig once in a school gymnasium somewhere in Fontana, California. But it's one of those things that I can't remember a thing about, beyond the fact that I saw them do it.

[At that time] I used to hang out – much to their resentment, I don't doubt – with The Seeds. I used to turn up at a lot of Seeds gigs and I've even got photographs of me with The Seeds and I'm sure they thought, 'Not that twat again', like you do, but they were always quite civil. It was around that time that they had the Sunset Strip riots, immortalised in that Buffalo Springfield song *For What It's Worth*. There was a place called Pandora's Box which was going to be closed down and the kids took to the streets – there was serious rioting.

[Pandora's Box] was notable for me because this band that I used to know in Riverside called The Misunderstood played there – one of the gigs that I do remember. Pandora's Box was incredibly hip, and they got up onstage and said, 'We're from Riverside,' which is a bit like saying, 'We're from Stowmarket,' and people actually tittered. But they were one of the best live bands I've seen in my life – I mean they were just devastating. Bearing in mind this was about 66, the bass player played slide bass and they had a steel guitar player called Glen Campbell and he was just unbelievable. I mean the technology again is a mystery to me, but I know that with the steel guitar sometimes you can use pedals and sometimes you can use it without pedals. And on nights when Glen was hitching up the pedals, the rest of the band would say, 'Wow, It's going to be a big night tonight, Glen's using the pedals!' So they came on, played this set and when they'd finished all the hipsters just stood back open-mouthed, which I'd never seen happen before. They just left their instruments feeding back on stage and all the groovers from Sunset Strip were just awestruck, as I was myself – they were wonderful.

ARTIST
Tractor

TITLE
Hope In Flavour

SOURCE
Tractor

LABEL
Dandelion

John Peel

The drumming sounds like The Way We Live, the rest of it doesn't. [Long pause] It does sound like The Way We Live. Once again, it sounds familiar but I can't put a name to it.

It's Tractor, from an album that was released on your own Dandelion label in the 70s.

Oh well, that's the same thing. The Way We Live is Tractor. It's the same people. They did their first LP as The Way We Live and then I said, 'That's such a crap name', so they changed it to Tractor, which wasn't much better. In fact I'm not sure that I didn't suggest Tractor. I'm fairly impressed that I recognised the drum sound, because that's a muso's thing that I wouldn't normally do at all.

What do you think of the stuff you released on Dandelion now? Do you think it stands up?

Oh no, but that's not the point. I'm not a great believer in things standing up. A lot of things I like now I'll probably find incredibly embarrassing – if I survive – in 20 years' time. And I kind of hope I do. I used to play records by James Taylor, for God's sake! Some of the things we used to play on the radio when we started in the early 70s were just utter crap. I've never claimed that I'm right. It's just stuff that takes my fancy at the time.

I think Kevin Coyne in the various bands he was in was worth the vinyl. Mike Hart was – *Almost Liverpool Eight* was one of the saddest songs I've ever heard in my life. If I play it on the radio, which I do about once a year, I always have to segue it into something else because I'm too choked to speak after it.

Medicine Head, I think, were worth doing. Stackwaddy, of course – miraculous!
I saw them at the Free Trade Hall in Manchester. They emptied the building.
They had no bass – they had a bass player – but they turned everything up
as treble as it would go. The singer was a deserter from the British Army or
something and used to wear a ludicrous wig and a beret. We got Jac Holzman
over from Elektra Records, because we needed the money to make more
records, and he was actually quite a nice bloke – I really liked the Elektra stuff
at the time, so we saw him as a kind of ally, we thought he would be a
pushover for all of this.

We arranged a gig at some college in North London and they were monstrous.
I loved them. I mean to me they represented the punk spirit before it
happened. And they turned up at this thing. One of them had had to drive the
van because they'd been stopped somewhere on the way down to London
because the driver was pissed – and this was like about four o'clock in the
afternoon, and he'd been dragged off to the police station. So they arrived in
a terrible temper because they were pissed as well but they'd had to drive.
And they got more and more pissed and the lead singer, John Knail, advanced
unsteadily to the edge of the stage, with lots of students looking up at him
thinking, 'Oh that's really beautiful', and he just got his dick out and pissed
into the audience. And obviously Jac Holzman almost haemorrhaged and we
thought, 'There go all those millions of dollars we reckoned on getting!'

ARTIST

SOURCE

Captain Beefheart

untitled bootleg tape

TITLE

The Key To The Highway

This isn't Son House at the 100 Club, is it?

I think it'll be apparent who it is when he gets going.

Is this Beefheart?! I really love Beefheart. I haven't heard him do this. Where
was this recorded?

**I've no idea, except it's pretty informal, just guitar and voice. It was before
72. There were no details on the tape. I don't know who the guitarist is.**

It's a pity that these things aren't better documented at the time. God, I've never
heard him do anything like this. If there has ever been such a thing as a genius
in the history of popular music, this is him. And it grieves me more than
anything that he's so ill.

I hired a car and drove him to gigs the first time [The Magic Band] came over
[1968], and actually found a tape of 20 minutes of the classic – in terms of
reputation – Beefheart gig which was on the first tour, when they played at
Frank Freeman's Dancing School in Kidderminster. When I told them, they said,
'Wow, it's a really groovy name.' I said, 'No, it's not a groovy name. It's a
dancing school run by a bloke called Frank Freeman.' Everybody played there
at one time or another. When you turned up, they were there with pots of tea
and cucumber sandwiches and stuff. They were really sweet people.

And again, half of the audience left during the first number, when [Beefheart]
used to play this extraordinary horn that he'd got from Ornette Coleman. If
you'd asked him to play *The White Cliffs Of Dover*, he'd not have been able

to do it, but he used to just blow in it as hard as he could and make this terrible racket.

I always find it difficult to analyse, describe, review, those things I care about most. And with Beefheart, to me he's so plainly in a class of his own and a distillation of all the wisdoms, as it were. I never forget sitting with him in a hotel in Edgware Road, just talking to him. He had a sketch pad and he'd come in and tell you about all these new songs he'd written, and he'd say it's going to be on the next LP, and of course it never was. He used to produce songs like most people piss, with that sort of frequency. And he'd sit there with a note pad as he was talking to you and [mimes drawing] he'd hold it up and you'd say, 'Oh, that's the waitress over there.' It wouldn't look anything like her, but you just knew that it was.

One of the first things he said to me was – almost by way of introduction – 'You have to excuse me, but I'm seven people away from myself at the moment, but I'm getting closer all the time.' At first you'd think It was hippy bullshit but then you'd think, 'I know what he means.' A lot of his things were almost like little jokes. Look at something like 'Big-Eyed Beans From Venus', which obviously at some stage he must have read as 'Bug-Eyed Beings From Venus' – he used to love all those little word-play things.

He was sort of intimidating but not deliberately so. It kind of diminishes him to present him as some wacko kind of bloke. He's just quite a funny man. He hated the record industry and assumed that he was being ripped off, which he was most of the time. And just brighter than most of us, frankly.

ARTIST
DJ Crystl

SOURCE
Drum And Bass Selection Volume One
LABEL
Breakdown

TITLE
Warpdrive

Oh, this is good. It's funny, I was trying to identify a record this morning. I played it on the radio and for the life of me I can't remember what it is. It's just a great Jungle record. It's got a kind of white voice on it; it keeps going, 'Reel and come again, selector'. Not in a Jamaican voice at all, and it's a mighty record.

I don't know what this is. You just lose track, so this could be something I've played on the radio, it could be something I've never heard in my life before. I like it.

This is DJ Crystl from the first *Drum And Bass* compilation.

I was listening to that this morning. I was skipping through it trying to identify the one with the 'Reel and come again, selector'. I'm not quite sure what it means: 'Play the same thing again', I guess, but it's just so attractive. It's a poetic way of saying, 'Play it again, Sam', and you think, 'That's terrific'. I just love that kind of use of language.

I was a latecomer to Jungle. I've never been to a gig, because I don't go to gigs much, but the music is wonderful. Those compilations are extremely handy to catch up, because it's evolved so much in a short time. And unfortunately now, as you're obviously aware, it's everywhere. It's in TV advertising and I'm sure that someone's getting ready *Neil Diamond: The Jungle Remixes*. It's out there somewhere. I don't doubt it.

ARTIST
Roxanne Shante

SOURCE
**Street Jams: HipHop From The Top
Part Three**

TITLE
Runaway

LABEL
Skanless/Rhino

I know this. Is this The Cookie Crew? Early Salt 'N' Pepa? Hold on, don't tell me. This is something I should know, because I've played it on the radio, I'm sure I have. The kids should know because I think it's on one of our holiday tapes! Is it one of the numerous Roxannes? Roxanne Shante?

I don't play rap now, very little of it, because I'm just so fed up with it because it's become such a parody of itself. I still get some of the records and listen to them in the hope of finding something that I want to play on the radio, but there's nothing there that does anything other than make me feel uncomfortable. It's just so kind of sexist and aggressive and pointless really. In the early days it was a lot lighter, some of it was funny and humorous, but also addressed real issues.

I wish I could remember the name of the record that I remember hearing about three years ago; a record that was going on – and rightly so – about the need for equality among the races and black freedom. But in the next verse or the one after, there was a lot of stuff about beating the shit out of your 'ho if she hasn't got a meal waiting for you when you get home. And you think, 'Can't you see there's a slight inconsistency here?'

You've been instrumental in introducing black music to a predominantly white rock-oriented audience, but I remember hearing that when you played reggae in the 70s you used to get threatening letters.

Oh yes, we used to get sent turds by the British Movement – we had some frightening letters. We had death threats and stuff but we don't get those now.

ARTIST
Miles Davis

SOURCE
Get Up With It
LABEL
Columbia

TITLE
Rated X

This is a complete mystery to me, I have to say.

The keyboard player [Miles] usually plays something else.

That's not much of a clue! Usually plays something else – Chris Waddle? Robbie Fowler? It's not another of Thurston Moore's bizarre. . . No. The beginning did sound vaguely Jungle-y, the percussion.

It's Miles Davis from _Get Up With It_, 1974.

Which I've probably got. . . I still do occasionally buy jazz records but more because I kind of feel they're good for me. And I listen to them and I know that people's passions are amazingly inflamed by what they hear and usually, I must admit, it leaves me pretty cold.

It's not the sort of thing you've played much.

I have a bit. I remember outraging John Walters [Peel's former Radio One producer] because both of us, oddly enough, had a kind of trad jazz period. I've got an enormous number of records by George Lewis – this isn't the trombone player but the clarinet player – and Bunk Johnson and obviously the British end of that: Ken Colyer, Chris Barber, Acker Bilk. I outraged John Walters by saying that the jazz that I like is in old black and white movies, when the bad guys used to run out of somewhere, leap into a DeSotto and put on the radio and there would be kind of hot, fast music spilling out. I don't want anything that requires too much intellectual effort, just something that's truculent and noisy. . .

Years ago, you used to play some of the more rigorous, experimental free jazz like Brotherhood Of Breath on your show.

Chris McGregor. Yeah, well that was kind of Walters's influence, because I was the victim of these same kind of uncertainties as the people who listen to the programme. I always see myself as being the listener's man on the inside really. And Walters used to persuade me that The Brotherhood Of Breath – and one or two other things besides – were the kind of stuff that we ought to be doing. It was actually OK, but you couldn't get into it like you could get into a Gene Vincent track.

Nucleus would be another one. Remember Nucleus? Ian Carr was an incredibly serious man and he used to come in and lecture Walters and myself on the inadequacies of almost every other musician apart from himself. And we were so frightened of him that when he said, 'How about a session for Nucleus?', we didn't like to say no.

ARTIST
The Fall

SOURCE
Totale's Turns

LABEL
Rough Trade

TITLE
Rowche Rumble

[Immediately] Ah, Gods, they bestride the world. I can't explain, I just adore them. If they made a bad record I wouldn't know. All they have to do is turn up and that's enough. The only person I would place on the same level as Beefheart would be Mark E Smith. It's almost impossible to imagine anybody else – especially in popular music, but in almost any area of activity – to be able to sustain your interest for that length of time without either veering into self-parody or becoming kind of safe and predictable.

To me they're like the great miracle of my musical life – no, it's true. I've said this a thousand times before but it remains true, they're always the same and always different and I just love that about them and look forward to their records more than any other. When I get a new Fall LP, I actually try to ration myself and say, 'Well, I'll listen to one track and one track tomorrow,' and I might be able to sustain that for a couple of days but then I go mad and listen to the whole record.

Considering they were in with punk from the start and ended up carrying on afterwards, do you see that as a. . .

Denial of the punk spirit?

No, more like an affirmation of it in that they carried on gradually mutating, whereas most of the other punks ran out of ideas or ended up reforming when someone waved money under their noses.

That's right. I don't blame them for doing that but I don't want to listen to it. I'm extremely grateful for the fact that they have continued, whatever the reasons. I don't bother to analyse, I'm extremely grateful that they have. I hope that they continue – I kind of measure my life in terms of Fall LPs. I like to feel that, with luck, I should have another 10 or 15 Fall LPs in my life. That's pretty wonderful and I'm quite happy with that.

ARTIST
Alemayehu Eshete And Shebelle's Band

SOURCE
Ethiopian Groove – The Golden 70s
LABEL
Blue Silver

TITLE
Tashanmanaletch

Is this Ethiopian? I only know it's Ethiopian because I got a bunch of Ethiopian 7" singles about 15 years ago and you can just recognise the style.
That's pretty much the time this was made. It was 77 or 78.
Andy [Kershaw] would know straight away but I can't remember the bloke's name. It's a great noise, though, because it sounds like it could be anything. Until he starts singing, it could be any place, any time really. It's lovely.
Did you play any of this stuff when it first came out?
Yes, I did, oddly enough. But so much of what you play on the radio is really dictated by what is made available to you. Because obviously I don't get every record that's issued around the world – I wish I did. So first of all there's the frustrating knowledge that there's hundreds, thousands of wonderful records that you're never going to hear.
A fellow phoned me up – it all sounded very questionable – but he offered me 150 Kenyan 7" singles earlier in the year and I just bought them on spec. I've only heard about a third of them, but there's at least 10 or 12 that are just magnificent, absolutely wonderful by any applicable standard. But it makes you realise that there must be so many more that you're never going to hear. That's really frustrating.

ARTIST
Ground Zero

SOURCE
Ground Zero
LABEL
God Mountain

TITLE
Euthanasia Drive

Well, the fellow doing the shrieking has got to be Japanese. Is that John Zorn squeaking away in the background? With Mick Harris on drums?
It's Yamatsuka Eye, Otomo Yoshihide on turntables, John Zorn and Uemura Masahiro on drums. They're collectively Ground Zero.
I was just bluffing on the drums. It's amazing, the stuff that goes on.
Does it hold any appeal for you?
Well, the confrontational aspects of it. I always like the idea of Gerogerigegege, the [Japanese] singer who masturbates onstage. Not that, I hasten to add, I'm much excited by seeing people masturbating onstage, but the confrontational aspect of that seems to be well-nigh irresistible. It's rather like you would like to see the faces of the people who are spectators at this extraordinary event.
I wouldn't want to sit down and listen to 70 minutes of it [Ground Zero] on the trot, but I like the idea of it. There's so much extremism in other areas of life,

most of it rather unpleasant, that I think that if you can sublimate it into something 'artistic', that's probably quite healthy. So I would approve of that on almost every level, really, as long as I'm not asked to listen to too much of it.

ARTIST
Head Of David

SOURCE
Nothing Short Of Total War: A Blast First Compilation

TITLE
Bugged

LABEL
Blast First

Sounds like Steve Albini on guitar. Does it sound like Steve Albini to you, William? [Confers with son who has just come in, who agrees] I'd swear that was Steve Albini on guitar, but not Shellac. It sounds like Big Black, I have to say.

It's actually Head Of David.

Is it?! Good Lord! They'll be jolly flattered, I would have thought, with being compared to Big Black. I saw them once on the same night I saw Nana Mouskouri in Brighton – it was one of the most bizarre evenings. I reviewed them both for *The Observer*. Head Of David were playing at the Zap Club and Nana Mouskouri was playing in concert. I was sitting at the Nana Mouskouri gig and there was so much cheap perfume in the air that I got a blinding headache. There was a row of middle-aged women in front of me and I tried to persuade them – as a middle-aged bloke – to come to the Head Of David gig with me, because I really thought their views on it would be interesting, but they obviously thought I was going to sell them into slavery or do something unspeakable, so they wouldn't have anything to do with it, unfortunately.

Do you think that Head Of David and Big Black have influenced the lo-fi bands or has that come from a different area?

It's impossible to say, unless you go look under people's beds and find which records they have in their record collection. That's why a band like The Smiths were so astonishing, because from listening to them you couldn't tell who they themselves had been listening to. I kind of like the lo-fi ethic but then you feel again – more so with Jungle – that it becomes a vogue, briefly, and then it's only a matter of time before you have the Liza Minnelli lo-fi double LP. It's the same thing that happened with punk, that happens with everything – when I get to know about it is about the time that it ceases to have any kind of meaning. When these things develop out of necessity or some kind of artistic motive, by the time they become the stuff of which Radio One radio programmes are made, that's not really the beginning of them so much as the end of them – or the beginning of the end, anyway.

ARTIST
Vaughan Williams

SOURCE
Orchestral Works

LABEL
Virgin Classics

TITLE
Fantasia On A Theme By Thomas Tallis

This sounds like the sort of thing that would be top of the charts on Classic FM, unless it's going to turn into something like *Songs From The Shows* or turns out to be an Andrew Lloyd Webber *Requiem* – which it might even be, I don't know.

I was very surprised to see that when Radio Three were having a debate – for reasons I never fully understood – as to who were the eight great composers of all time, and there was no mention at all of Chopin, which I thought was very strange. I wonder why Chopin had been left out of it? He wasn't even mentioned among the also-rans. Mainly because he did small-scale works.

When you were on Desert Island Discs you picked a few classical music items.

I like what Sir Thomas Beecham used to call 'Lollipops', in other words the classical equivalent of *All Time Golden Hits* – *Zadok The Priest* from Handel's *Coronation Service*. And then Rachmaninov's *Second Piano Concerto*. This sounds perfectly pleasant. I don't know who it is.

It's *Fantasia On A Theme by Thomas Tallis* by Vaughan Williams.

It's very English – it's got a nice kind of melancholic quality to it. The last thing I do before I go to bed at night is to walk to the top of a small hill – which by Suffolk standards is fairly mountainous – to take the dogs for a walk. When I get up to the top, I'm obviously on my own, so sometimes I'll sit on the road and talk to the dogs. It would be quite a nice piece of music to be playing at a time like that.

When did you first start listening to classical music?

At school. One of my best mates at my prep school was a fellow called Morrison. He was actually quite a good pianist. I've no idea what his first name was, because you never called anyone by their first names at all. But that's why I mention Chopin, because Morrison used to be particularly keen on Chopin. And so it's really standing next to Morrison as he played the piano when I first heard classical stuff. You have to be in the right mood for this and children coming home from school is not the right. . . [Shouts at excited dog] Stop it, Bridget!. . .

Coneyl Jay

185>

Born in London in 1964, saxophonist Courtney Pine first came to prominence as the face of 'New British Jazz' in the mid-80s. His 1986 debut album *Journey To The Urge Within* was the first 'serious' jazz album to make the British Top 40, notching up enough sales to qualify for a silver disc. This success followed teenage years spent playing funk and reggae sessions, as well as with his own hard bop group Dwarf Steps, and John Stevens's Freebop. In 1984 Pine formed Abibi Jazz Arts to promote interest in jazz among young British black musicians. This eventually spawned The Jazz Warriors big band in 1985, whose members included Steve Williamson and Cleveland Watkiss. Since then Pine has played with Art Blakey's Jazz Messengers, Elvin Jones and in Charlie Watts's Big Band. He has also worked closely with Soul II Soul, The Pet Shop Boys and as part of the jazz/HipHop project Jazzmatazz (instigated by Gang Starr's Guru). With time, Pine's own music has become increasingly broad in scope. 1990 saw the release of an instrumental reggae album *Closer To Home*, while 1992's *To The Eyes Of Creation* combined jazz with mysticism, ska, African and Asian influences. After touring with Jazzmatazz in 1995, Pine has incorporated techniques borrowed from HipHop into his music more and more: the process can be heard on the 1996 album *Modern Day Jazz Stories*. The Jukebox took place at Pine's North London home.

Alice Coltrane

Journey In Satchidananda

Impulse!

Something About John Coltrane

It's [John] Coltrane's *Greensleeves* bassline, but it's later. The bells remind me of Pharoah Sanders. It's like *Greensleeves* exactly, the arrangement, without Coltrane so far. The piano player's record?

Yes.

Not Stanley Cowell or something like that? It's quite spiritual, and the bells make it sound like something from the 70s. It's definitely not McCoy Tyner. Who is it?

Alice Coltrane.

[Bursts out laughing] Oh, man! I know this record so well. I like the album, especially the first [title] track. Wow.

We thought it would be a bit obvious to play you an actual John Coltrane track.
Until Pharoah came in, that would have been a mystery. It's interesting hearing the record without Coltrane. It's all around him. It's as if he's there but not there. Same sound. He'd be playing it exactly this way if he were there. I like the way she uses the tamboura in the background. She got into the more feminine elements of the music, adding those kind of sounds, the lighter sounds, the harp. Obviously John was trying to get more involved in that kind of thing, but he was still into the machismo, playing the saxophone at light speed. But with her you're getting a whole different thing; there's something slightly lighter, more feminine, to the whole thing.

The tamboura is used in an unusual context here, but works really well.
Very well. His music was so open you could almost use anything in there. There was one review of a gig where he had three saxophone players and he was playing bagpipes. But then he had two drummers and the reviewer said you couldn't hear the bagpipes, so he didn't know if he sounded good or not! That's the nature of his music, it was so wide that almost anything could be brought in and dealt with.

He didn't bring anything electric in, though, he stayed very much away. There was an instrument called the varitone, it's a saxophone that plays an octave above and below. Sonny Stitt used to play a lot of it. He [Coltrane] had one, but he didn't record with it. He was very wary of using electronic stuff in his music. Everything was more acoustic and natural.

Jacob's Optical Stairway

Jacob's Optical Stairway

R&S

Fragments Of A Lost Language

The intro could have been done in the 70s. There's so many similarities in the tone; but when the drums come in it gives it away. I don't know who it is. It's not 4 Hero? It's that [Fender] Rhodes sound. They use the exact same sound on [their remix of] my tune *I've Known Rivers*.

It is 4 Hero, but recording under the name Jacob's Optical Stairway.
The problem when you're involved in anything happening now, it's hard for it to have identity, because we know it as Jungle. So for me to say that's A Guy Called Gerald or that's Goldie – I've got Gerald's album and I've got Goldie's albums, so I might know bits of that. But the rest of it – especially when they're going under pseudonyms and using the same bits of equipment to make sounds – it's very hard. It's only that Rhodes sound that's very similar.

I like the idea of it being faceless as well, not having a focal point, a front person. 4 Hero have just sent me a mix of something which is totally out, totally different to any of this. So they're able to flex on either side. [The bassline comes in] There's a Fender Precision bass sound.

What do you think of musicians like Steve Williamson – or even yourself – working with the likes of Metalheadz or 4 Hero? Do you think it's a vital contribution to the music, or more an appropriation of jazz by the Junglists as a kind of cool surface texture?
It's hard, because the next generation to come along [will be] the ones who study Charlie Parker and programming at the same time. My generation are [points hand] that way in studying a jazz tradition and only 40 per cent in terms of programming. So I have to call somebody who knows what they're doing in terms of Jungle, and can do it – but I want to be in there, I want to be able to play, because I can hear how I would play on this. I would play differently on this than I would do on a jazz track or any other pop session. This has got so much variety and space for me to do whatever I want to.

It must be a challenge to play in a completely new musical genre.
I actually play *Rivers* live now in the set, and I remember two years ago saying to the drummer in the reggae band, 'I want you to play Jungle.' He said, 'What do I do? I can't play it.' But now it's a situation: 'Here it is, you have to do it, there's no choice, we're going to play it now.' And I can find my current drummer actually finding a style around it.

I have a friend who is a session drummer and he's trying to play Jungle manually. He uses three snare drums and two hi-hats and says he's almost there, but not quite.
The way I'm trying to do it is work with the record, with the DJs and the programming and after a while I'm going to take out the programming and just have the band playing. So we're learning to play it from the record like jazz musicians do; sit down and learn how to play the solo. If you can learn how to do Jungle on stage, then take away the record and just leave the band playing on the same level, you''ll hopefully get it that way. You look at the drummer and think, 'Oh, poor geezer.'

My nephews came over at Christmas and they're 15 and played some stuff which was ridiculous, 180 bpm – it was so out. And that's why I like Jungle, because it breaks the rules. I've been trained in this classical sense and this is nothing to do with that. It's like people in the States hearing stuff coming through the walls and then car noise outside and somebody shouting in the street. It's all that condensed onto vinyl or CD. If you were an alien and came down and looked at it, that's what it would sound like, and that's what these guys have unconsciously done. That's what music is supposed to do, reflect the sound of the period, and these are the first guys to actually do it for now.

ARTIST
Spontaneous Music Ensemble

SOURCE
A New Distance

LABEL
ACTA

TITLE
Tape Delight

First of all you're searching for the shape of the instrument – what is he playing? OK, we've got the hi-hat. Is this soprano saxophone? Yes it is, I think. Then you start looking for the style of playing, and the great thing about this approach to music is that you take yourself away from any style, even though to play free is a style. You're defacing yourself.

Which perhaps makes it more difficult to figure out who's playing.

Yeah, but that's what Jungle and free jazz have in common: elements of taking an instrument and doing things that the instrument's not supposed to do. The thing about free jazz is that it's now a style, a style from a period of time. As to when it's recorded, I couldn't tell you.

It was recorded in 94.

It's not Evan [Parker]? Lol [Coxhill]?

Spontaneous Music Ensemble with John Stevens.

I was going to say John because he has a strong way of playing and leading, and the whole thing started with drums. It did sound British. John had a way of saying, 'Get as close as dammit'; you know, get up there and play. And he had a really nice attitude, because he was into playing music for anybody. Anybody could actually take part in it. He wanted to get music onto that level.

You played with Stevens.

A long time ago. Various things. He used to do a residency at The Plough in Stockwell and he invited me down a couple of nights to play. Those were interesting. Those were nice for me, because it got me to know what it is to get onstage and play. When I played what I practised, he used to say, 'Forget all that, just play what you feel, stop practising on stage.' And he was the first to give me an opportunity to play in that kind of setting, to take a chance.

He was someone from the 60s and 70s who seemed active in bridging the gap between that era and the resurgence of British jazz in the 80s.

Oh, definitely, definitely, because he was doing these workshops during the day. He had this concept called 'Search and Reflect' – my wife saw an advert in the press and I went along and it was John Stevens. This was perfect for me because I was in Reggae World doing sessions and all that, but here was someone who played jazz who wasn't going to say, 'You haven't played *Cherokee* yet, so you can't play with me.' [He said] 'Just come and play, man.' That was John. He was into capturing a moment, just dealing with it and that was it. Songs would have no beginning and ending. There were times when we'd play and he'd have some structured things and after that he'd just go. It was really interesting for me to see that, because here was this English jazz legend; as far as I could see he'd seen it, done it, conquered it.

He had the band leader attribute to bring out the best in his players. He could see that I was going a certain way, so he'd sit down and talk about seeing John Coltrane playing in Germany and Elvin [Jones] came out hammering the drums into the floor. And then he would say, 'Let's play *Bye Bye Blackbird* tonight.'

So he had that way of tapping into what you had and forwarding it. But then after that he would just go off and just pull you in with him. So he had that positive band leader thing in terms of bringing players in and finding out exactly where they are and then pushing it and directing it in the way that you want them to be. He wanted me to play freer and not come on stage practising what I'd been playing during the day. He had that ability to nurture musicians. Rather than being safe all the time, it's a challenge, and when you come out of that challenge, you're a different person.

The last thing I heard about John was that he was in the studio doing a HipHop version of a song, so I'm sure he'd be involved with Jungle in some way or another.

ARTIST
Bootsy's Rubber Band

TITLE
Bootsy Get Live

SOURCE
This Boot Is Made For Fonk-n
LABEL
Warner Brothers

George Duke? Oh, hang on, it's [mimes slap-bass playing] Bootsy Collins. It sounded like Zappa in the first couple of bars but it's out there, funky like George Duke's albums. But as soon as the vocals came in and the bassline. . .

I spoke to someone who saw Bootsy live, and apparently when he spoke to the audience it was in the same tremulous voice that he sings in.

[Laughs] This is how he is for real? I met his tailor in Germany, a young lady, she just came up to me, maybe because I've got an afro, I don't know why. She gave me a card and said I must come and pay her a visit.

[Funkadelic's] *One Nation Under A Groove*, that whole sound in terms of being bass heavy, did a lot to affect the Jungle scene. You've got the same elements. In the Parliament thing, there were lots of things happening at the same time – it was so layered. Dennis Chambers said they were crazy, there were so many things happening at the same time.

What kind of music were you listening to when you were growing up?

I didn't listen to [Bootsy] that much. I was more into guys who were playing from a [jazz] tradition and then coming forward. If this was Stanley Clarke I'd say yeah, because Stanley Clarke came from Pharoah Sanders's band; but Bootsy, I would listen to it, but not in the same context. I wouldn't take it any less seriously but I don't have any Bootsy records in my collection, though I do have the Parliament stuff. [He looks at the sleeve] Bernie Worrell, of course. Maceo [Parker] and Fred Wesley. Every HipHop record sounds like them on horns. And they weren't playing to click tracks in these days. It's so tight from start to finish, no loops or anything.

Joe Harriott

Movement

Columbia

Beams

Unmistakable British 60s studio sound. [Laughs] You think of that guy who does *Record Breakers*, Roy Castle, those Dracula films, Pinewood Studios. [After a minute of the track] Whee, what a mood change. He was bad, y'know, my man on the sax there. It's gone now, don't say it. He started off playing this way, then he pulls you into another way.

The Jazz Warriors did a tribute to him, Joe Harriott. There's been lots of talk about who actually started freeform jazz. He claims that he started it, then Ornette [Coleman] heard him and took it back to America. I've read reviews — because I've been studying this guy quite a bit — and he said he started doing it in 58; which would make his stories kind of true. But because he wasn't able to get out of the country that much and play this kind of stuff, it was hard for anyone to actually date it — and this stuff is deleted.

Was Harriott an influence?

Well, he played alto and I don't really play alto, but the fact that he tapped so much into Charlie Parker, I was able to relate to how it was diffused into Joe Harrlott. I was influenced more by his political thing, in terms of how he was able to get by as a Jamaican/European: how did he get by? How did he get through the system? How did he get his records released? Obviously we have similarities, but I've got to learn from his experience. So he's an influence that way as opposed to trying to play like him. But he was a great player and a composer. You have to check out the *Indo-Jazz Fusion* [album], because that is incredible.

Gang Starr

Step Into The Arena

Cooltempo

Step Into The Arena

This relates to what you were saying earlier.

Yeah, because of Maceo, that sound is so right. Guru and these guys, they've got to pick it up. And even that [high-pitched sample] is a saxophone. It's like an evolution: you get that kind of sound, which is a bit of a saxophone solo, but looped and put in a different pitch so it doesn't sound like a saxophone, it may even be reversed. And now you've got to the point where you listen to a Jungle record and it's all like that; that's all you're hearing, as opposed to it being a little hook-line in a song. So we're getting more and more hardcore, more extreme in terms of the sound, the way we're altering the sound. With Jungle, it's gone so far that it's very difficult to decipher a record.

I went on the road with [Guru] in the Jazzmatazz thing and it was really funny because I had been on the road with Clint Eastwood and General Saint in the early 80s, and there were things that were going on in Jazzmatazz which were exactly the same as with Eastwood and Saint: frontman, doing this, back to the rock 'n' roll, and also two DJs and a rapper. It was the same thing but a couple of years later and with a different accent.

HipHop producers have been sampling jazz for years, but the way that you play it, the HipHop elements are used as a background texture, with the jazz element out front.

That's come from listening to all this kind of stuff and seeing it being done this way then thinking there must be another way. It was a conscious decision to try it from the other side, see how it works. But you have to have people with the right skills from the HipHop field, because jazz people don't know about HipHop. It might not have worked, the HipHop people might have been submerged in the jazz, but it's a matter of getting the right people who are strong enough on their instrument to play as hard as we do. I'm lucky enough to have met two individuals who are from the UK who believe in HipHop – that's [DJs] Sparky and Pogo. Just as much as I've studied in jazz, they've studied HipHop.

HipHop comes from the whole sound system thing and over here we have a big culture in sound systems, with [Jah] Shaka and all that, and they're able to have a more open opinion of what they're supposed to do than people from the States. When I say sound systems, they know what I'm talking about, but when I did the Jazzmatazz tour, I tried to get on that level with the DJ and it didn't work, he doesn't come from that kind of culture. There were two DJs [on the Jazzmatazz tour], Jazzy Nice and a guy called DJ Ski, and they're HipHop DJs. Nice is a bit more into the jazz thing but it's a different thing, they have a different way of looking at the music in terms of all the things that we want to do at one time. And the HipHop thing is just a part of it, but to them this is it, these are the rules. A lot of the Jamaicans were in New York and that's where they got it from, the whole toasting thing was Jamaican. So those parallels are very obvious. My parents are Jamaican and I was brought up here. I want to bring those parallels to light because there's something in it for me. It's important to me to know this knowledge of self. It makes me feel better about myself that my culture has influenced the rest of the world.

ARTIST
Tommy McCook & The Supersonics

SOURCE
Down On Bond Street

LABEL
Trojan

TITLE
Music Is My Occupation

[Instantly] Now you're talking, the house has come alive, this is what the house is used to. [Laughs] Whee! Probably Ernest Ranglin on guitar. Is it Don Drummond playing trombone? And it's either Roland Alfonso or Tommy McCook [on sax].

Tommy McCook.

I had the opportunity to be in a cab with Alfonso in Jamaica. We did a ska festival and I was in the band. And in between checking into the hotel, we were singing in the taxi and it was the first time we had the opportunity to talk. He liked my playing and he came straight to the point. Tommy McCook wasn't really into ska. He's a jazz man from Cuba and he went away, and it wasn't until he came back and saw [ska] being successful that he came and joined it. But they were jazz musicians. They were playing jazz in hotels for tourists, then went into the studio with Coxsone or whatever and did this kind of stuff, which were instrumental tracks for vocalists. Then what happened was the singers became famous and the musicians who created the music became session guns for hire. [Referring to the saxophone on the track we are listening to] He's playing *The Nearness Of You*. I played it today. [Laughs]

What was it like when you were doing reggae sessions?
I was going to school in the morning, I was a school monitor, and I was out at Brighton Top Rank, or Bradford, until two o'clock and they were saying, 'Play this and that.' You'd get Tappa Zukie shouting out, 'this song is da-da-da.' The songs didn't have titles, they were known as rhythm tracks, and they've all got some kind of unusual name for each rhythm, and then they sing whatever they want over the top of it. You'd have to know the horn lines by the name of the rhythm track, and you'd just have to learn quick. It was fun, you know. I was learning so much. A lot of those singers don't know what a key is, so it doesn't matter what tune the bass player plays as long as there's a drum pattern. Forget about the chords and the bridges, just have a drum pattern.

Island have just signed Buju [Banton] and they're doing a lot with him, trying to conform him to pop in terms of having some kind of Western-oriented thing. But in Jamaica you can just have a drum track and some guy talking about the weather and that's good enough for the territory.

It reminds me of Tricky.

ARTIST
Tricky

TITLE
Moody Broody Buddhist Camp

SOURCE
Pumpkin EP

LABEL
Fourth & Broadway

It is.
But I don't know the song. I know everything Tricky's done.

It's *Moody Broody Buddhist Camp* from the *Pumpkin* EP.
Yeah, OK. [Laughs] This guy is out. I think it was the combination of the chemistry, the components that he put together, and the way he's put it together that really got it for me. And also he does that drawl thing. Then the real drum kit and that acoustic guitar. This is almost like Björk territory, PJ Harvey territory, the lines between. PJ Harvey's on Island now, isn't she? [Pine used to be signed to Island.] You see all this stuff's happening when I'm not on the label. When I was on there who did I have to deal with? Mica Paris! [Laughs] As soon as I leave they get Tricky.

My album is totally influenced by his stuff. He's somebody I'd definitely like to see in the studio, in terms of how the stuff comes out. I don't know how he gets the results, a genuine programmer, if he's a DJ or whatever. But he gets good results. [*Maxinquaye*] really had a good flavour to it, very unique. He came from this group called The Wild Bunch, a Bristol band. I don't know if he actually came from it, but he's affiliated to Massive Attack [who did].

Like you say, his roots are in mid-80s British street soul: Massive Attack, Soul II Soul. Listening to that stuff at the time, it would have been hard to predict that it would develop into something like this.

It's just the way the whole thing has diffracted, lots of separate elements. I could draw a line between Julian Cope, PJ Harvey, maybe Björk, maybe you could connect that with Goldie, back down to Tricky to Massive Attack, Tracey Thorn. You can draw all these connections. I've worked with Soul II Soul – everything is connected in one way or another – but to predict what's going to come out next is very hard. Musicians: the way we work, you've got four things on in the house at the same time. You'll be walking up the stairs and hear something on the TV, and something being played upstairs, and suddenly they'll hit together and you'll think, 'Yeah, you can mix that acoustic guitar sound with that kind of drum sound and that kind of voice.' Who's to know what's to come next year or in five years' time?

The musicians who come through, the ones who I check for, are the ones who are successful not in terms of chart success but the ones who can reflect the climate best – that actually know. They've gone to ten different clubs, they can see what people are about to listen to, what tones are going on, what the latest equipment is, what people are going to talk about and they capture that sound and then put it out. And the record company has to be good enough to put it out straight away, and then it's seen as being ahead of its time, like this. This is a mixture of so much stuff. It's like putting it all in a glass and seeing what comes out – as long as the glass can hold it, and he [Tricky] can. That's why he's all right; he's bad, too, is Tricky.

Chris Cuffaro

Henry Rollins was born in Washington, DC in 1961, and came to fame after moving to California and joining the notorious and influential hardcore group Black Flag in the early 80s. Rollins left the group in 1985 and has since kept busy with The Rollins Band, spoken word gigs, a book company (2.13.61), the record labels Infinite Zero (run with Rick Rubin) and 2.13.CD, a fluctuating amount of freelance writing and acting (*The Chase, Johnny Mnemonic*), not to mention intense sessions of bodybuilding and tattooing. Rollins has become a controversial icon of deep integrity and passion, combining testosterone-fuelled aggression with an array of esoteric interests. Through his labels he has issued or reissued music he feels strongly about: from Gang Of Four to free jazz pianist Matthew Shipp; Devo, Tom Verlaine and Alan Vega to Mississippi Fred McDowell and Iceberg Slim. The Jukebox took place afterhours in 2.13.CD's New York office. Rollins admits to a far-from-encyclopedic knowledge of music, and the interview was less a test of his listening habits than a reaction gauge.

Funkadelic

Cosmic Slop

[Almost immediately Henry begins singing along with Michael Hampton's opening guitar solo] This is one of the greatest riffs for everybody coming up and jamming out for a while. Westbound has found a 1971 recording of Funkadelic, live in Michigan, with Eddie Hazel [*Live At Meadowbrook*] and they just put it on sale. They were going through, cleaning something out, unmarked, and just put it on and went, 'New release.' Someone should reissue [Hazel's] record *Games, Dames And Guitar Thangs*. I found a shrink-wrapped copy of that record in Providence, I think, for five dollars at a vinyl store. Years ago, we had the van pull up to the record store. We're all going through it. I said, 'God, I wish I had that record,' just because Andrew [Weiss, ex-Rollins Band bassist] had that on tape and we're all digging it. I just went over to the H section, I'm like [mimes astonishment], pull it up, shrink-wrapped, corner cut. I said, 'Hey, fellas!' Everyone went right up to the cashier, 'Do you have another one of those?' She went, 'No', and Andrew gave me the dirtiest look, like, 'You should have my fucked-up copy and I should have that new one.'

When I started Infinite Zero with Rick [Rubin], that was my first request to get out. We went to Warners and said, that record and all the Bootsy records, let's reissue all the Bootsy stuff. They said, 'We won't touch anything to do with George Clinton. It is a nightmare. We will not deal with George. You are out of your mind. We will not talk to you even another second. This conversation's over.'

The Grassy Knoll

Unbelievable Truth

I like that kind of processed, disintegrated, devolved thing, where they know it sounds like it's falling apart. Yeah, I always have time for stuff like this. It sounds like sampling Hendrix right there, it sounds like the beginning of *Purple Haze*. Yeah, this is cool, man. I like this. I'll pick this up.

I went to the grassy knoll [at the site of the JFK assassination] in February this year. I played in Dallas, a speaking date, and the lobby of our hotel looked right out at the book depository. Literally two blocks away. So I said, 'Let's go after the gig's over.' Me and my road manager went over there and sat on the grassy knoll and just kind of tripped out. It all looks the same as any time you've seen it on every documentary or movie or whatever, and it's heavy to kind of sit there. We were there at one in the morning, and there are people all over the place with their charts, pointing, doing their own little research. About eight people, different groups of people actively walking up and down and standing in the street and lining up positions and stuff. It was amazing that someone is still wondering.

Einstürzende Neubauten
Drawings Of Patient OT
Mute
Vanadium-I-Ching

[Immediately] Einstürzende Neubauten. *Patient OT*. I love this record. I have played this record so many times. Had it on vinyl, nearly wore it out. This is *Vanadium-I-Ching*. Not a second on this record that isn't get-down-on-your-fucking-knees-and-worship. There's so many great vocal effects on this record. Michael Mann used this for the *Heat* soundtrack, I think. [It was actually *Armenia* from the same album.]

I was in Holland last year doing a poetry festival and Blixa [Bargeld] was on the bill. I asked him if I could reissue *Kollaps* with the first single and the complete double 7″. *Kollaps* to me is one of the greatest records ever made. That record makes this record sound like Phil Spector produced it, it's so raw. It's like a power drill, a belt sander, a guitar, pipes and a spring for the bass, and on the back of the record it just shows them and their instruments on the ground at the Nuremberg Rally grounds. It's so intense. Blixa's doing vocals through a walkie-talkie, just screaming. Magic, that record, just total magic.

[Is that [*Patient OT*] the version with the EP at the end of it, with *Wasserturm*? Yeah. That's a dream Blixa had: hitting spaghetti and making music out of it. He got up, whipped out his Walkman, said the dream into it, and went back to sleep, and redid it. For the music they actually put contact mics on a water tower and played it. That's why it's called *Wasserturm*: Water Tower. I have about 50 or 60 live shows of Neubauten at home, stuff that they gave me. I've got great outtakes from *Halber Mensch*, alternate versions of *Sehnsucht* and *Letztes Biest (Am Himmel)*, them doing it really loud, really soft, just trying out all this stuff. Really cool.

Galina Ustvolskaya
Piano Sonatas 1–6
hat ART
Piano Sonata No 1

I don't know who this is but I like it. [Looks at CD] I love the hat label. They put out that [Albert] Ayler stuff, the German gig and the French gig on one record. Now, if you go to a record store, where do you find this? Is it jazz? Where do they put stuff like this?

Sun Ra
St Louis Blues
Improvising Artists Inc
St Louis Blues

[During improvised section] I like it when he's kicking this stuff. When it gets back into the yada-yada stuff, I don't know.

Do you know who it is?

I'm not very good at picking stuff out like that. I have an idea but. . . [I play another track: *Ohosnisixaeht*.] It sounds like Monk drunk at a party trying to play

Art Tatum. [Looks at the album] I heard this album once, found it cheap in England, played it once, haven't played it again. This [*Ohosnisixaeht*] I like. When he was doing the riffing thing, it just sounded cute or something. Yeah, this is cool.

ARTIST
Slayer
TITLE
Angel Of Death

SOURCE
Decade Of Aggression: Live
LABEL
Def American

[Immediately] Sounds to me like Slayer doing *Angel Of Death*. It is their best song. I like the studio version better. In fact, that is the only Slayer record you need, *Reign In Blood*. It's pure. I have a great story about that record. I was riding around with Rick Rubin one night and he said, 'You dig Slayer?' I went, 'I'd like to listen to it, because I've only heard bits and pieces.' I don't know much about this kind of Metal. He went, 'You ever heard my record, *Reign In Blood*, the one I did with them?' 'No.' 'Really?' 'No, I'm sorry.' We're driving. He just pulls into Tower. We walk in, buy a copy, he puts it in, we're in his Bronco, we go into Beverly Hills with *Reign In Blood* on at, like, 12. Him, me, and George Drakoulis power-driving through Beverly Hills, with the windows open and this thing melting the speakers. It's awesome. He says, 'This is all the rock 'n' roll you'll ever need. Here it is, 34 minutes, it kills what anyone can do in an hour.' And he's right. I have this album too, the live one. Those are my two favourites, actually.

I fell in love with this riff when I heard *Channel Zero* by Public Enemy, where they make the whole song out of this. That's one of the greatest riffs I've ever heard. I can't believe they leave it so quickly. Listen to how in-the-pocket this is. That's how the shit should be played. This is music that will make you kill your woman or something. Every time I go on tour and Slayer's been on tour, I always make sure I ask the house security what it was like, and they always say the same thing: 'Most violent shit we've had since Lynyrd Skynyrd, or The Allman Brothers.' If I was, like, 19 when *Reign In Blood* came out, that would probably be my favourite record, and I would have really hurt somebody at one of those gigs.

It's testosterone music.

I have a lot of that in me. When I was 18, 19, I had very little grip on it. I used to go to gigs in hopes of some university asshole picking a fight with me so I could pound a 40-hour week of minimum-wage frustration out on his face. I hoped for some Georgetown University jock to come to the gig to beat up on some punk rockers so I could just surprise him, that such a skinny bod could wreak such terror on a dude.

ARTIST
Miles Davis
TITLE
Theme From Jack Johnson

SOURCE
Agharta
LABEL
Sony

Sounds like they took part of Miles's band, the *Agharta/Pangaea* thing.

That's what it is: *Agharta*.

Immediately it sounded like the Miles thing, but I didn't hear anybody doing 'bab-bab-bab, bab-bab-bab, bab-bab-bab'. [Miles doesn't play trumpet until many minutes into the piece.] My favourite is *Dark Magus*. It's just brutal. It's him trying to burn out everybody, and the guitarist is really intense. I just love that record.

Apparently, Sony are working at putting out a box set of all Miles's 70s stuff.
Really? Sony was interested in my band, so I went up and met with [Sony executive] Donnie Ienner in his office and he's bragging about how he knew Miles and all this. So I said, 'You're Columbia, right?' He says, 'Yeah.' I go, 'Do you know how many Miles records you can only get Japanese imports of?' He went, 'Really?' I said, 'You don't know? I mean, this is your shit, right?' He says, 'Make me a list.' I said, 'You guys can't even put out *Live/Evil* in America? Come on!' He goes, '*Live/Evil*?' 'You discontinued *Big Fun*, that's a great record, *Live/Evil*, *Get Up With It*, *Dark Magus*, *Live At The Fillmore*, *Miles in Concert*. Those are all pretty cool records, why don't you put them out?' He goes, 'Well, I'll get right on it. OK.' It's so frustrating when you know the stuff is sitting down in the basement. C'mon, let it rip! It's amazing what America does to its greats, just erases them, or somehow enshrines them to a point where they're sterile.

ARTIST
William Parker's In Order To Survive

SOURCE
Compassion Seizes Bed-Stuy
LABEL
Homestead

TITLE
Malcolm's Smile

I like this a lot. I'm trying to figure out the sax player. Sounds like David Ware, or Charles [Gayle]. [Looks at the CD] I saw this one about an hour before you came in. I was looking at the Charlie Parker section at Tower and it was up on the shelf. Who's the sax player?
Rob Brown.
I saw [Parker] play at the Knitting Factory with Charles Gayle. God, he was terrifying that night. He was amazing. Both of them were great, but William really hit me hard. It really affected me. And Charles was playing so hard, I thought his head was gonna come off. I've never seen Charles play with more within-an-inch-of-his-lifeness than that show. I've seen him about four times or something, but that night he was just on some. When he pulls down on the [strap], I'm like, 'Oh no, he's gonna hurt himself. . .' I love it when he plays piano. It's great to hear him; it's amazing to watch him. He's all over it, making all these noises. It's really passionate, him and the piano together. It was amazing being in the studio when he did two piano pieces for [*Everything*, Rollins's 1996 spoken word album which featured Gayle and drummer Rashied Ali]. The one we used was one long jam at the end of the record. That was the high point of the night for me.
This is a great record. That's intense. See, I don't know anything about music, really; I don't know how the instruments work. But it seems to me, a lot of times when some [saxophonists] come to the end of their breath, and they fill back up again, they forgot where they just were. That's why I like John Coltrane's stuff. He must have had immense concentration skills, because he just never ever seemed to lose the thread. There's some stuff on *Crescent* where you hear

him trying to get somewhere, and it's like a dry gulch, you're like, 'John, turn around and go back, it's going nowhere', and he's like, 'Nope, no, it's there', and you hear him go, 'Nope, it wasn't there,' and he has to get out of it.

ARTIST
Cibo Matto

SOURCE
Viva! La Woman

LABEL
Warner Bros

TITLE
White Pepper Ice Cream

Is this the invasion of East Village Japanese punk rock girls? Cibo Matto? They practise down the hall at Context [a New York rehearsal studio used by Rollins], and every once in a while I stick my ear in the hallway. It sounds pretty cool. [After a few minutes] We heard *White Pepper Ice Cream*? Really cool lyrics.

ARTIST
Joe Henderson

SOURCE
Inner Urge

LABEL
Blue Note

TITLE
Inner Urge

It sounds like something Lee Morgan would've been all over. This sounds like it would be on *Sidewinder* or something. I'm not trying to guess who it is, I'm just saying that's kind of what it sounds like. Wayne Shorter? What year is it?
It's 1964.
Sounds nice. It sounds like Booker Ervin or someone. [I show him the CD case] Joe Henderson. Wow. The drums sounded very Coltrane-y [the drummer is Elvin Jones]. I knew immediately it wasn't Art Blakey; I'm waiting for that dat-dat-dat-dat on the snare rim. I don't have many Joe Henderson records, never listened to him a lot. This is great. I saw him play, couple of years ago in LA. He did a week. He had this young Canadian bass player with him who took these horrid solos in every single tune. And he would do really gross stuff like be playing and all of a sudden start going for something rock: 'I'm going to rock out, I'm a little upstart.' And [drummer] Al Foster was so pissed he put his elbow down on the rack tom, just playing like this [mimes bored, one-handed playing with head in hand]. And Joe came back onstage and [Foster] looked at Joe and went [mimes 'I am not happy' face]. This is beautiful. I'll check this out.

ARTIST
The Abyssinian Baptist Gospel Choir

SOURCE
Shakin' The Rafters

LABEL
Columbia/Legacy

TITLE
Said I Wasn't Gonna Tell Nobody

I wish I knew more about gospel music. All I have of gospel stuff is Rosetta Tharpe. Boy could she play guitar. Who's this? God, I love this kind of stuff! Can you pass me my bookbag? I want to write down some of this stuff so I don't forget it. I'm always looking for new stuff to listen to. I have an unending thirst for it. It's all news to me. There are a million good records under the sun. I'm just this big, open field waiting for the rain. I write it down and I go home and I check it all out.

ARTIST
The Buzzcocks

TITLE
Orgasm Addict

SOURCE
Time's Up

LABEL
Document

[Immediately] Yeah, I love this record. I like this version better, with Howard Devoto singing. When I first saw these guys in 1979 when they toured America, I had a cast on my arm. I stood in front of Pete Shelley when they played this and went [makes pseudo-masturbatory motion] thinking he'd be like, 'Yeah!', and he was like, 'Umm . . .' So I tied his shoelaces together and he gave me a look like, 'You untie those fucking shoes right now.' So I retied them for him. We played a festival with them in Belgium in 90 and the next morning him and his partner were at breakfast and I went up to him and went, 'Pete, my name is Henry Rollins, I was on the bill yesterday.' He's just giving me total stoneface. No hand, no smile. So I said, 'In 1979, it was a long time ago, but I never had a chance to apologise to you, remember when you played in DC and there's that obnoxious guy in the front row tied your shoelaces together?' And he looked at me and he remembered. 'That was me. I was just a dick, I'm really, really sorry, and if you remember, I tied them back.' He was like [mimes deadpan expression]. 'OK, I'll see you later.' I don't think he said a single word. He just nodded slightly, and that was it. I skulked out of that place. [Laughs] My meeting with Pete Shelley!

I bought this on vinyl in 1979 or 1980. I wonder if it's a bootleg? This is the kind of stuff I want to put out. I met Howard Devoto once. He was cool to me.

201

Adam Lawrence

One of the most wilfully independent figures in British music in the last 20 years, The Fall's Mark E Smith remains an outsider and maverick. He formed the group in Manchester in 1977 while he was working at Salford Docks as a customs clerk. First heard making a contribution to the 10″ compilation album *Short Circuit: Live At The Electric Circus*, the group has gone on to release an album a year ever since, as well as taking part in numerous side projects, such as providing music for the dancer Michael Clark. Fall cover versions testify to Smith's broad music tastes, ranging from 60s garage punk to 70s disco hits to a version of Frank Zappa's *I'm Not Satisfied*. Smith is both The Fall's one constant presence and its charismatic focus, delivering his pitiless lyrical chronicles with a withering sneer. At the time of the Jukebox, the group consisted of two drummers, plus bass player Steve Hanley, who first joined the group 16 years ago, and Smith's American wife, guitarist Brix, with whom he briefly reunited after several years of estrangement to record the 1996 album *The Light User Syndrome*. The jukebox took place in the central Manchester offices of The Fall's Cog Sinister label.

Captain Beefheart & His Magic Band

Mirror Man

Castle Communications

Mirror Man

[Almost immediately] Captain Beefheart . . . and on guitar.

It's some kind of outtake, I think.

It's *Mirror Man*. The Captain used to lock [The Magic Band] in a room until they got it right. The drums follow the guitar parts instead of the bass part like usual rock. I like Captain Beefheart. I got *Strictly Personal* because it was a budget LP. When you're poor and taking acid, *Strictly Personal* is the one. There was no alternative in those days, and it was 99 pence. I like all his stuff before he went to Virgin; all the 65, 66 stuff is really outrageous, and a lot more jazzy. *Trout Mask Replica* is a brilliant LP.

What appeals to you about it?

It's like nothing on earth. It's freeform but with discipline. There's a method behind it. The Magic Band worked hard; you could tell that. And The Mothers Of Invention did too; I used to think they were better than Frank Zappa actually.

Johnny Burnette Trio

Rockabilly Boogie

Bear Family Records

Drinking Wine Spo-De-O-Dee

I've got this by The Pirates. . . What is it?

It's Johnny Burnette.

Johnny Burnette. Fucking great. He wrote *Jingle Bell Rock*, which we were going to do on *The Word* at Christmas, funnily enough. Johnny Burnette's great. This is recorded on one mic; you can tell. Guys like Johnny Burnette, they thought that Buddy Holly and Elvis Presley were sell-outs. That's the mentality they're coming from.

Singing songs about the pleasures of drinking wine all day was outlaw activity in 1956.

For sure. Speed freaks. I love rockabilly. The ones I've got are just one-offs, compilations. I got one for my birthday, all the classic trucker songs. It's got *White Line Fever* on it and Caffeine, *Nicotine And Benzedrine*. I always buy that stuff when I'm touring America. We always go to the truck stops because you can get the best food there, and the tapes they sell are amazing.

This sort of sound is still alive there?

You won't get any Suede cassettes in those joints, no.

Nick Cave & The Bad Seeds

Helpless

Various Artists: The Bridge

Caroline

Nick Cave or Bono or someone?

It's Nick Cave. It's a Neil Young song.

It's a Neil Young cover version? What's it called? *Hopeless*? [Laughs] The Bad Seeds always play so slow. . . It's just slack. I've been to so many Bad Seeds gigs like this. . . And I've never liked Neil Young's stuff. I used to class him with James Taylor and all those other nuisances. They killed rock 'n' roll. I find it hilarious, all these groups aged 21 and their favourite LP is *After The Goldrush*. I used to go to parties and trash that LP when I was 16. It was the enemy.

Elvis Presley

American Trilogy (Medley)

Elvis At Madison Square Garden

RCA

Dixie by Elvis Presley. [Elvis whoops and Smith laughs] It's a comedy number; he's taking the piss. The best stuff of this period [early/mid-70s] is things like *Suspicious Minds* and *Poke Salad Annie.*

This is part of a medley.

And it's terrible. One of the worst things he ever did. He's obviously on drugs and he feels he has to keep connecting with his roots, but the band are bored to death. I was always a big fan of Elvis. The first Sun LP used to keep me going for months, and at that time you weren't allowed to like Elvis because he was fat and a fascist and all that crap. I used to say it doesn't matter; if you like it, you like it. You don't have to look like Elvis or behave like him. People have lost that; now you've got to look like what you like.

And the next one is a prime example of that. . .

Morrissey

National Front Disco

Your Arsenal

EMI

Morrissey, isn't it? Is it new?

No, it's old. It's *National Front Disco.*

I've never heard it before. [We sit trying to make out the lyric]

He seems to have a fascination with rough boys.

I'll say this; all closets have a fascination with Nazis. That's a fact of history. It's like the Hitler Youth in their little shorts. I've got no fascination with rough boys; I put one on crutches last week!

Whatever the sentiments in the song, the music is so dull, and even more reactionary than the lyrics.

205

Mark E Smith

Session musicians. Such a shame The Smiths broke up, just as they were getting good. . . I don't identify with that English thing about being fascinated by rough types and skinheads and that. I can't relate to it. It's funny because I'm usually seen as that kind of hooligan, working-class idiot, but I think they're all closets. I don't have anything to do with them.

The myth is that football hooligans, or whatever, are somehow more authentic.
Well, anyone can go to Dublin and cause trouble. What makes me laugh is they cause trouble in the softest parts of the world. They always start in Copenhagen or Amsterdam, or they're tough in Dublin. In Dublin they'll let you into a match without a ticket, they're so nice and easy going. The Italians had them sorted out. There was no trouble in Italy because the Italians told them: 'If you ruin our game of soccer, we'll machine-gun you.' It's easy to throw a few sticks at some Dublin kids; pseudo-hardoes, like bouncers or something. I have this trouble with road crews when I'm on tour; they get to Amsterdam and they have a bit of pot and see a few prostitutes and they go off the wall. It's embarrassing.

Morrissey defended this song by saying, 'I don't think black and white people will ever get on.'
It's bollocks, isn't it?

ARTIST
The Buzzcocks

TITLE
Boredom

SOURCE
Spiral Scratch EP

LABEL
New Hormones

[Immediately] The Buzzcocks. Best song they wrote.

And when punk arrived in Manchester how did it affect you?
I saw The Buzzcocks and I thought, 'I better form a group, I can do better than that!' I actually remember coming out of the gig at [Manchester's] Lesser Free Trade Hall and thinking that.

Did you consider The Fall a punk group when you started?
No, we were into garage. We were punk, but not as it was known then. Our idea of punk was mid-60s: The Kinks, The Seeds. Well, my idea of it was anyway. . . The Buzzcocks were very good, better than The Vibrators and all that shit. They had an avant garde touch. Also they paid for our first recording.

ARTIST
Public Enemy

TITLE
Bring The Noise

SOURCE
Bring The Noise 12"

LABEL
Def Jam

I quite like Public Enemy. I like the slower ones, funnily enough. I like NWA; they're very sparse and hard. This, to me, has no content. I used to buy rap compilations. The early rap stuff was quite good; they used to talk about ghosts and original subject matter, like in Northern Soul. Now it's all about, I've got a car and I fuck lots of girls. . . It reminds me very much of reggae. Reggae in the late 1960s was fucking great; just at the interim period between bluebeat and Rasta it was excellent. And then there was Bob Marley and Island Records and Virgin Records and it got all technical and It just lost it.

Prince Buster was great, Big Youth was great. They were hard.

ARTIST
Velvet Underground

TITLE
Rock 'N' Roll

SOURCE
Live MCMXCIII

LABEL
Sire

[Immediately] *Rock 'N' Roll* by The Velvet Underground. From *1969*.

1993, live in Paris.

1993? We played Glastonbury with them and this was the best thing they did, but I didn't like them at all. I think Lou Reed was doing it for the money, to be honest, and you can't blame him for that. I'm a *White Light/White Heat* person – one of the best LPs ever made. I don't like Lou Reed's recent stuff; too topical. The thing about Lou Reed is that he was dead simple and original, but now he's talking about Third World Wars and CND and it doesn't suit him. I wouldn't knock him, though; I think he's great. I think he's just got fed up with being ignored. You used to have to really hunt for a Velvet Underground record in Manchester in 1972 and 1973. In the 70s Eric Clapton would be selling millions of records, and The Velvet Underground couldn't get in the Top 200.

That seemed to fuck him up.

I don't blame him. I would be outraged.

ARTIST
Can

TITLE
Pinch

SOURCE
Ege Bamyasi

LABEL
Spoon

It's Can, isn't it? Off *Tago Mago*. . . Off *Ege Bamyasi*. *It's Pinch*. It always clears the room at parties when I put this on. It's fucking marvellous; the drums are great. It's a great LP. All their drum beats are like rave music, or disco; it really fucking moves.

Your song *I Am Damo Suzuki* (off *This Nation's Saving Grace*); what was that about?

It was about Can, and [the group's Japanese vocalist] Damo as well. He's a good mate of mine now, actually. He doesn't believe in making records anymore. He still plays, but he makes cassettes; he makes about three cassettes and he sends one to me. He still works with Jaki Liebezeit on the drums. If we play Cologne or Essen or somewhere he comes to see us play. He's one of the heroes of mine who've actually lived up to expectations.

ARTIST
Orbital

TITLE
Philosophy By Numbers

SOURCE
Snivilisation

LABEL
Internal

[Two minutes of foot-tapping] I've no idea.

Orbital.

Is it? I like Orbital. They remixed *Middle Class Revolt*; they were halfway through it, but I put a stop to it. They're good, Orbital, but too machine-orientated. There's not enough feel.

What current music do you listen to?
Just Italian rave really. It's got a lot of guts to it. Visnardi and stuff. . . The thing about stuff like this is that you can hear it's been done by a machine and you can tell there isn't going to be anything coming up. They should use technology to make it heavier; that's what I try and do. The problem with these is that they're not musicians, they're DJs. They don't really know much about studios and they don't really respect musicians because they're used to working with Primal Scream. The Drum Club were like that. They did tracks for us, but I didn't want it released. It was just a machine and me in the middle going 'middle class revolt'. It's not like you're in your bedroom anymore, you're in a studio and you've got to record it. People like Johnny Burnette knew that; professionals. He'd just put the mic there, put the amp at this level, and do it in one take. Now you go in a studio and it's like *Star Trek*; it's like going into the Starship Enterprise.

ARTIST
Scarface featuring Ice Cube

SOURCE
Hand Of The Dead Body 12″
LABEL
Virgin

TITLE
Hand Of The Dead Body Goldie Remix 12″

It's great that. Great sounds. The bass sound is excellent. What is it?
Scarface, a Goldie mix. It's hard to hear Jungle like this anywhere; you have to search for it.
Yeah, and you go to clubs and the DJs don't even know what the records are; it's all white labels. It's good, it puts the shits up the corporates. This is excellent. You'll have to do me a copy.

Dan Burn-Forte

209>

Sonic Youth formed in New York in the early 80s, during the dying days of that city's 'No Wave' era, when ugly noise and confrontation were the rule in the music. Guitarists Thurston Moore and Lee Ranaldo rose from No Wave's cohorts: the guitar armies of academic rockers Rhys Chatham and Glenn Branca. With bassist Kim Gordon (now Moore's wife) and drummer Steve Shelley, they explored similar drone-rock territory and post-punk psychosis on a series of low-key independent releases, before being championed by Paul Smith of the British Blast First label. This association produced the classic late 80s quartet of *Bad Moon Rising*, *EVOL*, *Sister* and *Daydream Nation*. A subsequent deal wiith Geffen Records allowed the group to expand their fanbase during the 'Grunge years' of the early 90s with minimal dilution of their abrasive guitar sound. Their most recent tour found them stretching out tracks from their 1996 LP *Washing Machine* into elongated, improvised guitarscapes. In 1997 they launched their own independent label, SYR, issuing two EPs of their own music.

Ranaldo and Moore were both eager to be tested, dubbing the encounter 'Stump The Stars'. What's more, they insisted on testing the interviewer in return (he failed to recognise any tracks!)

ARTIST
Rhys Chatham

TITLE
Guitar Trio

SOURCE
Die Donnergötter

LABEL
Homestead

TM: [Instantly] Bush Tetras
LR: No, it's Rhys
TM: Rhys Chatham, *Guitar Trio*.
LR: We played this piece, how could we not know what it was? Seeing that music live was my first impressive New York music experience.
TM: Bush Tetras were playing that kind of music also at the time. They had a song called *Too Many Creeps* that kind of ripped off Rhys Chatham. Much in the same way Sonic Youth ripped off Rhys Chatham. He was a piano tuner and a harpist and a musicologist who worked under LaMonte Young, and he was a young kid and kind of eccentric, and he loved rock 'n' roll – although his body didn't. He was enlightened by The Ramones.

ARTIST
Sun Ra

TITLE
The Cosmic Explorer

SOURCE
Nuits De La Fondation Maeght

LABEL
Shandar

TM: [Very quickly] Sun Ra. That's great. I'm sure it's, what, late 60s?
Later than that, I think.
LR: It was great.
TM: That's definitely my favourite period of Sun Ra, when he was getting into electronics, a late 60s kind of freak-out.
What's he like now? Didn't you just play with him?
TM: We played with him this summer, a free show in Central Park. I had met him before, when he was lucid, and he really loved to talk, about parallels and anagrams and all kinds of word play. It was really interesting, although you couldn't really have much of a straightforward conversation with him, because he was on these abstracts. But he had a stroke last year, and he's somewhat debilitated, somewhat paralysed, somewhat in pain. He was in a wheelchair.
LR: He's since had another one.
TM: His performance was fine. He's still doing that Fletcher Henderson tribute stuff, which is cool. He was rubbing his hands like he was in pain with the stroke. But he still seems very positive. We were talking to him. He doesn't respond, he doesn't talk, but he'd kind of smile. He still has orange hair, which is cool. I have 120 Sun Ra records.

ARTIST
Black Flag

TITLE
Life Of Pain

SOURCE
Damaged

LABEL
SST

TM: [Instantly] Black Flag!
LR: Black Flag!

TM: This is the riff we copped! We played this riff on [unintelligible]. *Life Is Pain*, right? Black Flag are crucial. Black Flag is the group to us that in the mid-80s were really important.

Because of guitarist Greg Ginn.

TM: Because of the whole chemistry of that band, the whole approach. They were basically coming out of a punk rock thing, and they were really open to discovering anything new, not just a teenage hardcore thing. Plus [Henry] Rollins was like a secret weapon, this kid from DC.

LR: He was at least as integral, when he was in the band, as Greg was.

TM: The original band at this period was Chuck Dukowski on bass, Dez Cadena on guitar, whoever they had on drums. It was frightening. If you'd ever seen them, the records are hardly, well, *Damaged* comes close, but at the same time you just wouldn't believe some of the things they were doing [paces excitedly out of microphone-range].

ARTIST	SOURCE
Derek Bailey	**Guitar Solos 2**
	LABEL
TITLE	Caroline
The Lost Chord	

TM: [Instantly] Derek Bailey. Derek Bailey? Is that him vocalising? Wow. I don't know this one. He's my favourite guitar player in the world. Only because . . . well, I never really thought so by hearing his recordings. I listened to his recordings for years, and they were so abstract, so really improvised, and I wasn't quite sold on what he was doing, though I was really impressed. But I saw him play live in a duet setting, with [drummer] Paul Motian, and he was incredible, really sublime, really interesting, just totally, absolutely super intelligent. It was so pure and simple. Unlike other free guitar improvisors, [Fred] Frith or whatever. It went through a volume effect, but that was pretty much it. He reminded me of those chess-playing musicians, like Warne Marsh. That kind of logic.

It's funny, we do all these interviews with *Melody Maker* and *NME* and the fanzines, and we try to talk about this real underground of London, improvisors like Evan [Parker] and Derek, Lol [Coxhill], [Louis] Moholo, the whole African contingent – and of course none of them have ever heard this music, there's no way they're going to write about it in the music weeklies. It's kind of a bummer. It's such an underground music. It's very serious, but it's also very humorous. It's very alive. In America now, especially in New York, there's a lot of interest in that music, a lot of people searching for information – and there's a lot of it out there, but it's so small that you can't find it very well.

I think people brought up with a kind of liberal, punker kinda thing, getting into this music in their 30s, there's a lot of these people out there, scavenging for these documents.

Carcass

Forensic Clinicism/
The Sanguine Article

Necroticism: Descanting the Insalubrious

Earache

TM: Slayer? DSI? Is it from Clearwater, Florida?
The UK.
TM: Bolt-Thrower?
LR: Napalm Death?
TM: I don't know what it is.
Carcass.
TM: Oh, Carcass. I mean, after a while we would have guessed it. Just run down the names. I mean, nothing to say about that.
LR: There's nothing to say.
TM: I love Slayer, for what it's worth. They inspired a generation.

Hans Reichel

Avant Lore

Guitar Solos 2

Caroline

LR: Adrian Legg.
Hipper than that.
LR: Hipper than Adrian Legg?
TM: It's on vinyl.
LR: Henry Kaiser?
TM: Henry Kaiser? Is it American?
It's German.
TM: Hans Reichel. As far as electric guitar, he's really interesting. Because not so many people are doing things with electric guitar that's really experimental. He definitely is. He's cool. I liked the thing he did, *The Angel Carver*, with [cellist] Tom Cora. He had one FMP record that was really cool, I forget the name of it. I saw him play once, and he had this quartet, and this woman singing doll sounds. I had to leave, because it was like bad Performance Art. It was like all you really dread about art music onstage. It was a shame.

Ut

Brink Over Chicken

Early Live Life

Blast First

TM: [Very quickly] Ut?
LR: That's unbelievable, that you called that one!
TM: That was an Ut rhythm if I ever heard one. Ut were one of the coolest bands. We were associated with them when we first started.
LR: Cool, and obscure as hell.

TM: I saw Ut's very first gig, when they were a New York band. It was still totally atonal, a sort of square-wheel rhythm thing. It was at Max's, still during the No Wave, when it was waning. I remember No Wave people coming to see Ut, and they were so like hard and weird-edged that the No Wave people left – they couldn't even deal with it. After that they became interesting, really musical. Then I think they got into this rut of trying to maintain what they were doing. But the older they got, the more disillusioned they got with the rock 'n' roll scene – they weren't really a rock 'n' roll band. They were way more far out than that. There was really no forum for it in a way.

ARTIST
Neil Young

SOURCE
Arc-Weld

LABEL
Reprise

TITLE
Arc (excerpt)

TM: Caspar Brötzmann? Last Exit? Fat? The Splatter Trio? Slaughterhouse? How old is it?
A year.
TM: It's a brilliant track. Where are they from? New York? LA?
I don't know where they live.
TM: Blind Idiot God?
LR: They wish!
TM: Sun City Girls?
LR: A Zorn thing?
TM: What is it? We didn't guess this one.
It's Neil Young. It's from _Arc-Weld_. [A release including a CD-full of feedback noise and improvisation – which Sonic Youth, on tour with him at the time, persuaded Young to put out. They find the fact that they didn't get it hugely amusing.]
TM: That was really good. I never listened to that track before. A good Stump The Star! You win on that one.
LR: Because we were certainly at that gig! The most inspired choice yet!

ARTIST
Mars

SOURCE
No New York

LABEL
Antilles

TITLE
Helen Fordsdale

TM: [instantly] Mars. That's the greatest. One of the greatest tracks ever. What is it, _Puerto Rican Ghost_?
No, it's _Helen Fordsdale_. So what happened to them, when they were so obviously great?
LR: It's the same as Ut, except even more so. They were so obscure that nobody related, nobody supported it.
TM: I remember seeing them at the time and just hating it. You'd go and see Patti Smith or something, and Mars would be on the bill. Or Talking Heads, summer of 77. They started really early. I guess they were even more twisted when they started. They were arty, came from art schools, Florida, Minneapolis,

converging on New York, that whole No Wave scene. Mark Cunningham [Mars guitarist], like James Chance, really had this background of interest in Albert Ayler-type jazz. Which nobody else had. Johnny Thunders surely didn't.

ARTIST
Lou Reed

TITLE
Metal Machine Music B-2

SOURCE
Metal Machine Music: The Amine-Beta Ring

LABEL
RCA

LR: [Instantly] *Metal Machine Music.*
Which side?
LR: Side four, the best side. Side four? I even got that right! We used this, though, on *Bad Moon Rising*. That's how we know it. We used it behind *Society Is A Hole*. Can you get it on CD?
Yes, but everyone says it's not as good.
TM: I wouldn't want it on CD. It's way too layered.

ARTIST
Black Sabbath

TITLE
Rat Salad *and* Fairies Wear Boots

SOURCE
Paranoid

LABEL
NEMS

[They'd guessed this earlier, when I first put the tape in the wrong way round. We played it again anyway.]
TM: Sabbath Sabbath Sabbath Sabbath.
LR: Which record is it? I'd only recognise *Paranoid*.
TM: This must be when they were just getting into Yes! It's funny, someone wrote a piece in *Village Voice* about Black Sabbath all of a sudden becoming the third major influence for underground rock 'n' roll. There was always Stooges and Velvet Underground. Now it's like Black Sabbath have become the big third. Which is really funny, that they're suddenly validated. That tempo they played, especially on the first few records, so primitive, but also so effective. But this article also said how all these bands that exist now acknowledge them, except for Sonic Youth. Which is totally wrong in a way.
LR: No, musically we don't acknowledge them at all!
TM: I do. In a lot of chord-playing. Especially on a song like *Chapel Hill* – it's totally a rip-off.
LR: You're crazy! *Chapel Hill*?
[Moore sings the riff to *Chapel Hill*].
LR: Oh, I guess so, but that's not the main part of the song, that's a little riffmeister kind of thing.
TM: It's part of the main centre of the song, right there. That kind of half-step chording, that all comes from Sabbath.

Ali Farka Touré was born in 1939 in a remote village near Niafunke, in deepest Mali. In his late teens he took up the guitar, joining The Niafunke District Troupe – a travelling group of musicians and dancers – during the 1960s. He worked as a sound engineer for Radio Mali before beginning to record a series of solo albums for Sonodisc in the early 80s. In 1988 he started a fruitful contract with the World Circuit label, releasing *Ali Farka Touré*, *The River* and *The Source*, the last-named featuring guest appearances by blues artists Taj Mahal and Rory McLeod. Although often described as blues influenced, his three-fingered picking style, first perfected on the traditional monocorde guitar, owes nothing to Western tuning or chord progressions; Touré remains a fierce champion of the notion that American blues has its origins firmly rooted in central Africa. His most successful album to date has been *Talking Timbuktu*, a collaboration with Ry Cooder released in 1994. The Jukebox was conducted in French through an interpreter.

ARTIST
Boubacar Traoré

SOURCE
Kar Kar

LABEL
Stern's Africa

TITLE
Santa Mariya

[Immediately, before Traoré has begun singing] It's *Kar Kar* [Traoré's nickname]. It's in keeping with the Malian musical tradition, but different from the music I play because it's from another region – Bambara. It's like the difference between English and Scottish music. It's very, very good. I like it a lot because it is original, truly African, music.

To Western ears at least, Boubacar Traoré's music has a strong blues feel to it. What does the 'blues' mean to you?
I don't really know the word blues, but what you're talking about comes from a traditional feel of original music which then influenced the music that became known as the blues. If you imagine a tree, then the blues is the branches of that tree; Malian music, not African music, and not even West African music, is the roots. American blues, to me, just means a mix of various African sounds. It's not American music, it's African music imported directly from Africa, and when I hear 'the blues' I don't hear America, I hear Africa.
Kar Kar was one of the first West African artists to use and adapt the Western guitar rather than playing a traditional instrument. I respect him for this; I'm very proud of him.

ARTIST
John Lee Hooker

SOURCE
Blues Brothers (Recordings 1948–51)

LABEL
Ace

TITLE
Boogie Children

Is it Lightnin' Hopkins? Or John Lee Hooker? I've listened to quite a lot of his music, but I don't know this. Generally I don't listen to American music; I listen to French and Arabic music. The first time I heard John Lee Hooker was when a friend brought back a tape from Paris. I didn't actually think he was American. He sounded as if he came from Mali; the only difference was the language. As I was listening to him I picked up my traditional guitar and played exactly the same thing, and it was after that that I thought I should do more with my music because he was producing something second hand. I decided that I should show people where this music really came from. When I met John Lee for the first time, in Paris last year, I invited him to come to Mali to hear the origins of his music. As yet, he hasn't taken up the invitation, but I'd love to play with him because he would learn a thing or two. He could learn the roots of his music. I'm not being big-headed about this, it's just the truth.
John Lee gave me the idea to take my music further. Think of it this way: I had the sugar, but he made me realise how sweet it was. And he is unique in his field because he is authentic, he hasn't moved too far away from the tradition.

ARTIST
Baaba Maal/ Mansour Seck

SOURCE
Djam Leelii

LABEL
Rogue Records

TITLE
Lamtooro

[Immediately] Baaba Maal.

Do you know who the other guitarist is?
No, I don't. Even though Baaba Maal is from Senegal, this is not Fouta or Senegalese music, it's 100 per cent Malian. Everything he does is taken from Malian music – this is not his composition or invention. This song is a Malian song that everyone plays. All the same, I like him very much because he is the best Senegalese musician, even better than Youssou N'Dour.

In Africa, all musicians have a line or style in which they play. They may sound different, but you can recognise that line regardless of what they are playing. Baaba Maal is like this. He may have studied music, been to college and become a professional and master, but the root, the line, of his music is Malian. He has taken the sounds and melodies of Malian music and changed them, changed the language. But Baaba Maal is a noble musician, and when he goes into the Fouta region of his country he is an idol of the people, a leader.

ARTIST
Bo Diddley

SOURCE
Chess Masters

LABEL
Magnum Force

TITLE
Bo Diddley

I don't know this. I have never heard of Bo Diddley. But I liked it very much; I like the rhythm and the music even though I can't understand the words. I can tell you the origin of that rhythm [he plays along to the record, tapping out the beat on the table]. It's a hunters' celebration dance, played on a Hari drum, which is used to welcome a chief or nobleman.

ARTIST
Bill Frisell

SOURCE
Lookout For Hope

LABEL
ECM

TITLE
Lookout For Hope

I don't know who it is and I can't find anything of interest in it. Nothing. It's like the high music of the Sorbonne; it has nothing to do with Africa and there's nothing particularly African about it.

Does that mean that music must have an African ingredient in it for you to like it?
Music must have some significance to me. It must mean something to me. This doesn't. It was just sound – it didn't seem to come from anywhere or have a message. In Mali, music is always talking about something – history, legend, family, this animal, that tree, this river, those flowers. The American music I like – John Lee Hooker, Lightnin' Hopkins, Sam Cooke – says something to me even though I don't understand the words.

ARTIST
Oumou Sangaré

TITLE
Diaraby Nene

SOURCE
Women Of Wassoulou

LABEL
Stern's Africa

[Immediately] That's Oumou. She may sound very different from the way she sang at the beginning of her career, but her music is still typically, traditional. Her words and music are very significant and educative. She sings about life, and the good and bad in all of us, be we European or African. She says that everyone's future is not in their own hand, but in God's, and destiny's. For the Wassoulou people she's an idol and hero, and for that I hold her in very high esteem.

ARTIST
Jimi Hendrix

TITLE
Voodoo Chile (Slight Return)

SOURCE
Electric Ladyland

LABEL
Polydor

[Immediately] Jimi Hendrix. Listen [he blows his cheeks out], he sounds like a toad [he makes toadish sounds to accompany Hendrix's wah-wah guitar]. I like Hendrix very, very, very, very much, but this track is a little too strong, little too heavy for me. He doesn't always move my heart, but I respect the fact that every guitarist in the whole world has tried to imitate him at some point. I have even met Africans who have tried to copy him – and they have made themselves ill doing so. They have tried to use his tricks [he makes a thinner weedier sound]. People have never been truly able to imitate Hendrix because it's God which gave him his unique talent.

He's a black American who's never been to Africa, but he's a phenomenon. He speaks with the guitar; he makes it do exactly what he wants.

ARTIST
Robert Johnson

TITLE
Kindhearted Woman Blues

SOURCE
Robert Johnson: The Complete Recordings

LABEL
CBS

I don't know him, but he sounds as if he's the same generation as John Lee Hooker.

No, he's a little earlier; this was recorded in 1937.

This is not, and never will be, American music. It is African, truly African. When black Africans were taken to America they had an African spirit, and a spirit of African music, but then they became immersed in another language. Then when they were liberated from slavery they had to find a way to earn a living and a lot of them did that busking. This maintained their connection with Africa because that lifestyle of playing on the streets or in bars to earn a living is similar to what people do in Mali. I like this because it's rare to find a black American who sounds like he knows his roots and where he has come from.

ARTIST
Salif Keita

SOURCE
Amen

LABEL
Mango

TITLE
Kuma

Hearing this makes me want to go back home. Salif is our Jimi Hendrix. He's the idol of Mali. He is a nobleman. God has given him his voice and his music and there is no one to compare with him. We both started playing music at roughly the same time – and I was an engineer on some of Salif's first records – but Salif always played in the clubs, whereas I would play in the studio with the National Radio Orchestra Of Mali.

How do you feel about Salif's more recent albums?

I don't like them. Now he is producing music that is primarily influenced by European and American music, not African. To me, Salif's music today has no significance. He has lost his way. You have to keep to the path and not deviate; you have to know the direction you're going in. It's important that we don't play European music because otherwise we will lose the original, the roots will be lost forever. And there are always problems when African artists collaborate with Americans or Europeans. On my last album I recorded with Taj Mahal and there were many difficulties because Taj couldn't really keep up or understand what I was doing. I have the way I play; I have my own tuning. I like playing with black American musicians, but they don't always understand the tradition, they haven't learnt what I know. To me, Salif doesn't play African music any longer. I've told all this to his face.

And how did he respond?

Salif certainly told me what he thought, but that is between him and me.

Paul Weller was born into a working-class family in Woking in 1958 and was in his first group by the age of 14. With Bruce Foxton and Rick Buckler he formed The Jam, and for six years from 1976 the group were one of punk's most celebrated and idolised units. Splitting the group in 1982, Weller surprised many in the 80s with the ersatz jazz and R&B of The Style Council, formed with keyboardist (and ex-Merton Parka) Mick Talbot, and his overt support for an array of political causes, particularly the pro-Labour Red Wedge movement. In 1989 Polydor refused to release his 'Garage House-influenced' fifth Style Council album and terminated his contract. He then had two children with his wife, former Wham-ette and Style Council backing vocalist Dee C Lee, before releasing a debut solo album on Go! Discs in 1993. At the time of the Jukebox he had just released the *Wild Wood* album, a record which would secure his critical and commercial rehabilitation as the Godfather of Britpop. He claims his favourite pastime is sitting in a room listening to music.

Curtis Mayfield

Back To The World

Curtom

Future Shock

Curtis Mayfield. *Back To The World*. *Future Shock*. That's a great album – one of his best. I was playing it the other day funnily enough. It's a really underrated album as well. I don't know why because every track is great and the lyrics and arrangements are brilliant. The melodies go hand in hand with the lyrics – the deeper the lyrics go, the deeper the melodies go – and you've just got to follow it. And that sleeve design! Don't you think the roots of Soul II Soul, that sound, that beat, that swingy sort of drum sound, is in this? I do like some of his earlier stuff with The Impressions, like *Check Out Your Mind*, but I prefer this solo stuff more. And his voice is funny, isn't it? Sort of a fragile falsetto, so small, but so sweet. He's definitely an influence, mainly lyrically I think because he's just so positive about things. I'm really bored with these HipHop and gangsta lyrics – all that 'bitches' and 'niggers' and 'guns' and the rest of that crap. It wasn't any better for Curtis's generation, in fact it was probably worse, but 20 years ago Curtis, Gil Scott-Heron, Stevie Wonder, Marvin Gaye, they were saying 'Let's clean up the ghetto'. I'd sooner hear that. I don't see the point in wallowing in the shit we're in; let's talk about how we're going to get out of it.

The Style Council seemed to be heavily influenced by Curtis Mayfield.

What, *Kind Of Loving*? The one everyone hated. It didn't have that sophistication and it didn't have very good melodies, so I think the comparison fails by a long shot. But he did mix a track on that album, and he was brilliant to work with. The vibe you get from him is that he is really at one with himself and the world. And I did this other thing with him, interviewing him for a video of his gigs at Ronnie Scott's. That was brilliant.

But it's true most of your influences are American R&B.

Yeah, probably 60 to 70 per cent. Basically my tastes are black music in most forms and English 60s pop which comes from that R&B source. I can't think of too many exceptions – maybe Syd Barrett or early Pink Floyd, but even Floyd started as an R&B band playing Chuck Berry.

Traffic

John Barleycorn Must Die

Island

Freedom Rider

[Before the vocals] Traffic. *John Barleycorn Must Die*. *Freedom Rider*. I like Steve Winwood. I think he's great; great voice. He's just got that R&B sound, and he also developed something more, something else in Traffic. When he first started with Spencer Davis it was just pure Ray Charles and it was just so weird to hear a 15, 16 year old white kid from Birmingham singing like that. It didn't even seem to be mannered; it seemed quite natural, it just flowed out of him. I suppose I like him because he was kind of a role model for me in that he was English and into R&B – it showed me a way of taking inspiration from other people's music, but also of trying to add something of your own as well. The playing is great on these Traffic albums – not necessarily technically, but they just had a great feel, which is more important.

Do you think anyone sounds as good today? Mick Hucknall?

Mick Hucknall? What a load of old bollocks. He doesn't compare in any way. These people [Traffic] were making real music, and they could outplay any of us lot today. I've been playing a long time, but I'm only just getting there. These people were doing this shit when they were, how old? 20, 21?

Some people have accused you of lauding the past too much. Doesn't your new album sound just a little too much like Traffic or The Small Faces circa 67?

If it does I take that as a compliment. I don't get hung up on that retro thing because I don't think I'm doing what Lenny Kravitz is doing – and no disrespect to him. If people say it sounds like an old record then that suits me fine because they're my favourite records – they sound the best to me. That is my time; that's what I come from. I've been listening to this sort of music off and on for a long, long time now and it's an important part of my character and my music. These records still sound fresh – I defy anyone to say otherwise. They will always invigorate and inspire me.

All the same, don't you think music must keep innovating, moving forward?

But I think it is. I'm still adding to the music – it's not just straight plagiarism. I think I'm still interpreting the past, still adding something to it, something fresh, something new. Why are so many people hung up on originality? What is original music? Is it Techno? If that's truly original music I don't want to know about it, I don't want no part of it. I mean, on [*Wild Wood*] we just tried to cut the tracks live in the studio as much as possible, tried to keep the mixes rough, tried to make the drum kit sound like a fucking drum kit, and the guitar like a guitar. I don't know what's wrong with that. That's how I like sounds to be.

ARTIST
Jamiroquai

SOURCE
Emergency On Planet Earth
LABEL
Sony Soho Square

TITLE
Hooked Up

You might have got me here. [After hearing the vocals] Oh, Jamiroquai. They cut a lot of this stuff live as well apparently. I know he's getting a lot of criticism right now, but I say leave him alone and let him fucking develop in his own time, because Jamiroquai are bringing real music to people, to younger people, and if it makes them backtrack and get into Gil Scott-Heron and Stevie Wonder then that's got to be a good thing. And he's pretty up-front about his influences. I've never seen him try to deny his influences – he's giving credit to the source – so what's the fucking problem? We've had five or six years of people saying pretty much nothing, and it's good to see people with attitude, people getting back into saying something.

Can't you have too much attitude? Can't attitude sometimes backfire and get in the way of the music?

Well, it can definitely backfire on you, but does that mean you shouldn't still say it. Lennon said it,? Marley said it, Stevie Wonder said it; why shouldn't Jamiroquai say it? He likes that sort of music – what's wrong with that? My generation, and his, have had more than 30 years of black music and culture in this country. It's part of us now – you and I probably wouldn't be sitting here now if it wasn't for black music. Just because he's white doesn't mean he has to follow Iron Maiden or be in a Heavy Metal band. Not every white kid has to be into Heavy Metal or white chunky rock bands.

ARTIST
Jimmy Smith & Wes Montgomery

SOURCE
The Dynamic Duo

LABEL
Verve

TITLE
James And Wes

Kenny Burrell? It's not Jimmy Smith. It's not Grant Green. Wes? But it's not Jimmy Smith, is it?

Actually it is.

I should have known this because I've got this album – although admittedly I haven't played it for a long time. I didn't recognise it was Wes Montgomery until he did those octave runs. I got heavily into Jimmy Smith around 1980/81. His music was the first thing that got me into jazz, but then I heard a lot of other organ players who I liked a lot more – more funky, gritty players like Jimmy McGriff and Freddie Roach. I started buying lots of the Blue Note reissues: Herbie Hancock's first LPs – *Taking Off* and *Empyrean Isles* – a lot of Stanley Turrentine and Lee Morgan. But with Wes, and I know this might horrify some jazz pundits, I find some of his stuff too MOR. Maybe you just have to know the right albums and obviously I don't. Who's the drummer on here? Yeah, Grady Tate – he's great.

Didn't the idea for The Style Council come from the Hammond sound?

Yeah, but not from Jimmy Smith. It was more from Ian McLagan of The Small Faces. He was probably the first influence on Mick Talbot, even though it was in a roundabout way because McLagan got it from Booker T.

What do you think about the change from The Jam to The Style Council now?

It's just what I wanted to do at the time. There was no great master plan or anything; I just had aspirations – or pretensions, as some had it – to make other kinds of music.

You've gone back to playing the guitar more on this new CD.

Yeah, I lost confidence in my playing in The Council. I wasn't interested in that Rickenbacker sound any more, and I didn't know what else to do, where to go from there. It took me time to get over my hang-ups – I'm nowhere near as good as any of these guys – but I know what I can do now, and I'm getting somewhere with it, which is an incentive.

ARTIST
The Sex Pistols

SOURCE
Kiss This

LABEL
Virgin

TITLE
Holidays In The Sun

[After a few seconds] OK, that's enough. Pretty dated, don't you think? I find it hard to listen to a lot of this punk stuff now to be honest, including my own stuff

– I just can't fucking handle it. It seems like a million years ago. But it was necessary at the time for me. I thought the 70s was a very, very dull time – all that Yes and ELP and Progressive rock stuff. I didn't like the way they looked, I didn't like their attitude, I didn't like the music. So it was great to see The Pistols – they had attitude and they were aggressive and the music was loud and furious, and there were the clothes and the hair. For me the punk scene only lasted for a very short time – by the time all the bands had been signed up it was over, it had become diluted. I hated what it all developed into – I mean the records were fucking awful after a while. But I got off on the energy and the fact that people were up there saying something and getting people excited.

Why do you think you – unlike many from that era – have survived? Johnny Rotten, for example, is washed up in LA. . .

Yeah, doing Schlitz adverts. I tend to think, and this isn't me blowing my own trumpet, I just think this is a fact, that I can actually sing and play, and I can actually write songs. Not everyone's going to like them, but I don't think anyone can deny that I can do it. I think John, bless his heart, would have trouble doing that, and I'm sure he doesn't even want to. I'm still making music and still doing what I've wanted to do since I was a kid. The Pistols were for that moment and what they generated was good at the time, but it doesn't stand the test of time. Every time I hear it now it just makes me laugh.

ARTIST
Elvis Costello

TITLE
Tramp The Dirt Down

SOURCE
Spike

LABEL
Warner Bros

I don't know this. [After the vocals start] Is it Elvis? But I don't know this album. I don't know much of Elvis's stuff – but I liked the words.

The career of Elvis Costello seems an interesting point of comparison. You both came to prominence in the punk era, you've both been very political at stages in your careers, you're both singer-songwriters, and you're both still around. Yet his credibility has always remained untarnished.

It has seemed that way, yeah.

The same can't be said about you, though, can it?

No. Not at all.

What do think about that credibility gap?

I don't know how to answer it. From my perspective I've got to make mistakes to be able to see what I can do and what I'm good at and what I'm not good at. I don't want to put Elvis down or anything, because I respect the fact that he's lasted, but he's made pretty much the same record – apart from that Country album – since he started. Whereas I, good or bad, have tried to do different things. Sometimes I've miserably failed; sometimes I've succeeded.

What about The Style Council name? Was that a mistake? Didn't it rather imply image before content?

Well, the press seemed to assume it, didn't they? But that's their problem. If you can't look beyond a word or the name of a group then are you fit to judge the music? If you're not prepared to dig a little deeper, if you just look at it all at face value. . .

But doesn't the word 'style' inevitably lead to certain preconceptions?

Yeah, but what I'm trying to say to you is that if you looked a bit deeper, there were plenty of other things to counteract that, that it evidently wasn't just about style or clothes. You only have to read the lyrics or read some of the sleevenotes – especially on the early Council records.

Going back to that political period, do you have any regrets about it now?

Yeah. I wish I hadn't got involved in the Wedge. We were manipulated by the Labour Party. I think I should have remained non-partisan to it all. We as a group should have carried on doing what we felt was right and doing the benefits we agreed with. We shouldn't have belonged to, or looked like we were part of, the Labour Party. We got swallowed up – inevitably because they were a bigger machine than us. It has put me off politics now.

You said recently that during parts of the 8os you were quite a long way up your own arse.

Yeah. Ego's a very, very dangerous thing when it's running rampant. And now, sitting outside of it all and seeing what it is, I can see it in different artists around me.

Anybody spring to mind?

Well, Bono's got to be careful, I think. He's making outrageous claims. Bono's putting both his bollocks on the line, whereas I only had one of mine on it. But Elvis has never had any of his on the line – he never wanted to join in the Wedge – and he was probably right as well. He had it sussed. But it was a growing period for me and I still hold a lot of those ideas, I still believe in socialism. Maybe it needs a different name these days or something, a revision, a new idea. People don't seem interested anymore. And the international establishment have pretty much done away with it, pretty much stamped it out.

ARTIST
Suede

TITLE
So Young

SOURCE
Suede

LABEL
Nude

Who the fuck's this? The Banshees? Suede? I don't know enough of their stuff. I liked *Animal Nitrate* – I thought that was a really good single – and I really liked their version of *Brass In Pocket*, but I'm not crazy about Brett [Anderson]'s voice. I'm not a massive Bowie fan, never have been. I can't get with too much of this kind of teenage angst thing – I tend to think it's all a bit staged, a bit mannered.

He wants to be a star, that's all. He's going for it. I can't really knock that – we've all been there at some point or another. He's obviously a big Bowie fan, but I don't mind that. As I've said, I don't mind the retro thing. It's like saying: did the first Jam album sound too much like The Who? Of course it did, because we just plundered it, but mainly out of enthusiasm, because I just love that sound. But this just isn't particularly my sort of music, that's all.

Well, I was trying to play you something you wouldn't like.

You've succeeded.

What would it have taken to really annoy you musically? George Michael? Nirvana?

Well, Nirvana would have done the trick. They sound like The Police. Or a Sting track would have done it as well. But it's nothing personal, I just ain't into those sounds. Although I like the guitarist on this, Bernard [Butler]. Whatever happens to the band, he'll do all right. Like Johnny Marr in The Smiths – there's always one music man in a band.

ARTIST
Stevie Wonder

SOURCE
The Jazz Soul Of Little Stevie

LABEL
Motown

TITLE
Square

Who the fuck's this? Larry Adler? It's got to be him or Stevie Wonder. Which album's this from? I've never heard this.

It's from his first album – recorded when he was just 11. As well as harmonica, he plays piano, organ, drums and bongos.

He's a genius, isn't he? He really is. Not in a press-hype way: more like the way people talk about Mozart, about being a child prodigy, he's the same thing, a pure one-off.

But it's difficult to talk about Stevie Wonder. You've got to watch what you say about Stevie Wonder. I'm always loath to criticise him because Stevie Wonder will always make a great track every now and again. He's made some duff albums, like *Square Circle*, but then you've got *Overjoyed* on that album, which ranks up with his best ever. I'll tell you what I think he needs to do, if I dare say this. He needs to get behind the kit again, get rid of all those fucking drum machines and all that Swingbeat crap and start playing again. Because that's what everyone wants to hear, I think, including all the HipHop kids who love all his earlier stuff, because no one plays kit like him. It's sort of wrong technically, but it's so right as well. And he needs to cut that kind of real rough album again. If you ain't got a good drummer, you ain't got a good band, simple as that. I'd just like to see some of these guys get back into some more raw recording, away from all this digitised bullshit we've had for fucking ten years or more.

Why did your drummer, Steve White, leave you at the end of the 80s?
He got fed up, because we started working with drum machines and synthesisers. He couldn't handle it.

But you were also quite difficult to work with during that period, weren't you?
Yeah. I lost the plot. I don't know what to say – sometimes you lose it, sometimes you don't. I don't believe any artist is so consistent that they never put a foot wrong. We all make duff albums now and again. No one's brilliant all the time.

ARTIST
Al Green

SOURCE
Al

LABEL
Beechwood

TITLE
Tired Of Being Alone

Turn it up. [He moves his chair back for maximum stereo effect] I want to listen to this one all the way through. His voice is just phenomenal, fantastic – and the drummer, Al Jackson, is really great on that track as well.

I went to see him recently at [London's Royal] Festival Hall, and I feel really bad about saying this, but I just couldn't handle all the cabaret shit. As soon as he started doing the 'Jesus, Jesus, Jesus' thing, I had to go to the bar and get with some other kind of spirits. But he's so brilliant as well, of course, and he's too great to put down, it's just that I don't like cabaret, I don't like showbiz. I like things raw; I like to see people just do their thing. I would like to see Al Green with a small band, so you just get his voice and none of the rest. I love his voice. It's a similar thing to Marvin Gaye, it's almost as if their voices are a separate entity from their bodies. Do you ever get that vibe? And at least he's still making albums; I wish Marvin Gaye and Marley and Lennon were still around making records. I miss these people more and more.

You seem quite moved listening to that track?
It was lovely, yeah. It's because I haven't heard it for a while, I suppose.

Dean Belcher

Born John Wardle, Jah Wobble got his more exotic name when a drunk Sid Vicious attempted to introduce him to a friend. As one of the gang who hung around Sex, Malcolm McLaren's shop on London's Kings Road, in 1975/76, Wobble might have joined The Sex Pistols alongside his friend John Lydon, but he was, by his own admission, too much of a yob. When The Pistols split up in 1978 he joined Lydon's new group, Public Image Ltd, where he formulated his booming dub-influenced bass style. After he left the group he worked on projects with Can's Holger Czukay and Jaki Liebezeit, U2's The Edge and formed The Human Condition. In the early 80s Wobble dropped out of music altogether, first driving a minicab, then working for London Underground. He made a surprisingly potent return with *The Invaders Of The Heart* in the late 80s. A hit single with Sinéad O'Connor, 91's 'Visions Of You' raised Wobble's profile further, and his burgeoning taste for eclecticism found him collaborating with a diverse cast of musicians on the subsequent *Without Judgement*, *Take Me To God* and *Heaven And Earth* albums. In 1995 he collaborated with Brian Eno on the *Spinner* album.

In 1996 Wobble composed the orchestral *Concerto for Chinese Harp And Orchestra*, with Wobble's partner Zi Lan Liao as the soloist. Other projects include the albums *The Inspiration Of William Blake* and *The Celtic Poets*, which highlight his interest in spoken word. The Jukebox took place In Wobble's East London home.

The O'Jays

Back Stabbers

Philadelphia International

When The World's At Peace

Sounds a bit New Orleans. Allen Toussaint? I'm hearing people who have checked out a lot of music from the past. It could even be from the past, remixed, regular R&B thing. Who is It?

It's actually an original item. It's The O'Jays, from 1972.

Oh right, so it's the authentic thing. I used to check all their stuff out. The O'Jays – that's fine by me. Sounds good. Not the best thing I've heard them do.

Were you influenced by Philly soul?

Yeah, yeah, the sound of Philly: MFSB Orchestra, *I Love Music*, *Back Stabbers*, all those old tracks. They had good bass playing, and it was one of the first times you could distinctly hear the bassline in American music: the bassline was an absolute entity in its own right. There was a lot of good soul in that mid-70s time. The sound of Philly directly influenced me with how chords can make an atmosphere, with the strings and stuff. Lots of suspended chords, that real high stuff, which implies a sort of tension. I'd say more than inspiration, that was a direct influence. It was so simple: bassline, sustained chords and all that.

I would never have thought that was The O'Jays. It was chunky sounding and Philly's generally smooth. When you have a real smooth thing happening with wonderful harmonies and stuff, it elevates your spirit, takes you closer to God. Funnily enough, in that way a really smooth Philly track would affect me as much as a Renaissance tune, polyphony and voices swelling. The real masterful thing is to have that smoothness and have a groove there at the same time. What I liked about The O'Jays was you had a lot of congas up in the mix. That's why I always had congas for years, because of Philly. I thought it was amazing.

Arvo Pärt

Tabula Rasa

ECM

Cantus In Memory of Benjamin Britten

[Immediately] Ooh, fuckin' hell, I like that. This [the Jukebox] has started off better than I thought. I thought there'd be a load of crappy pop music, but you've brought old man's music. Well done!

[Referring to the track] Somebody's been listening to Shostakovich, with the strings and the use of the bell, so he's been listening to *Babi Yar* or something. It would be nice for it to develop a bit more. I like it when you're not aware of the sequence starting. You listen to Górecki's [*Symphony*] *Number Three*, I love that stuff, it never stops. It's wonderful writing, very mature and understated.

Don't tell us, let's have a guess who it is. Play us the track after [ie *Fratres*]. European? British or central Europe? Hungarian-ish? Czech? Polish? Yugoslavian? It's not Arvo Pärt, is it? I've heard a couple of bits by this geezer before and the geezer's a fantastic composer, as are Tavener and Górecki. 20th century classical music brings as many tears to my eyes as anything from the 19th or the 18th century. It's the business. This stuff, I love it; paints such a beautiful picture. This is shivers, the shiver test. It's doing that. I thought he was Hungarian.

He's from Estonia.
Oh, right. We're doing a bit of classical now, it's all that we're doing. It's not a thousand miles from this. It's a definite style.

When did you start composing in a 'classical' style?
I always have fairly big bands and when you've got over five players you're going to get into arrangement territory. Then you're dealing with six and seven, then you're building it up – you get the horn player while he's there to do a little counter part. You chance your arm with arrangements and surprise yourself how good they sound and develop your own style. So the stuff becomes more orchestrated and then it lends itself naturally into writing with a very orchestrated feel to begin with, rather than orchestrating afterwards. Then lo and behold, suddenly you're sitting down and writing parts for 70, 80 people, suddenly you're walking like that [Wobble imitates balancing on a tightrope]. I've got a [compositional] style that's grown naturally from the music I've played over the years, but it's also very 20th century.

I was just wondering as you were talking if you ever had aspirations to do orchestral work when you were with PiL. I would guess not.
Not in a million years did I think that. No way. That would have been the same odds as becoming a Tornado pilot.

ARTIST
Sly & The Revolutionaries

SOURCE
Black Ash Dub
LABEL
Trojan

TITLE
Cocaine

Right, give us a clue. First of all, is it a straightforward dub album? Versions from vocal cuts? I'm hearing it's old style. I'm hearing right dodgy old space echo, which I love, so that's a very old technology. But the quality of the recording is very good, the separation and everything, which would suggest it's fairly contemporary, or a remix of old 70s stuff, because it sounds very clean to me.

It's Sly & The Revolutionaries from the late 70s.
You got certain trademarks with reggae, like with Lee Perry's stuff. You'd hear phased reverb, which I've noticed some of the rave groups are using these days, so you get that phasing that kind of goes round in a circle. You'd notice certain trademarks in the arrangement. This one, I don't know what studio it would be out of. L China Smith on guitar?

It's recorded at Channel One.
[Wobble looks at the album sleeve] Sly [Dunbar]. So it's Robbie Shakespeare [on bass]? All I can hear is it's the classic 70s sound. It's got that rounded feel, so I was thinking it's probably Robbie Shakespeare.
Sly was always economical, not so many rim shots as someone like Style Scott, just groove. Channel One: there's a certain sound with the vocal cuts. What I

like with Shakespeare is he really had his sound. Again, you're playing something that was a direct influence. This bass playing was the bass playing that turned me on. It was simple, well organised music, very well played. It was allowed to breathe with a top-to-bottom thing happening rather than having too much mid-range.

In the 70s there was a strong affinity between punk and reggae. Why do you think that was?

Well, for me it was really simple: before the punk thing came I liked reggae from a very young age, when it was called bluebeat, even before the days of ska. That was in the days of skinheads, 67, 69. At the time you could distantly hear the bass, but the first thing was simply 'chagga, chagga, cha cha', the ska guitar patterns: chops, basically. That made perfect sense to me. I remember it was considered brutal, primitive music at the time by people who were into Progressive rock: it wasn't worthy of being looked at. Then when it developed into the 70s they brought the bass to the fore. I was a bit of a tearaway when I was a kid and I'd go out and about to places and end up in blues [dances], sneaking in and, 'What's this fuckin' music?' Very simply, you'd be standing there with the bass going and be transported somewhere else. This was music of heaven, it was music of the stars, it was mystic. I'm not gilding the lily, it's true. It would be total music: it was beyond music, it had a direct physical effect. I think it had a healing effect. I think it is very healthy, because you got a sense of space, in the same way as those 20th century composers. It ultimately has the same effect. I got into music as I'm neurotic as much as anything else, and that simple thing happens: you forget your neurotic self.

ARTIST
Leftfield with John Lydon

SOURCE
Open Up EP
LABEL
Columbia

TITLE
Open Up (Full Vocal Mix)

This could be anyone so far. [After a brief vocal line] I recognise that voice, I think. Do you know what? That sounds like Johnny Rotten.

It is him, with Leftfield from 95. This is a Sabres Of Paradise remix.

Oh, right, yeah. I quite like that as I recall: really well done production. My only experience of this sort of stuff is when we've played clubs, where before and after they've got what I still call the disco. This one, you see it come on, the people will be E'd up and they'll go mental. It sort of makes sense, because John's a pretty wild character, and he's got a real edge to his voice and somehow it works. It's basically intense: that hi-NRG thing happening behind his voice.

You're right, it has got a hi-NRG feel.

His voice is so uncompromising, it's got a certain cut to it. There's always a certain anger in there, so it makes sense to take that simple element and put another simple element behind it that's really full-on.

Do you keep up with what he's doing? Are you still in touch?

I see John every few years, we run into one another. Last time I seen him was a couple of years ago. The only other times I hear anything is if I see things in the paper, where he slagged off the Royal Family, which I quite like. I think that's great. You asked me, do I keep abreast of what he's doing? Well, I don't because I don't hear much. I don't know if he's releasing records. My view is he should have been doing more. The geezer's got something to offer and should find the right people to work with.

ARTIST
Omme Kolsoum

TITLE
Charraf Habibal Alb

SOURCE
La Diva II
LABEL
EMI Arabia

Well, that's the real deal. Omme Kolsoum. Shiver.

I don't know when it was recorded, maybe the 1930s?
Yet again, big thing in my life. I listened to Radio Cairo on the short wave and it was all [Wobble makes a phasing sound]. And it's natural phasing: it goes up to the stratosphere and down, so it's the biggest phasing you'd ever have. It was better to have it with all that shit going on, it suited it, seriously. You'd hear these tremendously long introductions where you'd hear the band walk on, all these people clapping – imagine loads of clapping with a phase on it. Then you'd hear somebody warming up on an oud, then the darbuka kicked in and the band would start up. There'd be this cheering and they'd play these most gorgeous motifs, very classical, very complicated stuff. Then it would die down and then you'd hear the crowd go fuckin' mad and obviously you know the singer's on stage.

When did you first start integrating Middle Eastern elements in your music? Was it a conscious decision?
A mixture. I had this unconscious thing, this connection basically with a 3/4 thing that was untutored, that was hard-wired in, as Aristotle would have said! Aristotle said we were born knowing certain things – in modern parlance I was hard-wired. The other elements, the chromatic scales, were sort of in there, but I had to listen to a lot of Arabic music because you've got something there – I think people make the mistake of being very exact, and to me it's not a case, strictly speaking, of geography. What it is, you've got music sung to the glory of God and to the cosmos, if you like, and it's also very related to the culture: the state, the music and the religion and the people are all very connected. All that stuff's remained through religion, because when spiritual values are kept there's a structure there. Arab music's wonderful: fuckin' honour it. If I was forced to only listen to one kind of music, it would probably be North African.

ARTIST
Masaki Batoh

TITLE
Yoo Doo Right

SOURCE
A Ghost From The Darkened Sea
LABEL
The Now Sound/Ghost House

[After a minute or so] All I'll say at this point is it needs Jaki Liebezeit to come in on drums. It reminds me slightly of a Can riff. [After the vocal line starts] This has now reminded me of Can, with the vocal, and also a bit Dr John. Can had a lot of that deep thing in them like a New Orleans thing, but this is too linear to be out of America. It's like *Yoo Doo Right*. It's got that kind of a feel.

It's a cover version of that song.
Oh, I got it. YES!

I'm surprised you got it because it's a lot different from the original. Even the lyrics are different.
I'll tell you why: it's because I play a lot with Jaki and I can hear Jaki's rhythmic pulse in there. No one's got a rhythmic pulse like that. That's how I knew that.

It's by a Japanese musician called Masaki Batoh.
Of course, this would be Japanese, like the geezer who imitated Miles Davis for years. I tell you what, it was fuckin' good. He really understood it. I couldn't believe it when I heard it. It was just about spot on.

How did you get into Can?
I'm not actually a Can fan. Everyone claims to be Can fans now. I'm a Jaki and a Holger [Czukay] fan. I like the groove things with Can; I didn't like the bluesy or rocky things so much.

[Liebezeit] is an incredible geezer. Every time he comes over – he comes over once or twice a year – his playing style's a bit different. It's still Jaki. [Adopting a German accent] 'Well, you have to develop or it's pointless.' This is amazing: this geezer's getting on for 60 and thinking of changing and developing for the sake of changing and developing. He's a fantastic player that hardly anyone knows. If you're a drummer, he's a master.

ARTIST
Don Cherry

SOURCE
Brown Rice
LABEL
Horizon

TITLE
Brown Rice

It sounds like someone's been listening to gamelan. Nice funky bass. They're also listened to Miles Davis – the bassline's like something off *Bitches Brew*. I wonder if it's Michael Henderson on bass? Dr John [influence] again with those high vocals.

The bass player's Charlie Haden. His playing here reminded me a bit of you.
Yeah, it's got that flow, that relaxed, loose quality.

[The track ends] The leader here isn't playing his usual instrument, or at least not so you'd notice, but that's probably not much help. It's from the mid-70s.
[After a pause for thought] OK, at that time the kind of people that were merging – it was the original World Music in a way – were people like Don Cherry.

It's Don Cherry.
When you said it was somebody not playing their own instrument: Don Cherry then, unless the trumpet was going through a wah-wah. That's where the term World Music comes from, and I loved the way they used it because I hate the term now, but they used it in a really unified sense. And [Jon Hassell's] Fourth World music – it was a real integrity thing.

What do you think of the concept of World Music now?
I think it's a real ghetto in a way. You go where your heart tells you and you go where the music takes you, always. But you also have a view to how you

present yourself, and the area I'm very keen to avoid is 'World Music', which is a shame really, but it's become a lumpen mass. In any scene it will always be reduced to a lowest common denominator. It's also a hybrid in the wrong way because the best elements are missing a lot of the time. There's a lack of understanding of the rhythmic element which is to really access that thing of losing the 'one'; it doesn't have that mystical feel; but before it gets to that it fails because it doesn't function. It's basically not serious.

ARTIST
Jin Yong Uen

TITLE
Bow To Avalokitesvara Bodhisattva

SOURCE
Buddhist Chants And Peace Music
LABEL
Music Club

Cuu-Jeng. It's either Cuu-Jeng or the Japanese version, the harp. And Chinese bamboo flute. Right. Fuckin' hell. This reminds me very much of a mantra to this woman. [Wobble shows a picture of the Bodhisattva] It's the female version of the Buddha. Is it Cantonese? Very Chinese, just hanging in the air, beautiful. It's Buddhist temple music, it's a mantra. Wait a minute, I might even have a tape. Fuckin' hell, yeah. Hang about. [Increasingly excited, Wobble goes to look for the tape. A bell rings on the track we are listening to. Wobble turns his attention back to the music] Now the vocals come in, right? [After a very brief pause the vocals do indeed come in. Wobble punches the air] YES!

Wait a minute, hang about. [Wobble phones his partner Zi Lan Liao on her mobile. Speaking to Zi Lan:] I've forgotten the name of the female deity, the female Buddha. [He puts the handset against the speaker] Check it out. What is it? Tell the journalist. The geezer's come to play me a load of stuff and I've got to guess who they are. I can't believe he played me this one. I showed him the picture, tell him who it's about. [Wobble hands me the phone and Zi Lan explains the story of the Bodhisattva Guang Yin].

I can't believe that, it's my favourite Chinese track. [To Zi Lan] Oh, you're in a petrol station? I dialled the wrong number, spoke to some bird in Manchester. I should have said, 'Hey listen, you don't know me, but check this out!' All right, darling, speak to you later. [Wobble puts the phone down] Honestly, it's the Divine Mother working, mate, meeting of minds and all that. It's amazing, honestly.

The sleevenotes say that 'Traditional Buddhist music is, of course, acoustic. The recordings on this collection represent the more modern form of the genre presently popular in China and Taiwan.'

Well, to an extent. Don't go thinking that you go all over China or Taiwan and you'd hear that everywhere, because what you'd hear is pop music, their version of Madonna. But I go to the temples. Buddhism's taken a few knocks but it's still very much alive in China.

I'm totally blown out by that [track]. The last time I heard that was in Canton.

Michael Heffernan

237>

In 1973 Robert Wyatt fell out of a window at a party and suffered an injury which left him paralysed from the waist down. Although it effectively ended his spell as one of the UK's most inventive drummers, his musical career continued – he happened to be one of the UK's most inventive singers, songwriters and arrangers, too. Beginning as a drummer and singer in The Wilde Flowers in mid-60s Canterbury, Wyatt went on to a famous five year stint with Soft Machine. In 1972 he formed the more spontaneous, and equally acclaimed, Matching Mole. Post-accident, Wyatt found his true voice and recorded his best work, starting with *Rock Bottom* in 1974. The same year, his version of The Monkees' *I'm A Believer* made the charts – a feat repeated eight years later with the Elvis Costello song *Shipbuilding*. In between his own releases, his collaborations have been many and various, from Brian Eno to Mike Mantler, Working Week to Ultramarine. Wyatt joined the Communist Party in the mid-70s and his work became increasingly political throughout the 80s. After a five year hiatus, he re-emerged in 1991 with *Dondestan*, his best work for 15 years. An instrumental mini-album, *A Short Break,* followed. In 1997 he released the highly acclaimed album *Shleep*. The interview took place in Wyatt's home in Louth, Lincolnshire.

Charles Mingus

Haitian Fight Song

The Clown

Atlantic

I never saw this band. I do think he's underestimated in importance as a bass player: it's good that you've got one here where he starts on his own. I think he's probably my favourite ever bass player. Apparently he used more fingers than other bass players. He used three fingers of his right hand, which is why you get rather uneven walking lines, using the middle finger and the first finger. What I like about his solos is that they're the most like speech patterns of any bass player, so that makes him the most remarkable.

This has got a strong melody and even though it's just a quintet, it's like a whole group feeling – not just soloists and a rhythm section, a real group. [Looks at CD] It's from *The Clown*! My God, that is going back.

In your biography you mention a lot of bass players as major musical influences.
It's what drummers work with – we're both in the engine room, so they're the ones you get to know, and that can be the crucial thing. Also, when I'm making a record, it's the one thing that I can't do myself, so I have to get in a bass player.

One of the things that influenced me about Mingus is the compositional thing. There's a tendency in jazz, and it can be all right, for each composition to be a vehicle for the soloists to do their stuff – that's the only reason that tune is chosen. Whereas with Mingus, each piece has got its own character and it's very particular. And even with a small group, an informal set-up like that, they're playing that piece, not some other piece – that's what I like. Because he came from the West Coast and not the East Coast, he got involved in a lot of his early workshops with a mixture of all sorts of strange people that he might not mix with in some other context. But the first groups he had were extremely academic sort of intellectual exercises, the Mingus Workshops. He gradually got bluesier, but his bluesiness had a terrific intellectual authority because he'd done all this technical homework beforehand. So he was in total mastery of time signatures and harmonic complexities and so on.

The Raincoats

Fairytale In The Supermarket

The Raincoats

Rough Trade

It's English anyway. Could it be The Slits? Is it Palm Olive? I really think she's good – let me get in a plug for Palm Olive as a fellow drummer. I once said [to The Slits], 'If you ever want me to drum on your records I'd be happy to come,' but they never asked me. I was very hurt by that, but never mind, I got to play with The Raincoats instead. It's not The Slits? Blimey, I'm pleased I recognised the drumming. It's Palm Olive and somebody. Yeah. Go! Go!

It's from The Raincoats' first album, with Palm Olive on drums.

I did the last gig in my life [in 1981] with The Raincoats. We did *Born Again Cretin*, which they did very well. I really enjoyed it. . . I didn't know [this] was The Raincoats because I didn't hear their first record. To be fair, that definitely wasn't Ari Up singing. What threw me was that distinctive drumming style that I associate with The Slits – that's my excuse. Very nice. I liked that.

How did you come to play with The Raincoats?

I think they were on Rough Trade and we met around Rough Trade. It was a fairly loose set-up where people were listening to each other's stuff and clocking what each other were doing.

You played with other post-punk troups and musicians – Scritti Politti, and Epic Soundtracks from Swell Maps. Few other musicians from your generation got so directly involved in that area.

Well, it surprised me, to be honest. If I was asked and I could do it, on the whole I would. I liked the attitude round then. There were a lot of people I got on with better from that eruption than from that early period in the 70s, that I might have been expected to identify with. I liked the rough and ready approach. It's like somebody said about me: I'm like Jimmy Sommerville on valium, and I haven't got his get-up-and-go, I've got a lot of get-down-and-stay. But apart from that I really liked all the people I heard from that period.

I didn't think rock 'n' roll was so precious that it had to be played in tune. It never struck me as the essential ingredient in the first place. In fact by having that strange detuning that they all seemed to do – that slightly untuned desafinato that they had – it gave a bit of harmonic interest to a music that normally doesn't have any at all. The music I'd been involved in listening to before, the jazz, had gone into a tailspin of rejection of organisation anyway. So quite a lot of pop groups at that time were a sort of electrified version of a free jazz revival – which to those of us who were accustomed to these things was quite nostalgic really.

ARTIST
Cornelius Cardew

TITLE
Smash The Social Contract

SOURCE
Cornelius Cardew Memorial Concert

LABEL
Impetus

Oh, it's Communist Party, brackets, Marxist-Leninist, close brackets. Could it be Laurie Baker, the composer? I think I recognise that pianist. Oh, that's very interesting that, because Cornelius Cardew used to write a lot of pieces, but I don't think that is Cornelius Cardew. Although he did take on the attempt to write popular songs, that would have been in the era when I don't think he specifically dealt with things like the Social Contract. The things I remember by him at the time were more Internationalist, but it may be.

It *is* composed by Cardew, a performance from his memorial concert in 82.

Is it really? Oh, that's interesting. It could have been Laurie Baker on drums. [He looks at the sleeve] Laurie Baker, there you are.

One thing to say about Cornelius Cardew, before anybody says, 'What a load of crap', or anything like that, is he was the most stunningly knowledgeable musician. One of the few in this country that had that really encyclopaedic knowledge of music, that we associate with non-English figures like Pierre

Boulez and people like that. And had he lived he would have been recognised as one of the giants of music, just because of the breadth and depth of his knowledge. What people object to, of course, is the way that he channelled that vast knowledge into certain disciplines; but I think that's very heroic myself, and it was very interesting to hear it.

ARTIST

Hatfield And The North

SOURCE
The Rotters Club

LABEL
Virgin

TITLE

Fitter Stoke Has A Bath

Oh, that's Richard [Sinclair]. What a lovely voice, it's so true. On *Rock Bottom* he and Hugh Hopper really held it together [on bass]. In the mid-6os – he actually came from a musical background, his dad was a musician – although he was younger than us, he always used to sing in tune which I thought was pretty avant garde at the time, and actually I learnt to do the same. It took me a few years. A musician that he liked even when he was a teenager was Nat King Cole, who *nobody* listened to in the 6os. Nat King Cole: people don't realise why singers like him so much. It's because he's so in tune, so accurate. That's half the battle really – and Richard always was.

Hatfield And The North were one of the most fêted groups from that whole Canterbury Scene of the 6os and 7os. Was there any sense of a 'scene' at the time, or has it just become labelled thus with hindsight?

The first time I heard of the Canterbury Scene was in an article. It was invented by that bloke who does family trees [Pete Frame] and in order to do family trees, you have to have families. If I hadn't been told I was in a thing called the Canterbury Scene, it wouldn't have occurred to me. It surprised me that such a thing came to pass and it was interesting how these history books eventually get written. It makes you wonder about them. [Laughs]

I had a very, very unhappy and unsuccessful time at school in Canterbury, during which time I actually lived nearer Dover. I think in the long run, despite some very nice and, to me, now seemingly essential associations like Hugh Hopper, I was unhappy in Canterbury. I know Dave Sinclair [Ex-Caravan and Matching Mole] is very affectionate about it. I never had that kind of ruralist affection. I was taken to the country at about the age of ten, simply because my Dad had a terminal illness and retired early, somewhere where he could take it easy for a few years. As far as I was concerned, my life was shut up in my room doing little paintings and listening to records. Highlights were saving up enough money to go to London to concerts, or buy an Ornette Coleman record. I wasn't primarily interested in music for a start, and secondly, I certainly couldn't play. People have put out demos and tapes from that period from the 6os which I'm on, and I just find them so ridiculous, I can't believe anybody wants to listen to them.

King Crimson

In The Wake Of Poseidon

Island

Cat Food

I'm trying to work out where that bassline comes from. Oh, what is that? People do that, use a classic bassline and it throws you. You spend the whole time trying to remember what it is. Oh, John Lennon. It's from a Beatles . . . that one they did on the roof. It's very interesting indeed. They can all really play. [Wyatt later identifies the bassline as coming from The Beatles' *Come Together*.]

It's King Crimson from 1970 with Keith Tippett on piano.

I was going to say, the pianist was particularly good. [Laughs] Michael Giles on drums? He's a terrific drummer, I should have guessed it from that. To be honest a lot of bands came up around 68, and in 68 we [Soft Machine] were in America. What I heard of the other bands at that time were Big Brother & The Holding Company, Sly & The Family Stone and The Buddy Miles Express, and Larry Coryell playing in the smaller clubs. American groups, basically, and of course we were with Hendrix. I didn't really know much at all about English bands who would have been considered our contemporaries. I don't remember ever actually going to a rock concert that I didn't have to play at.

This is an example of the meeting ground of Progressive rock with experimental jazz of the era. Both King Crimson and Soft Machine used Keith Tippett's horn section [Marc Charig and Nick Evans]. King Crimson also collaborated with South African exiles like bass player Harry Miller, while you collaborated with brass players Mongezi Feza and Gary Windo.

The connection is very simple – Keith Tippett's personality. A West Country bloke with a great big heart and completely unlike the Old Boy Network jazz mafia that was the London scene at the time. He had all barriers down, listened to everybody, open-minded, never put anybody down, and one of his things was to get all these different musicians from different genres together – particularly the South African exiles. He would get together these bands and get us into them and then we'd meet each other. So really you could put a lot of that down to one man.

I think Mongs [Feza] and the South Africans we knew anyway, because we used to go down to Ronnie's old place and see The Blue Notes when they came to London. Although I didn't know them personally then, it would certainly have helped getting acquainted with Keith Tippett and Gary Windo and all those people. Alfie [Wyatt's wife] knew Johnny Dyani and Chris McGregor, and when we got together in 70–71 I also got to know her friends as well, so that would be another connection. It was Alfie, Evan Parker pointed out, who introduced him to John Stevens, for example. Chris McGregor was another one with a big heart.

Nina Simone

I Put A Spell On You

Mercury

I Put A Spell On You

[Immediately] Ah yes, this is nice to hear. [Sings along] There's a fantastic saxophone solo on this but I don't know who it is. It's so great. [Sings along to the sax solo] Yeah! Then she picks it up and he keeps on going, he keeps pushing it. *Now* he's finished. Cor, that's the stuff. The saxophone solo is like some of the players who played with James Brown: Maceo Parker.

Didn't you used to sing this with The Wilde Flowers in the mid-6os?

I think I used to sing it but I have a hard time remembering more than about 20 years ago to be honest. But certainly Nina Simone was very important. In fact most of the singers that I was influenced by were women, funnily enough. I seem to have more affinity with women's voices than with men's. That's because my voice never broke really.

I think she's a great singer, not just a good one. I'd put her up with Ray Charles. The thing is, she doesn't quite belong anywhere. Really she belongs in the continental tradition of chanson singers, Jacques Brel and all that sort of thing, Edith Piaf – that dramatic presentation of songs. It partly came out of a folk tradition of music hall but not the jokey side of it. Oscar Brown Junior was that as well. It's not pop and it's not jazz, it's not any of the categories that now exist. It's more intimate, more nightclubby. Amazing presence. When she's in Ronnie [Scott]'s she makes the place look really small. It's like having a real queen in a room, the real nature's aristocracy. By the time I saw her, she was no longer hitting the notes. She just sort of intimated them, sketched them in the air. And it was all you needed if you knew the songs.

ARTIST
Public Enemy

SOURCE
It Takes A Nation Of Millions To Hold Us Back

TITLE
Party For Your Right To Fight LABEL Def Jam

Robert Wyatt

Sounds like they're sampling Sly Stone. NWA or something like that?

It's someone equally well known.

Not by me, evidently. It's not Public Enemy? I'm trying to work out what they're sampling. Oh well, I know this one. I think that's one of the great lines: '*It takes a nation of millions to hold us back.*' It completely inverts the whole notion of dissidence. It's very close on from The Last Poets, the first people who did this kind of thing, without a rhythm section, just a cappella.

What I like about [rap's] kind of talking – in posh music it's called *Sprechgesang* – is that for some reason it liberated words. There's been a problem, I think, in black pop music since Motown. Even in some of the stuff I really love, the lyrics are a bit like rhyming soap operas. What's nice about all this black *Sprechgesang* is that it actually liberated the language that you could use on a pop record. It was a shame because in all this time, the black Americans were reinventing the English language every five years and made a massive contribution throughout the century, probably even before, to revitalising the language, then you get the Motown pop songs that sound great but they all just go '*Ooh Baby*'. It was a waste of all that fantastic vocabulary that's been cooking in the streets.

Although Public Enemy get their message over without any compromise, there's some witty interplay going on between Chuck D and Flavor Flav.

I used to listen a lot to Peter Tong's rap sessions on Radio 1 and there is some very funny, very witty stuff going on. As for the stuff that people think is terminally defensive in attitude, I don't think that anyone who hasn't been to America and been around on the streets. . . I don't feel you can talk about it unless you've been there. It's a long time since I've been, 25 years, but I found white American racism made me feel ill and I wasn't even particularly interested in the subject at the time. But if I lived there, I think I wouldn't really be answerable for what it would do to my brain – and that's just me. So what it must be for someone who's in the firing line, I can't imagine.

ARTIST

SOURCE

Sly & The Family Stone Stand!

LABEL

CBS

TITLE

Don't Call Me Nigger, Whitey

[Immediately] Oh, that is Sly Stone. [Wyatt drums on the table] Yeah, there's one thing about Sly Stone that I really like: it's like Mingus, there are lots of dimensions in it – a foreground, a middle ground and a background, and there's something happening in all of them. It's very beautifully spaced. Also that Mingus thing of each piece is a whole world of its own. [During the wah-wah harmonica break] Another thing is, I was very influenced by him in this business of the wordless 'vocal guitar solos' [Wyatt's trademark scat style].

Funnily enough, I was listening to this track this morning and it suddenly became apparent that it's like your own vocal style.

That's it. Almost like harmonica solos with your mouth right up to the mic [he cups his hand over his mouth to give a wah-wah effect] and you take a breath. Wonderful. And I thought, 'Yeah, I can play solos now!'

The record that most knocked us out when we [Soft Machine] were in the States was *Stand!*. That was as good as rock music got at the time – absolutely amazing. And the singers he gets in – that woman's a fantastic singer. He got ever such good players.

I read somewhere that you're a big fan of [Sly's bassist] Larry Graham.

Yeah, absolutely. One of the great bass players of all time and a great singer, deep voice, when he had his own band after he left Sly Stone. Very weird, strange person – they all were, but fantastic musicians. There's so much going on, you can't quite tell. . . Nowadays you can get effects with vocoders and stuff, you can sing through synthesisers and get instrumental effects and so on, but this is before them and better than all that really. It could be a vocoder thing [Sly] had been a disc jockey and knew a lot about studio technology. It's very good, led onto Bootsy and all that sort of stuff.

On some of the singles – specifically *Dance To The Music* – the bass is very loud.

They had very eccentric mixes. They'd make aesthetic decisions on each track, where to put things, who to have doing what, things coming in and out of each tune. They're great art, Sly Stone's records. And having been a jazz fan, it's nice hearing rhythm sections as good as the first one you played. If you're brought up on rhythm sections like Mingus and Dannie Richmond then rock can seem a bit pedestrian by comparison. A rhythm section like that has got the dimensions of the ins and outs that make it more interesting, more organic.

Pink Floyd

Masters Of Rock

EMI

Apples And Oranges

Is it Barrett? Is it Jerry Shirley on drums?

It's Pink Floyd, one of the last things Barrett did with them.

I thought it was the second [Barrett] solo LP. That bassline's just a major scale going downwards. It is one of the great tunes, the major scale! [At the line '*Thought you might like to know*'] See, that's another Beatles influence, it's exactly *Sergeant Pepper* – or it's just as likely to be the other way round: Paul McCartney used to listen to them [Pink Floyd]. That's lovely, it's really good. As you can gather, sometimes with English musicians, I know the people without necessarily knowing the music. I didn't collect records or go to the concerts. I was never a consumer. I really like them, and there again liked them individually as people. I'm biased because they were very kind to us and to me. In the early days, they got us out of some horrendous tight spots when our equipment blew up, and they would lend us some – and groups don't do things like that. And they were very generous when I had my accident. [Pink Floyd organised and headlined a benefit concert for Wyatt in the same year]

Musically, it's very refreshing to hear that. I'm ashamed to say I didn't know it but I don't actually have rock records to listen to particularly. I see rock music as a boy-next-door activity. Rock doesn't have any romantic associations for me. It's what people like us used to do [laughs], the kind of things we got up to. That's all I feel about it, but having said that, I thought it was very inventive. I enjoyed it very much.

The Canterbury Scene we mentioned before has acquired a sort of mythic status over time, but not as much as the 67 UFO Club scene. Was it really as exciting as it's been made out to be?

Well, you have to forgive the people involved if they're subjective. The subjective facts are I couldn't play in the 60s. It took me a long time. So I associate the entire decade – if there is such a thing as a decade – with excruciating embarrassment on my own part. That's bound to colour what you think about a place or a time.

Objectively, I'd say it was good, yeah. It was good in the sense that the groups weren't the only thing, just part of what was going on.

It was almost like having a big indoor market, really. We [Soft Machine] used to go down there and play, and sometimes they'd have Monteverdi playing, and the atmosphere would already be perfect. All you'd need was Monteverdi playing and people wandering about, or lying on the floor and things like that, and Mark Boyle's and various other people's film projections all over the walls, and already that was it, the atmosphere. And then there would be the groups. It didn't rely on the groups. It was a place to be anyway. As a stage, the audience were all in the play. And except for a few stars in the old style, like Arthur Brown, who was wonderful, most people were fairly anonymous. They would just be there as part of making the scene.

I think at that time I was still too much of a jazz and blues fan to quite be able to tune into what they [Pink Floyd] were doing. The bands I knew in London before them were Zoot Money and Georgie Fame. I was more used to the Ornette Colemans and the Sun Ras, and compared with what was going on [in jazz] by the mid-60s, even the most non-poppy pop groups seemed fairly tame to me, and fairly commercial. That's not a criticism, it's just a fact.

ARTIST
Miles Davis

SOURCE
ESP

LABEL
Columbia

TITLE
Agitation

[During Tony Williams's long drum solo introduction] Sounds like Elvin Jones. It's not? Good Lord! He was very influenced by Elvin Jones – School of Elvin Jones. [Trumpet comes in] Well. Oh, in that case it's Jack DeJohnette.

It's not actually.
Hang on. OK. It's Tony Williams. Stupid, I am! Oh God, shoot that man. What a funny mistake to make. But that's a really interesting mistake, because I'd never thought of Tony Williams as being anything like Elvin Jones. But that early section and the business of stumbling over where you expect the bar-line to be, is such an Elvin Jones thing. And it's a much deeper sound than I associate with Tony Williams: he usually has a much lighter, crisper sound. It was a very important time for Miles Davis. He never really recovered from the loss of Coltrane and he nearly went under then, I get the impression. But it was finding Tony Williams and doing a whole new thing that put him back on track. I don't know this one, I have to say. This is terrific, I really like this.

It's from *ESP* from 1965.
I should have this, let alone know it. Miles Davis started recording when I was born and he's been there all my life. And if someone asked me what was my very favourite voice sound ever, I'd have to say Miles Davis.
Miles Davis is one of the great jazz philosophers. It pisses me off when people list great philosophers and only list great philosophical writers, because to me some of the great philosophers weren't writers, they were people who did other things: Thelonious Monk or Miles Davis.

ARTIST
Brian Eno

SOURCE
Nerve Net

LABEL
Opal/Warner Bros

TITLE
My Squelchy Life

I was going to play you another piece [i.e. Eno's *My Squelchy Life*] but it seems I've recorded over the tape by mistake.
You'll have to hum it! [After about 20 seconds of me humming] Ah, hang on, that could be Johnny Rotten. Don't tell me, because I know who that is. That's stupid – I just remember him saying something about sex once that that reminds me of. Of course, it's Brian. I think Brian would be very amused, first of all that you sang *My Squelchy Life* and I said 'Johnny Rotten'. And secondly, I would think this is only acceptable if you point out that we've broken new ground here, in that you've not actually played the record and I commented on it. I think it's appropriate; Brian would really appreciate that.

I have no objective opinion of Brian at all. I just consider him a great friend and an utterly good bloke. What else can I say? Brian and I used to spend a lot of time together in the 70s just talking and hanging about. Which, despite this thing about various scenes I may have been on, I don't remember doing with musicians on the whole. We used to have such fun. That's why it's so appropriate you didn't play the record, because we used to have fun imagining things that there could be. In the 70s we thought, wouldn't it be great to get all these records that we were listening to from all around the world, totally nothing to do with pop or rock 'n' roll or jazz or American music, anything like that, anything to do with Europe at all, and you could find tracks that would appeal to people and just package it like pop music. It's difficult to explain now that kind of idea has become commonplace, in fact hackneyed, how exciting it was at that time to draw up these sort of thoughts. He was a very enjoyable person to think with. I find that thinking out loud with Brian is incredibly good exercise for the brain.

You performed on *Music For Airports* in the late 70s, which is now regarded as a landmark in Ambient music. The idea that it was equally valid to listen to or ignore the music seemed very radical at the time.

That's perhaps why we got on well, because I do like that thing that he does and we both do, which is, 'What if you turn the situation upside down, whatever the assumption or premise might be?' You're banging your head on the wall to try and do something to grab people's attention – what if you do the opposite? [Laughs] Ideas circulate and I'm very loath to attribute ideas solely to one person or anything. This question of authorship wouldn't really be a battleground [for Eno]. Although he is a fountain of ideas, he wouldn't promote himself necessarily as such, because he's interested in the circulation of them, and they go through various processes.

I remember a thing that I'd come across from Miles Davis. He [Miles] was talking about how to arrange things in a piece of music. And Miles Davis basically wouldn't tell anybody what to do – his arrangement was the choice of musicians you had in the first place. And Brian thought that was terrific and went on to do some things like that, where you wouldn't tell anybody what to do – the arrangement was choosing the musicians. And so that idea you can't attribute either to him, or to me, I think you'd have to attribute it to Miles Davis, but the point is, the idea was very illuminating.

Eno always used to describe himself as a 'non-musician'.

I don't know what it means in rock 'n' roll, frankly. [Laughs] As opposed to who? Dave Clarke? What are we talking about here? But that's good. It's the great saving thing about pop music. There's a lot of pop music you only have to be able to hear in your head to be able to do it. But that only makes it like conversation. There's nothing wrong with that – doesn't mean it's crap.

Selections

Selections